accept no autism!

Our Family's Story of Recovery

---

tatianna dickens

Jebaire Publishing
Snellville, GA

Accept No Autism!: Our Family's Story of Recovery

Published by Jebaire Publishing, LLC

ISBN-10: 0-9786796-4-4
ISBN -13: 978-0-9786796-4-4

Supervising Editor: Shannon Clark
Copyedit: Fran D. Lowe

Cover Design: Jebaire Publishing (In-House)

To Zack, Jacob and Abbie – for growing my heart
beyond my wildest dreams.

To James - for standing faithfully by my side when
a lesser man would have fled.

To our team (family, friends and professionals alike) – for
your tireless prayers, supports and efforts.

And to the Father above –
for sustaining, teaching and protecting me, and for granting me
the honor of taking part in Your miracle.

CONTENTS

Foreword

I'm glad you've picked up this book. I give out bad news to concerned parents all too frequently, and it is far from easy. I am currently employed as a medical psychologist at a family practice residency center as the behavioral faculty of the program. Presenting a family with their child's diagnosis is always a heart-wrenching experience, both for them and for me. There is no exception. The rules for relating difficult news are set by professional guidelines: give the objective facts in a way that helps clarify what is likely to occur; provide options and choices for the disorder; share the prognosis for the condition; offer the risks and benefits of treatment versus non-treatment; and last but not least, make sure that, if there are viable options, you leave them with hope. I know it sounds pretty clinical and detached—like one could eventually grow accustomed to the process, perhaps even narrow it down to a science —if only it worked that way.

For both the professional and the families, this situation creates an emotional roller coaster; unfortunately, the medical/early intervention system sets forth only a vague road map to follow. When a family hears a diagnosis like "autism spectrum," it often tears them apart. The medical providers, in an attempt to separate their own feelings when relaying difficult news, often leave the family to interpret the medical jargon on their own. It was under these circumstances that I met Tatianna Dickens and her family.

This book is written with a firsthand understanding of what it's like to get an autism spectrum diagnosis for one's child. It provides specifics of their intensely structured day, with the day-in and day-out details required at every level of every day. These massive efforts are designed to maximize every potential resource for a developing brain in order to change the course of the disorder, and ultimately, the child's life. If you continue on, you'll get to read a book by one of my heroes. She's one of the reasons why I keep working in this field on a daily basis. I can't promise that what worked for the Dickens family will work for every family, but I can tell you that it worked for them because I've seen the proof. Having a complete foundation of information will help you make the best choices for your family.

Read on and find hope.

Robert Mayfield, Ph.D.
Medical Psychologist

Acknowledgments

Contrary to popular belief I am not a strong person. In fact, I am quite the opposite. Without the generosity of others, our family would not be celebrating the miracle of Zack's autism recovery. Without the hope and strategies offered by licensed, prescribing psychologist Dr. Robert Mayfield, we never would have set out on this journey in the first place. Without the dedicated pursuits of skilled therapists (Jennifer Travis, Chelsea Smith and Dehlia Jornigan in particular) and many teachers, we would have buckled under the burden. Without the love, encouragement, prayers and financial support freely given by family and friends we would have given up long ago. Without the editorial gifts and time invested by my close friend and confidant Barbara Toth our story would be far less eloquent. Without the deep desire of Jebaire Publishing to glorify God and share His wonderful works, I'd still be awaiting this divine provision.

Most importantly, without the grace and protection extended by the Lord God Almighty our family would be in ruins. For all these blessings and more, I am and will forever be thankful.

What you see and hear depends a good deal on where you are standing; it also depends on what kind of a person you are.

—C. S. Lewis

1

Denial: Stop! Your Child Needs You

Wake up: This is not a dream. This may be a nightmare but not a dream. Before one can make headway with a problem, one must first admit that there is a problem. This is true with all struggles in life, and autism is no exception. It is excruciatingly difficult for a parent consumed with love for a child to take the first step and admit that there is something very wrong with him or her. The problem, however, is that denial will not remedy the situation. The child with autism will not just grow out of this or that worrisome behavior. This is not a phase but a devastating disorder that demands immediate action.

Our son, Zack, started exhibiting odd characteristics when he was about 23 months of age. (At the time, my husband, James, and I also had a three-and-a-half-year-old son, Jacob, and would soon be welcoming our new daughter, Abbie, into the world.) One day, as I was relaxing in the comfort of my rocking chair, Jacob was proudly showing off his latest and greatest Tinker Toy creation. Suddenly, Zack picked up a long rod from the pile and began to whack the futon repeatedly. Concerned about the furniture, I asked him to stop, but my request made no noticeable impression on him. Trying to spare myself any unnecessary movement, I tossed a pillow in his general direction, hoping to gain his attention, but this effort failed as well.

My family was visiting at this time, and I distinctly recall having an unsettling conversation with them about Zack. With Abbie's arrival imminent, I was even more emotionally charged than usual. Even so, I tried my best to stay composed as I prepared myself for a lecture about Zack's recent display of disobedience; instead, my parents shared their distress over Zack's unaffectionate and extreme behavior. According to them, each attempt they made to lovingly touch him resulted in violent screams and tantrums. I thought to myself, "What do you mean he screams when you touch him? He doesn't scream when *I* touch him. *Look*!"

Because Zack had suffered during the first year of his life with Gastroesophageal Reflux Disease (GERD), an unrelated digestive disorder, I had held him and fed him almost constantly in an effort to make him feel better. He bonded so closely with me that I was able to touch Zack how and when I wanted, but I was the only one. Even James tried to convince me that he could only touch Zack on his terms without risking a screaming session. I couldn't believe it was true; or rather, I didn't *want* to believe it was true.

Then John, my father in-law, came to visit. Like all grandparents, he wanted to take lots of pictures of his cute grandkids. At three and a half, Jacob was a ham through and through, and he loved to have his picture taken. Questions arose, however, about Zack's uncooperative disposition—every time John ventured to take his picture, violent screeching tantrums resulted. Well, I couldn't argue with this one. No one could tune out Zack's hissy-fits on these occasions, yet I continued to make excuses. I had witnessed the camera flash sending him frantically over the edge many times, so I figured there had to be something wrong with his eyes. I had often caught him squinting, even on cloudy days. Thus, I concluded that the bright flash must be responsible for Zack's ultra-sensitive response. I assumed that he subsequently transferred his fear of the flash to a fear of all circumstances surrounding cameras, whether a flash was present or not.

A few months later my mother-in-law, a nationally certified

teacher, came to visit. Extremely worried about Zack, she was the first to push us toward getting an evaluation. She told us there was obviously something seriously wrong with him, and we needed professional advice. I definitely wanted to hear nothing of the sort! Along with her concerns about his sensitivity to touch and light, she pointed out two additional disturbing behaviors to us: Zack appeared to be obsessive/compulsive about pounding things with his favorite stick. Also, he failed to look her in the eyes and answer to his name when she called him. In her opinion, his development was significantly delayed.

Again I was poised, ready, and willing to offer an explanation for these behaviors. "Boys love to hit things with sticks," I told her, "so this is not a bizarre activity." Of course, it wasn't the activity she took issue with; instead, she was concerned about Zack's intensity level. I reiterated my theory about his eye sensitivity, thereby justifying his reaction to cameras as well as his poor eye contact. Addressing his unwillingness to answer to his own name, I suggested that he was merely too distracted by the television or too fascinated by the cool toy he was taking apart and putting back together. I even borrowed from that old adage, "He *is* a boy after all; boys *do* develop slower than girls."

Then Abbie was born, and we experienced the wonderful distraction of the "new baby" phase. We noticed right away that Zack not only ignored his baby sister, but he also refused to acknowledge the rest of the family—even me—when we were holding her. Since Zack was extremely attached to me before Abbie was born, I had anticipated that he would have a difficult time adjusting to any situation which required him to share me. So, yet again I made an excuse for his increasingly introspective and introverted ways. I told myself he would eventually come to terms with the fact that we had a new child in the family and understand that he was no longer the baby.

Also, we could hardly be expected to address any of Zack's jealousy issues while we were in the midst of the "new baby survival mode." We were all too exhausted to do anything until everyone was sleeping through the night, which finally happened when Abbie was four months old. Zack was now 28 months old himself, and he was still no closer to coming to terms with having a little sister. His acting-out and temper tantrums had also escalated significantly during this short period of time. I surmised that Zack had finally grown into a typically defiant "terrible two."

At two, Zack had been able to say about 20 words fairly clearly. Our oldest, Jacob, spoke only about 10 words when he was two, but James and I were not overly concerned because we have a family history of late-talking on both sides. We had tried unsuccessfully to teach him some sign language at that age. Six months later, however, when Jacob finally recognized that the sign represented a word, he suddenly began talking in very complex sentences. He's been talking our ears off ever since. At 28 months, Zack had lost all but about five words from his vocabulary, and the remaining ones were not as clear as they had been before. Because of our dismal experience with Jacob, it never occurred to me to teach Zack sign language. Also, I wasn't especially worried about Zack's limited vocabulary because of Jacob's amazing verbal leap from a few words to complete sentences. Little Brother was sure to follow in Big Brother's footsteps, right?

One incident in particular confirmed in my mind that Zack was fine. He was about 27 months old at the time. We were visiting family, and he had thrown his treasured stuffed frog, Soggy Froggy, into a tomato planter protected by chicken wire. It was too tall for Zack to simply reach in and retrieve Soggy Froggy. Using those wonderful brain cells of his, he stuck his hand through the small opening, grabbed the frog, and elevated the toy the best he could. Then, alternating his hands, he methodically and purposefully worked Soggy Froggy up the inside of the wire. Zack stayed on task, lifting him up, one inch at a time, until his cherished stuffed animal was rescued. "You see!" I said to myself. "He is a creative and intelligent child! There is nothing wrong with him!" Of course, this awesome example of problem solving did not require the use of language or a human connection at all, so this exercise was right up Zack's alley.

To have a well-rounded pleasant life, however, Zack needed to engage in social interaction and conversations with others. Strangely, this skill appeared to become more challenging for him to demonstrate with each passing day. It was around this time when his poor pronunciation really started to grate on my nerves. I knew that he had been able to say some of these words before and pronounce them with much more clarity.

Rather than saying "please," for example, Zack had begun to say "pwease." Why all of a sudden was he refusing to cooperate? Whenever Zack asked for something with a "pwease," I always insisted that he say it correctly. I felt that he was being lazy and disrespectful, and I was not going to tolerate it one little bit. We would get into what I presumed to be huge battles of the will over his "pweese," when actually he was no longer capable of producing the right sounds. (*With the regressive form of autism, skills previously mastered disappear before one's very eyes.*) Unfortunately, I had absolutely no idea about what was going on. He would get so incredibly frustrated with me—and me with him. Why was my little cutie-pie torturing me so? Did I have a reason to be concerned? Or was my impatient nature caving in to the pressures of motherhood?

Shortly after the "pwease" issue began, Jacob came down with an ear infection. I loaded up all three kids, and off we went to the doctor's office. Our pediatrician, Dr. Tim, is a nice, caring individual who takes his job seriously. After confirming Jacob's infection and writing the prescription, he asked me if I had any questions. As I revealed my uneasiness over Zack's limited language and uncooperative ways, Dr. Tim asked him a couple of questions, to which he responded as any two-and-a-half year-old would: with words, a smile, and great eye contact. He asked Zack for a high-five, and my son obliged—again, just as one might expect from a toddler. Dr. Tim told me I had nothing to worry about. There is no simple blood test for autism, and Zack had behaved impeccably, giving the doctor no cause for concern. As relieved as I was to hear those words from a doctor I trusted, I knew that Zack was having a *really* good day. Dr. Tim did not see the Zack I knew—the Zack who was throwing tantrums and not talking well, the Zack who made me anxious when I didn't want to be anxious. For as long as I could, I held on to those lovely, comforting, encouraging words: "I have nothing to worry about. I have nothing to worry about."

Then one day, despite my intense attachment to Dr. Tim's reassuring words, I was forced by the circumstances to release myself from them. I could no longer reasonably ignore the fact that there was something terribly wrong with my precious little boy. Given Zack's very limited vocabulary and his failure to consistently point to objects, I was finding our kitchen routine increasingly frustrating. Over the course of those first few months with Abbie, Zack talked less and screamed more every time he was hungry or thirsty. He would stand in front of the pantry or refrigerator and just scream. I would open the door and track his eyes in my vain attempt to determine what he wanted. Most of the time when I tried to get him to point, he refused and threw a tantrum. The same was true if I tried to get him to say the name of the food or drink item. After several minutes, which usually felt to me like an eternity, I would eventually decipher what he wanted, and the screaming would stop. . .until the next time.

Once Abbie started sleeping through the night and I regained some energy, this kitchen scenario became more and more of an issue. My patience was quickly fading. During one particularly infuriating morning, I just snapped. I remember thinking, "This is no way to live! I can't do this anymore! My child can't even make his simplest, most basic needs and wants known to me!" Then it all hit me like a ton of bricks: "MY CHILD ISN'T OK AT ALL!" Desperation closed in on me, and I immediately experienced a harrowing physical reaction caused by my mounting anxiety and dread. All of the distressing comments from others I had managed to suppress came flooding back to my mind. We had to get help and get it fast! I clearly wasn't able to fix Zack on my own. He had only been getting worse, and I knew that I couldn't handle it if things got any worse than they already were. Little did I know that things would get far worse before they got any better.

It seemed as though everyone around me had recognized Zack's need for an evaluation by the time I was ready to come to terms with that fact. Several months earlier, a friend had suggested contacting our local non-profit Birth to Three agency as a means of evaluation. This organization also provides a multitude of services for children with disabilities. With an all-consuming urgency, I made the disquieting phone call. It was such a discouraging thing for me to hear that it would be four months before they could fit Zack into their busy schedule. There were no other comparable evaluative or therapeutic resources available in our area, so we were at the mercy of their calendar schedule. I was finally willing to acknowledge that my son needed some immediate professional help, but I was expected to wait for four months? Overcome by feelings of desperation and sadness along with confusion, it never occurred to me to seek help elsewhere.

I began to say to myself, "If only I had been proactive from the first onset of symptoms. . . .If only I had known more about autism and the early warning signs. . . ." Nine months had passed between the time Zack displayed the first noticeable characteristics and the unofficial autism diagnosis from our Birth to Three agency. Nine months were wasted before early intervention therapies began—nine months that could have made all the difference in the world to my son were gone forever. What kind of a mom was I? I waited so long and did nothing! Looking back, I realized I had known deep down in my soul that Zack needed help. How could I have let my own denial continue for so long before coming to my senses? My perception of guilt was all-consuming during that four-month period leading up to Zack's evaluation.

Remarkably, even after I had received the first unofficial diagnosis of autism, I still convinced myself that the experts must have missed something: perhaps there was just something wrong with his hearing. Zack had screeched so frequently during the first year of his life due to the discomfort of his bout with GERD. I reasoned that exposure to the constant barrage of intolerable noise could have damaged the ears of our entire family, and Zack had been screeching much closer to his own ears than to ours. Also, James and I both had a family history of hearing issues. I convinced myself that this, if not the screeching, could be the real culprit responsible for Zack's unresponsiveness when his name was called. This would also explain his very poor receptive language scores. I thought, "He just can't hear adequately. That's it! As soon as we get his ears taken care of, all will be well." Of course, in order to accept that rationale, I had to intentionally overlook the fact that Zack could hear the refrigerator door open from two rooms away. (That wasn't exactly indicative of hearing loss, but this wasn't at all relevant to me. I just didn't want to entertain the thought of more troubling alternatives.)

The evaluation reported that Zack was severely delayed in almost every area, including fine motor skills, self-help skills, coping skills, oral motor skills, cognition (thinking and learning), receptive language (understanding), expressive language (communication), and social/emotional development. My heart sank as I heard the results of the testing from the agency therapist. Not only was he severely delayed in language and social skills, but he was also severely delayed in many other areas we hadn't even considered. I didn't really know anything about autism, but Zack's deficits were so diverse and alarming.

Sobbing uncontrollably, I began to wonder, "Could this be my beautiful boy's lot in life?" Choking on the horrible words I didn't want to ask or have answered, I somehow managed to spit out, "Does our child have autism?" Our local experts were not at liberty to use the dreaded "a-word" because they didn't have a medical doctor on staff to complete their diagnostic team. (*An official diagnosis of autism requires that a complete team of professionals be in agreement.*) Despite their noncommittal answer to my question, they also did not reassure James and me with, "Get out of here! Your child is normal."

Even without an official diagnosis, it was still inherently clear that Zack had many very serious deficits to overcome. This was not what James and I as parents had desired for our precious son. Yet, even though it was enormously heartbreaking, we were still unbelievably desperate for help. Four years later, words still fail me when I seek to describe how overwhelmed we felt.

It would have been far too easy to beat myself up for waiting so long to take action, but I was already thoroughly devastated over our current situation. For the sake of my mental health, I decided to focus on the present and not dwell on the past. This was a vitally important insight for me—one that served as the impetus for the work that lay ahead. Wallowing in guilt about the past simply was not productive; on the other hand, pouring the energy of that guilt into my son's future could and would be productive.

Therapists at our local agency were swamped with children graduating from their program to the public school system; therefore, they could offer us no immediate assistance. So that first month I was entirely on my own. After allowing myself to mourn for three days, I picked myself up and got to work trying to help my little guy. All the self-pity in the world wasn't going to help my Zack; instead, I dedicated myself to helping him the best I could.

The experts sent us home with the following suggestions:

1. *Transition Zack from the sippy cup to an open cup and/or straw;*
2. *Try to gradually increase the variety of textures of his foods (Good luck!);*
3. *Attempt to improve his eye contact (and base vocabulary) by naming objects while simultaneously bringing pictures of these objects up to your face;*
4. *Encourage turn-taking;*
5. *Promote alternative play instead of allowing obsessive/compulsive and self-stimulatory behavior (otherwise known as "stimming"); and*
6. *Encourage mirror play and the naming of body parts.*

My attempts to implement any of these suggestions caused Zack to throw a tantrum and screech beyond belief. There were many additional areas where his skills were devastatingly sub-par, and it felt like there were a million different details I needed to work on with Zack: Where should I start? How do I stop the tantrums and screeching? Would my sweet Zack ever be able to tolerate another person's touch? How could our family survive this seemingly unbearable burden? How could the child we love have autism? This couldn't *really* be happening to us, could it?

Still refusing to face reality, I couldn't bring myself to believe that Zack's receptive language was actually so severely delayed. I began to quiz him as the evaluators had done to see if I could elicit a different response. Surely he knew more than they were giving him credit for—he just *had* to! Much to my dismay, all this exercise did was confirm my worst nightmares. Zack understood so little about the world around him, and the worst part was that he didn't care in the slightest. He would have been perfectly content pounding his stick every minute of every day for the rest of his life. But then again, he would also have been perfectly content screaming every time he wanted a drink or a snack. Boy, was his world about to turn upside down! So was mine, for that matter.

As unbearable as it was trying to come to terms with the prospect of living with a child afflicted by autism, it was even more unbearable to imagine myself sitting back and doing nothing. I was determined to save Zack by doing everything humanly possible, now that I knew what I was dealing with. I made myself and my son a promise—no longer was I going to get in the way of Zack's future. *This* was a promise worth keeping!

"A woman who can cope with the terrible twos can cope with anything." - Judith Clabes[1]

"Then you will know the truth, and the truth will set you free." (John 8:32)

1 Copyright 1995 Cook Communications Ministries. God's Little Instruction Book For Mom by Honor Books. Used with permission. All rights reserved.

2

People: Searching for Support

Having a child with autism can be painfully lonely. I felt as though no one could truly comprehend the devastating heartbreak I was living through. Frankly, one actually can't understand such misery unless they have lived through it first hand. I wish this wasn't the case, but it is. During the midst of these trials with Zack, I never asked, "Why me?" because I know that we live in a fallen world as a result of sin. Also, I firmly believe that everything happens for a reason, even if we can't fathom the reason at the time. There were many times, however, when I did ask, "Why not someone else, too?" I know this sounds terrible, but I desperately longed for a friend to share my deepest darkest fears with—someone who could really empathize with my tragic ordeal. As it was, I think that sharing my all-consuming sorrows was hard on my friendships. Because it was so draining, I had the sneaking suspicion that those close to me were avoiding me—just kidding. . . well, sort of. I have friends who cared deeply and wanted to help, but they had no idea what to say to me to make me feel better. I'm not even sure that there really *was* anything they could have said to make me feel better. It wasn't their fault; I just wanted to talk to someone who could actually relate to my pain. My life situation was too far outside the experience of anyone in my circle of friends. The same was true with my family.

When we first set out on this journey, my dad told me that the very best thing in Zack's favor was having me for a mom. It was an extremely sweet comment, and I appreciated the love that inspired him to say it. His remark, however, only made me cry because an insurmountable task lay before me: my son's life was in my hands, and this daunting predicament was inescapable. The weight of this huge responsibility was pressing me down and crushing me to the point that sometimes I could hardly breathe. Giant waves of desperation washed over me on an almost constant basis.

All the while, I felt the added pressure of racing against the clock. Much of the literature I had read confirmed that significant gains needed to be made before the child reached five years of age. Because the brain begins to solidify around that time, it becomes less malleable and flexible. This makes it infinitely more difficult to build the new neurological pathways that are extremely necessary for the child's development.

After about six months of agonizing therapy, which to my mind appeared basically ineffectual, my dad tried to encourage me by saying that Zack would eventually turn out all right. Because stress was obviously taking its toll on his beloved daughter, he asked me to try to relax and take care of myself. I'm sure he was worried about me since I had lost too much weight, destroyed my molars by clenching my teeth, and frequently suffered migraines. In addition to these physical manifestations of my stress, I had also spent countless sleepless nights brainstorming about various ways to teach Zack more successfully. To say that I was a complete mess would be an understatement. As well intentioned as my Dad's words were, they didn't bring me any comfort. Instead I just kept thinking to myself, "Even if Zack, by the grace of God, does somehow manage to turn out all right, do you have any idea how much blood, sweat, and tears it will have required of me? Look what this has cost me already, and I've only just begun!" I realize these reflections sound extremely self-centered. However, they were formed under extremely excruciating circumstances; and my emotional state was very fragile at the time, so please read this graciously.

Trying to save your child from autism has to be one of the most difficult jobs on the planet because it continually and thoroughly saps your entire being from the inside out. I prayed desperately every morning for the strength to get through yet another heart-breaking, miserable, discouraging day with Zack. I prayed through every tantrum, every perceived failure, every awkward and embarrassing moment in public, and every instance in which I felt I couldn't bear this infernal situation any longer. There were many moments when my prayers consisted only of uncontrollable sobbing because mere words were incapable of capturing my pleadings. Out of sheer necessity I was forced to rely completely on my Lord and Savior who undoubtedly sustained me through these tremendously horrific times. Yet, even with this amazing grace covering me, I often felt as though I was barely surviving at all.

Having a child with autism can be so overwhelming that it is crucial to find avenues of support. The thought of anyone weathering this storm alone, or with insufficient assistance, is unimaginable to me. I would advise those of you who are parents of children with autism to strive for and acquire even more help than you think you need, if at all possible. Don't be afraid to ask for help. Beg if you have to. There is no shame in admitting you need help. The worst answer you will receive is a "no," and even then, there is always someone else you can ask. You may *feel* all alone, but you are *not* all alone.

Though my friends could not personally relate to our situation, it was extremely obvious that they wanted to help us any way they could. We attend a wonderful church with a very loving church family. When they saw us struggling so desperately, they took it upon themselves to bring us dinner every single night for six months. These meals were an amazing blessing to me: it was such a relief not to have to think about what to cook for dinner and then spend the time cooking it. With their thoughtful, practical help, I had more time to keep an eye on Zack and make sure he was engaging with someone—not just "stimming" in a corner.

I know that a handful of special brothers and sisters at our church have been praying for us every day since the very beginning of our ordeal. Now, more than four years later, they still pray for us daily. Never, ever, underestimate the power of prayer—the Lord can move all manner of mountains for those who pray. He performed a miracle on my son, saving Zack from autism. If that isn't moving a mountain, I don't know what is! I will never take the people who have faithfully prayed for us for granted. These prayer warriors are dearer to me than they could possibly imagine.

Spending seven to eight thousand dollars per year on therapy over a four-year period was a hardship for James and me, especially on a single income. We had no choice but to live paycheck to paycheck. Our extended family was exceptionally supportive, both emotionally and financially. My in-laws generously covered the cost of sending our oldest son Jacob to a private Christian school. This had been a major priority for us, but without discretionary income we were unable to afford the tuition. My parents agreed to foot the bill for a new washing machine when ours died. (Incidentally, this occurred at the precise moment our entire family came down with a stomach bug.) They also bought us a new dryer and helped out with the expense of new tires for our minivan. Because we had no safety net for unexpected expenditures, I don't know how we would have managed without their generous help.

We briefly considered leaving the community we loved to move closer to our family in northern New Mexico. This would have provided more options for respite assistance, but we decided against it because Zack would lose valuable therapy time as he transitioned from one household environment to another. We would also have had to find and develop new relationships with an entire new team of therapists. This process would have taken more time than we were willing to lose. So we decided to stay put, for better or worse. Thankfully, it turned out to be the right decision for our family.

About seven months into our intervention program with Zack, I heard about a local autism support group that met once a month. Finally, I had the opportunity to visit with other parents who understood the challenges we were facing. Even though every child with autism is so different, we were still able to encourage one other and brainstorm together about strategies for handling various situations. Laughing and crying about our similar predicaments was especially cathartic.

Another benefit of the group that I hadn't anticipated was being able to put into perspective the small gains and progress Zack was making. I actually found myself feeling grateful for little things: "Yes, I might be dealing with *this* right now, but at least I'm not dealing with *that*, or at least. . .not yet."

I talked to parents who were dealing with cases much more severe than Zack's. One of the children, for instance, had wandered out of the house at night and couldn't be found for hours. Another had seizures and wasn't responding well to the medication. Many of the kids refused to sleep through the night. One child was ten years old and still not potty-trained. We felt extraordinarily blessed not to have to deal with all these issues. It wasn't that we didn't have our own issues with Zack, but we were definitely made aware of how much worse it actually could have been. If we had been forced to deal with every possible frustration associated with autism, our lives would have been even *more* harrowing. The ability to feel blessed during this difficult time has been a remarkable benefit to me, and I try to hold on to that appreciation—that spirit of thankfulness— wherever I go.

Our hometown has a local, government-sponsored organization that offers assistance to children with disabilities. If you live in a moderate- to large-sized city, you most likely have access to a similar agency providing relatively comparable services. There may also be private companies and resources available that provide information on a multitude of important topics, such as implementing an effective intervention program, training, dealing with bureaucracies, and preparing for the Individual Education Plan (IEP) meetings with public school systems. One such agency is Autism & Aspergers Consulting, LLC. They can be reached via the web at www.aactnow.com .

Federal law requires that all states provide an information and resource center regarding special-needs educational issues for their residents. In New Mexico this organization is Parents Reaching Out (PRO). You may contact them at (800) 524-5176 or on-line at www.parentsreachingout.org. In addition to supplying resource materials, our local organization has worked in conjunction with our universities to design a class in which students pursuing degrees in teaching, early childhood development, and pre-med can interview parents of special needs children. This experience provides the students with a unique opportunity to more fully understand each family's struggles and successes. Potentially, they can then apply what they have learned to their future careers. Both the families and the students find this exercise extremely rewarding.

The Cure Autism Now Foundation and DAN! (Defeat Autism Now!) are two good resources for addressing your questions and concerns as well. Both provide much information on the latest scientific studies and bio-medical options available for your special child. I feel the need to warn you, though: Don't get so involved in the research and bio-medical treatments that your pursuit for assistance comes at the expense of your child. Don't waste valuable time chasing a magic pill or solution, because there is none. The only tangible hope for your precious young one does not come in a nice, neat little package but a horrible, very messy, monstrous one. Nevertheless, *here* is where some hope abides. Hope *does* exist for children with autism!

One of my greatest desires is to share this hope with those of you who may feel hopeless. I know how priceless hope is to a family dealing with the innumerable challenges of autism. Grief-stricken families need to know that they are not alone and there are people in the world who truly care and sincerely want to help. There are some kindred spirits among you who actually do have a true appreciation for what this tribulation entails. Some may have survived this onslaught of autism years ago. They may be ready, willing, and able to minister to you. Let them comfort you and offer you refuge. Don't drown in despair. Allow those around you to help so that you may keep your head above the extremely troubled waters.

The way each day will look to you all starts with who you're looking to.—Unknown[1]

"Come to me, all you who are weary and burdened, and I will give you rest."
(Matthew 11:28)

---

1 Copyright 1995 Cook Communications Ministries. God's Little Instruction Book For Dad by Honor Books. Used with permission. All rights reserved.

3

Therapists: Finding the Right Fit

One of the first things parents of a child with autism have to come to terms with is their inability to take on this battle alone. The fact is, a child affected by this devastating disorder requires constant therapy. There is a very real possibility of multiple deficits, including speech difficulties, occupational/sensory challenges, physical issues, and other severe developmental delays; therefore, having a team of professionals is a necessity. We worked with Robert, a fabulous lead psychologist who never steered us wrong. Not only did he give us great advice, but he was the only professional on our team that offered us any hope whatsoever. We will be eternally grateful for his encouraging words. Our team also included a speech pathologist, an early intervention expert, and an occupational therapist. Thankfully, Zack had no physical therapy needs.

Although our local Birth to Three program didn't have the authority to officially diagnose autism, we went ahead and began our early intervention program when Zack was 32 months old. Unfortunately, without a formal diagnosis, we were unable to get anywhere near the help we needed. Initially, we were given only six hours of help per week, and this only occurred during the utopian weeks when all of the therapists arrived as scheduled, which was seldom the case. I do realize that people have lives of their own, and sometimes they had no option but to cancel their appointments with us. However, the frequency of missed appointments became a phenomenal drain on my psyche. It interrupted the continuity that Zack and I were beginning to depend on, and being so exhausted and overwhelmed, I found myself deeply resenting every cancellation.

All of the autism literature states that the earlier you start therapy, the better. Moreover, if you want a shot at a positive outcome, the average recommendation is a minimum of six hours per day. Despite the fact that we only qualified for six hours of therapy *per week*, I took this suggestion very seriously. During the remaining 37 hours, I acted as Zack's primary therapist. Even during times not officially designated for therapy, I diligently redirected his "stims" and encouraged him to practice the skills introduced during the therapy sessions. My determination to provide non-stop therapy was absolutely draining in every respect.

After a few months, our agency mentioned to us that they could conceivably give us many more hours of professional help if we went to the Early Childhood Evaluative Program (ECEP) affiliated with the University of New Mexico and received an official diagnosis. So, when Zack was three years old, ECEP evaluated him and gave us the choice of either Pervasive Developmental Disorder Not Otherwise Specified (PPDNOS) or Autism Spectrum Disorder (ASD). They felt that his level of disorder fell somewhere between the two. Zack had every single characteristic of autism except the echolalia (*an automatic repetition of words spoken within one's presence*), but he was not as severely affected as he could have been. We chose PDDNOS because it sounded somewhat less scary to us, but we were told that Zack would qualify for the same services regardless, since both diagnoses fell under the autism spectrum umbrella.

Our team at the Birth to Three organization couldn't believe their ears. The entire group (except for Robert) thought that Zack's case was much more severe than ECEP's extraordinarily generous diagnosis of PDDNOS would indicate. Only Robert was greatly encouraged by Zack's ability to bond with his dad and me, but even he recognized that Zack had a multitude of problematic issues to overcome. The others thought that Zack was obviously a full-fledged, clinically autistic child. Even an ASD diagnosis, which carries with it an assumption of a spectrum with varying degrees of severity, would have fallen short in the opinion of the experts who were spending the greatest amount of time with Zack. They told me in no uncertain terms that Zack must have had the evaluation of a lifetime for them to even offer us PDDNOS.

I don't suppose the name really mattered one way or the other, though, since the odds of success with any diagnosis on the autism spectrum are minimal at best. In fact, studies indicate that high-functioning cases (usually those with higher IQs) tend to have better outcomes. This distinguishing criterion did not apply to Zack, however; ECEP determined his IQ to be 50 during his first evaluation. Whether he was PDDNOS, ASD, or clinically autistic, it honestly didn't matter one iota. No one who knew Zack at the time could have disputed that even with a monumental amount of work, the chances of noticeable improvement were practically non-existent.

Now that we had obtained a formal diagnosis, our agency was able to offer us 17 hours per week of various therapies. They doubled the amount of time with the speech therapist, occupational therapist, and early childhood developmental specialist. In addition, they provided a dance therapist, a nutritionist, a preschool class, and a feeding class that addressed his issues with eating. Four hours per week of respite services (temporary relief or rest for parents) was also offered to us, as well as an additional psychologist to gauge my emotional well-being.

There was another condition (aside from the official diagnosis) placed upon the implementation of these additional services. I was required to participate in all of the therapy sessions in order to learn what needed to be done the other 25 hours per week. I couldn't use that time to clean house, do laundry, or prepare meals. Those kinds of chores had already become a very low priority: Zack's therapy took precedence in all instances. Nevertheless, this stipulation was just fine with me because I really wanted to learn these skills so that I could help Zack as much as possible.

In fact, I became so knowledgeable that I was able to teach Jennifer, our wonderful respite provider, how to provide therapy for Zack. I paid her for additional hours of help because she did such an amazing job with him. When I just couldn't push him any longer, she was still able to press on.

Easy therapy sessions were non-productive for Zack; pushing him to the verge of a meltdown was the only course of action that produced real results. Trying to get his brain to form a new neurological pathway was like trying to shove sand into a balloon—not an easy endeavor, by any stretch of the imagination. Those extra hours of help kept me sane, especially on the weekends. Jennifer was a lifesaver for our family, and we will never forget her.

Of course, some therapists were definitely better than others. Certain ones really connected with Zack on a personal level. They were able to draw him out of his "stims," attention deficits, noncooperative tendencies, and—most importantly—out of his tantrums. All the while, they still pushed him to learn. Unfortunately, other therapists were a poor match. One of them didn't have a clue how to connect with Zack, so he would just sit and watch Zack disappear into his own little world. He would just tap his chin and suggest that we reschedule for a time when Zack was more willing to "cooperate."

The problem was that Zack was never in the mood to engage and cooperate. He had to be forced to do these things, or he never would. I would get right in Zack's face and insist that he get involved. If I had to participate in all of the therapy sessions, then by golly, Zack had to participate in them too. I wasn't about to let a precious hour of therapy slip away without a fight. Sometimes

Zack was brought out of his own world with minimal resistance, but most of the time it was a major struggle, accompanied by our all too familiar "friends"—Screeching and Tantrums.

Another therapist suddenly decided to drop one of our hours of therapy per week because he felt Zack didn't need it any more. Even if he had discussed it with us before-hand we would not have consented. The number of hours of one-on-one engagement was so very important to Zack at this stage. Even if he *was* making progress in this particular area of therapy, we still needed more help. Besides, a therapist lacks the legal authority to change services without parental consent. This particular therapist often failed to show up at the house without calling to cancel and reschedule, which was quite irritating. So I had quite a dilemma on my hands. What was worth fighting for? Should I pursue more hours with this therapist when I wasn't very satisfied with the job he was doing? Instead, I decided to focus my energy on those things I could actually change.

Our Birth to Three program normally provides services only until age three. Since Zack's birthday falls in October, he missed the cut-off point and was therefore eligible to receive help for another year. The following spring, after having worked with the agency for about a year, we decided it would be more beneficial for Zack to transfer to the public school system during the summer. This would allow him to have four half-days per week of summer school during the entire month of June. Continuity and structure were essential for Zack to avoid skill regression, so summer school appeared to be our best option.

By this point, I also felt equipped to train several more college students to help make up for the loss of therapy hours. College students are an exceptional resource—one I highly recommend to everyone presently living through this ordeal. We really benefited from their youth, enthusiasm, and willingness to learn and gain real-life experience. Perhaps most importantly, we really appreciated their willingness to work for $10 an hour. Private professional therapists for autism are not covered by most insurance plans, and some charge $200 or more per hour. When your child needs a minimum of 42 hours a week of therapy, the cost for sessions can get out of hand in no time. Many families go into a great amount of debt or are forced to take on multiple extra jobs to try to pay for this therapy. I even know one couple who divorced, agreeing that custody should be placed with the non-working parent , just so the child would qualify for and benefit from Medicaid and SSI services. Yes, some parents are *that* desperate for help! We consider ourselves very blessed that we were able to get by without that degree of upheaval in our lives, financially or otherwise. But we definitely could not have done this without our college students.

Chelsea, our phenomenal young psychology major, had worked at a reputable autism clinic in Maryland before coming to work for us. She required no training whatsoever. Not only was she experienced, but she was also a natural—no question about it. She mentioned to me recently that she wants to adopt a child with autism when she is through having kids of her own. Now *this* is a person who is truly called to work in the field of autism! She had an extra-special way with Zack and could get him to cooperate and absorb more material than the rest of us could ever hope to achieve. What a blessing she was to us!

Personality and temperament played a big role in how effective the students were in dealing with Zack. Some really connected with him and taught him a great many things as a result of that connection, demonstrating how imperative it is for a child with autism to form some kind of bond with a therapist. As with any interpersonal relationship, some combinations are far superior to others.

It was also necessary for me to feel comfortable with the work ethic of the students so that I could feel at ease to go about my housework or take a nap. One of our college students worked extremely hard but only when I was in the room. If I stepped out for even a moment, she allowed herself to become less engaged with Zack. She only lasted two weeks at our house because I needed someone who didn't require the constant monitoring of a babysitter.

Speaking of babysitters, there was an amazing one, Diane, at my Jazzercise class. Yes, throughout this extremely difficult time I still made the effort to go to Jazzercise. In fact, staying with this class for the sake of my own mental health was the first decision I made when we received Zack's diagnosis. My pent-up anxiety, anger, frustration, exasperation, and sadness required a physical outlet; and Jazzercise was the perfect opportunity to vent these emotions. Also, Diane was wonderfully patient with Zack, and she never permitted him to play in the corner all by himself. She planned arts and crafts projects, which helped Zack with his fine motor skills, and encouraged lots of social games such as "Red Light/Green Light" and "Simon Says."

To make things easier for Diane, I organized a packet of information all about Zack. I explained his numerous sign language approximations, provided suggestions for problem behaviors, listed current academic goals, and indicated his schedule for the week. This gave her the tools she needed when Zack acted out or pursued an unproductive tangent; in essence, she was as prepared as possible for anything he might do. Yet, there were still definitely instances when I was called out of class because he wouldn't allow her to change his diaper, or his tantrums were too much for her to take. These incidents, however, occurred only rarely by Zack standards. Most of the time, Diane handled him with much grace and maturity. We both understood that Zack was interacting with a new authority figure in a new environment filled with social activities where he was expected to behave himself. Besides the welcome benefits Jazzercise provided for my mental and physical well-being,

I counted each class as an hour of therapy for Zack, so I didn't feel any guilt about it whatsoever.

For a year and a half we also pursued speech therapy for Zack through the New Mexico State University Speech and Hearing Center. At this clinic, speech and language pathology students worked with Zack and earned practicum hours under the direct supervision of a professor/adviser. One of the professors was very agreeable and asked me for a lot of input and suggestions about what goals to work on, the direction of the therapy, and strategies to take home to practice. I found this relationship extremely rewarding because she recognized that I had a lot of valuable insight about my son and his needs, and it was important to me to feel as though we were working together as a team.

Regrettably, the other professor/adviser appeared to be unwilling to take any of my ideas into consideration. I assume she felt that she was the expert and therefore had complete control over his program. If she had made the effort to explain her strategies to me, I may have been willing to bite my tongue and take a back seat. But I still needed to feel included in the process so that I would feel competent taking these tools home to practice. With her, I definitely did not feel like we were members of a team working toward a common goal. Unfortunately, this particular professor was the main adviser for the program, so I was required to deal with her the majority of the time. Because it was quite costly and there was a sizable time commitment, I decided after a year and a half that I could no longer tolerate the situation and terminated our participation. I'm sure some parents are willing to just let the experts "do their job," assuming that their expertise is beyond reproach. In our case, however, I whole-heartedly believed that this sort of blind acceptance was not in Zack's best interest. Merely accepting the advice of the "experts" rather than educating myself would not have allowed me to provide Zack with the consistency I knew he required. Individuals with autism usually have difficulty generalizing concepts to multiple situations. Zack was no exception. Indeed, conformity across the various therapy environments was crucial for his success.

Doing what I believed in my heart to be appropriate for Zack helped keep me sane and motivated throughout the years of therapy. I didn't want to sit back and do nothing. Zack was my son, and he needed a lot of help. I was going to help him any way that I could, and it was this attitude that set me up for a particularly strange encounter. . . .

The day Zack graduated from our Birth to Three agency, the manager pulled me aside. She told me that I needed to learn to "tone it down a notch or two" and not be quite so intense and involved. Apparently several of the professional therapists had been intimidated by my overzealous participation in the therapy. I tried my best to offer them free rein at every opportunity; but when they passively sat there, watching and wondering what to do as my baby stimmed in the corner, I got involved. *Surely* I wasn't expected to allow the situation to continue on this way.

Advocacy for one's child is an absolute necessity with autism. If someone had felt that there was a problem with my actions, why didn't they bring it up with me instead of asking the boss to reprimand me? Also, all this came up after working with them *for over a year*! I strongly believe they should have aspired to do their jobs better so I wouldn't have felt the pressing need to intervene. If I did step on toes, I did so only because I had no other choice. What I desired most of all was to take a break from this insanity. I wanted help—not a power trip.

Remember, in the beginning the agency had insisted that I participate in all of the therapy sessions. Then, why were there complaints when I did just that? Furthermore, I am convinced that my high level of intensity and non-stop dedication were absolutely essential to Zack's recovery. I will never regret being there for my precious boy when he needed me the most.

Obviously, not all professionals receive specific training regarding strategies for the management of a child affected by autism. I always appreciated and respected those therapists who—out of a desire to excel in their field and provide the best care—learned as much as possible in order to help my Zack. This level of dedication is necessary for success, both on the part of the family and all the therapists involved.

So, if others are telling you to relax, take it easy, and not be so intense about this whole thing, my advice is to pay them no heed. There are "experts" who have actually suggested to frustrated parents in dire need of specific strategies and advice to "just accept it; it is part of the autism." Useless, hopeless statements should be ignored. Seek better counsel. There is a wealth of possibilities for you and your child. *Never* resign your child's potential to the opinions of the professional community solely because they are the professionals. Trust your instincts, learn all you can, and strive to help your child live up to his or her greatest potential. Without your active involvement, there is less hope for your child. *You* are the most important therapist your child will ever have. *You* are the one who lives with your child and can make sure their therapy goals are applied to daily living.

I know these comments add another level of pressure to you as parents of a child with autism. But I believe with my whole heart that your role in all of this is by far the most critical element in your child's progress. Do not be discouraged: a parent's love and commitment is a mighty powerful thing.

The strongest evidence of love is sacrifice.
—Caroline Fry[1]

1 Copyright 1996 Cook Communications Ministries. God's Little Instruction Book For Men by Honor Books. Used with permission. All rights reserved.

Tatianna Dickens

Let us not become weary in doing good, for at the proper time we will reap a harvest if we do not give up.
(Galatians 6:9)

4

Mary Kay: Sometimes a Woman Just Needs to Cry

One evening, when Zack was a little over three years old and we were knee-deep in therapy, I decided that I needed a night out of the house more than anything else I could imagine. A friend was hosting a Mary Kay cosmetics party for fellow stay-at-home moms, and this seemed like the perfect opportunity to unwind and stop thinking about autism for the first time in a very long while. Throughout my enormously demanding days with Zack, I often felt too busy to even breathe. Finally, I had the chance to pamper myself, a luxury long overdue. I actually managed to find the time to shower and transform myself into a relatively presentable individual, a rare occurrence during this stage of the game. My heart soared, full of expectation, as I headed for my relaxing party.

Little did I know that the ice-breaker question was waiting to pounce on my unsuspecting spirit: "Where do you see yourself in five years?" Seems benign enough, doesn't it? Well, it wasn't. As I started to contemplate this simple question, I was overwhelmed with feelings of desperation. "Five years? Five years? Where do I see myself in five years?" my mind raced. For the past six months I had been exposed to an endless supply of screeching, tantrums, and stimming. All the while, I was hoping against hope that somehow I was drawing my precious boy out of his own little world. There was also the looming possibility that there would never be an end to this heartbreak that was my life. "Five years? Five years? You've got to be kidding me," I thought. I had spent every waking moment over the last six months wondering how I was going to survive the next five minutes, and now I was expected to be able to look ahead five years? And I was supposed to answer this question with joy and eager anticipation?

I simply could not bear to continue down this path, dreaming about the future. My dreams were dead at this point because my existence was purely survival mode. At the time, I had no clue that there actually was light at the end of my tunnel and I would be able to happily dream about my life again someday. The prospect of answering this seemingly light-hearted, simple question was just too daunting. I could feel pain and heartbreak welling up within me. No longer could I just pretend to be graciously handling my adorable son's devastating disorder. I broke down, sobbing uncontrollably in front of friends and strangers alike. Choking on the breaths I had so longed for just a short while ago, my frantic fears and shattered dreams refused to remain captive any longer; they had to be released.

My friends were overcome with sadness and pity, and they did their best to console me but to no avail. The hostess even offered me a free vacation she had earned from Mary Kay. I appreciated her thoughtfulness, but I knew that I couldn't just drop everything and leave for even three days without it having a dramatic negative impact on the effectiveness of the therapy with Zack. Everything we worked on during the intense therapy sessions had to be generalized to daily living, so we practiced all of the drills continuously, even during so-called "down time." Repetition, review, and consistency of routine were crucial to maintaining Zack's current levels. A getaway of even three days was completely out of the question.

What I actually needed most was a good, long cry. But before too much time had passed, I realized that I had to stop crying because I knew what tomorrow had in store— another six-hour minimum day of intense one-on-one therapy. Whether I liked it or not, I would have to pull myself together and get to work. No matter how tired or sad I was, I felt like I was Zack's only hope for improvement. How I longed for a break, a chance to escape and regroup and recover a little bit. Despite my desire for some personal healing time, it simply wasn't practical at this point.

When Zack was a little more than three years of age, we were invited to go to Denmark to visit my husband's brother and new wife. However, we were very wisely counseled against taking such a long trip by our lead psychologist, Robert. Four months later, my mother-in-law, Karon, offered to watch all three of our kids so we could take advantage of the Mary Kay vacation gift after all. Her willingness to watch them, even our very hard-to-live-with Zack, was such a particularly selfless, incredible gesture. I was so thoroughly worn out that surely I wasn't going to be able to keep up these exhausting efforts indefinitely. Ultimately, we conceded and took off for three days. We hoped and prayed that this short jaunt wouldn't prove terribly detrimental for Zack.

I'm sure Karon did the very best she could, but working to maintain an intense level of interaction with one who doesn't care to interact is exhausting beyond belief. Trust me, I know. We deeply appreciated her desire to help, and it was an indescribable blessing to get away. Leaving the constant craziness behind, even if it was just for a brief time, was a welcome relief.

Unfortunately, our three-day vacation cost Zack many of the skills we had previously worked on and mastered. We came home to a little boy who had regressed so much that a month of especially excruciating therapy was necessary in order for him to regain his pre-trip skill levels. Regretting our decision to take off in the first place, I felt a great deal of guilt over what I had just "done" to him and myself.

After managing to survive that extremely difficult month, I felt like I deserved a reward for all of the hard work I had just poured into Zack. A friend of mine recommended a good massage therapist, so I eagerly scheduled a time for the first massage in my life. I could hardly contain my enthusiasm. "This will be great!" I said to myself.

Under most circumstances, a massage can be a wonderfully peaceful and relaxing experience; this was definitely the effect I anticipated when I set out for my appointment. In my case, though, it turned out to be far too much of a stress reliever. Once again, all of the fragile emotions I had been holding inside came bubbling up to the surface. I cried and cried throughout the entire massage, sharing little bits and pieces of my agonizing experience with the poor masseuse. She ended up feeling so sorry for me that she generously gave me the massage on the house.

It is amazing how many tears you can cry, even after you think you are all cried out. When the last thing you ever want to do is shed one more tear, crying is usually the one thing you can do with ease. I feel as though I've cried enough for two lifetimes. Occasionally when I look back over my experience with Zack's autism, I wonder if I should have considered taking antidepressants for the sake of my other two children, because they saw me cry so often. Had I not been such a mess, I think that this period of time may have been significantly easier on them. Thank the Lord, kids are remarkably resilient. When I ask my oldest, Jacob, what he remembers about teaching Zack to talk, he only mentions the multitudes of therapists who came to our house. Any images of his distraught mom were now too distant to recall. The Lord was not only looking after Zack and me but protecting Jacob's memories as well. God is so very good; His loving works are all around us.

A parent of a child with autism never takes even the tiniest developmental milestone for granted, at least I never did. I would share my little moments of excitement with anyone who would listen: "Zack initiated an incomplete phrase with me." "Zack had a moment of good eye contact." "Zack had a breakthrough with sharing and pretend play." Sometimes, when I revealed such hints of progress to our therapists, they would roll their eyes in disbelief and say, "Yeah, sure. He did that. Uh-huh. That's fantastic." These comments were made to me, the "deluded and desperate mother," with no inflection whatsoever. The flat responses clearly portrayed their unwillingness to trust my enthusiastic depictions. I can't say that I really blamed them, but it would have been nice not to have to face such obvious expressions of doubt. The therapists knew that with every ounce of my being, I wanted to see Zack achieve these milestones. Perhaps they thought that in my sleep-deprived state I was hallucinating about his steps forward. With autism, skills can take a very long time to develop, and they aren't usually consistent while they're in the process of becoming solid. Sometimes Zack wouldn't show off the new skill he mastered until months later. Then, and only then, was I able to prove my earlier claims and justify the excitement I had displayed.

I marveled at every little bit of progress Zack made, and in one sense, that progress inspired me to renew my dedication toward our therapy goals. Even on these good days, though, it was still very easy for me to slip into depression. The fact that I took delight in every small improvement only brought to my attention how dismally far behind he really was. Each of those incidents was also a painful reminder of the immense—no, the completely insurmountable—amount of work yet to be done. Discouraging thoughts ran through my mind over and over: "My son is never, ever going to come close to catching up with other kids his age. We are running out of time, too! Zack will be five before we know it. If he doesn't make significant gains by then, all will be lost!"

My feelings of desperation would overwhelm me once again, and I would burst into tears for the millionth time. I detested the fact that I cried so much, but I just couldn't seem to help myself. One girlfriend told me that she was through with crying over her boy with autism. She was going to make herself stop, once and for all. I remember thinking, "Wow! What strength! What determination! How is she going to be able to pull that off? What is her secret?" I wanted in on that kind of emotional stability! Unfortunately, try as she might, she was unsuccessful overcoming this challenge, just as I was. Such is the toll of autism.

I have a faith that teaches God never gives anyone more than he or she can handle without His help. I firmly believe this to be true. It's easier to trust this truth now that I am not presently living through the anguish of having a child with autism. But when we were in the midst of it, I remember asking God more than once if He was sure I could handle this. I often felt that I couldn't take it for even one more minute.

I recall thinking, "This would all be easier if Zack had a terminal illness!" At least I felt like there would be an end in sight if that were the case. I know how horrible it sounds, but this entire experience was so awful that at times I just wanted it to end. Running away was also a fairly common daydream: "If I could escape, surely life wouldn't be so painful!" I also remember thinking how much easier it would be just to end my life. Even though I knew such an action was unacceptable to my Creator, I just wanted my pain to cease. But then, who would be there for Zack? So many times I felt trapped in inexplicable agony that no one else could even come close to understanding. I felt completely alone and isolated.

For the first year and a half, I woke up every morning exhausted and in tears. As I cried and prayed, I begged God to release me from this burden because I knew He had the power to do it. If that was not His will, then I would need Him to carry me throughout the day. All hopes of recovery required Zack to participate for a minimum of six hours of therapy, seven days a week. I had nothing left within me to give him, so the Lord *did* carry me. He performed a miracle on my son and even used me in the process. I am totally convinced that I was sustained solely by the strength of His all-consuming, unfailing love. I know that I would never have survived this experience without Him.

In retrospect, I can actually look back and see Zack's autism as a huge blessing. It was by far the worst experience I've ever lived through, and at times it nearly killed me. Nevertheless, the Lord's strength prevailed through my weakness, and He used Zack's autism for His glory. I have grown so much from this experience—as a Christian, a wife, a woman, and a mom. I am not the same person I used to be, and this is a very good thing. Now, I never take even the smallest achievement for granted when it comes to any of my kids. I see God's wondrous works all around me. Life is amazing, and He made it that way. Now I don't mind it at all when I cry, for they are happy tears that flow freely as a result of the miracle that is my son.

A mother's love is patient and forgiving when all others are forsaking, and it never fails or falters, even though the heart is breaking.
—Helen Steiner Rice[1]

Those who sow in tears will reap with songs of joy.
(Psalm 126:5)

1 Copyright 1995 Cook Communications Ministries. God's Little Instruction Book For Mom by Honor Books. Used with permission. All rights reserved.

5

Tantrums: Surviving Wal-Mart

Having a child with autism forced me to do some real soul-searching. I used to be one of those people who looked disparagingly at parents whose children were out of control. Why couldn't they make their children mind? I assumed that they just didn't know how to be firm with their kids or teach them proper behavior. Basically, I thought they were bad parents. I thought to myself, "When I have kids, they will never act this way! I will be a *good* parent." There was no conceivable instance in which I could imagine myself tolerating their bad behavior. Regrettably, now I recognize that I was far too judgmental and carried myself with an air of undeniable superiority. That was then. Now I know what it is like to live with the anguish of autism. When I see a parent in distress over their child for any reason, I no longer offer a disapproving glance or word. Instead, I reach out in sincere sympathy with a genuine desire to help in any way I can.

One common expression of autism involves the child throwing unbelievable temper tantrums that make an ordinary two-year-old's conniption fits seem insignificant by comparison. This was true in our case. Self-injurious behavior is often an element of these tantrums. We were fortunate that Zack only banged his head twice before he came to the conclusion that it hurt too much to continue. Unfortunately, his tantrums included intolerable ear-piercing, high-decibel screeching.

Every time Zack was asked to engage with someone when he

didn't want to, he screeched. The same was true when someone touched him; when there was something on his plate that he didn't like; when the plate, utensils, and cups were not green; when he wasn't wearing green; when the book didn't have a frog in it; when his routine changed; when we insisted that he be flexible if we changed the rules or structure of a game; when someone took his picture; when he was asked to stop his self-stimulatory behaviors (stimming); when he was frustrated; when we insisted that he point to a picture in a book; when he was expected to use his sign language to communicate; when he had to transition from one activity to another; when he was asked to grasp a writing utensil; when his hands were dirty; when he was hungry; when he was thirsty; when his grandparents tried to hug him. . . .Zack's tantrums occurred with such frequency and intensity that I was afraid to leave the house. The prospect of going out in public with him, even to run the simplest errands, mortified me. Judgmental looks and the lack of understanding from others, along with the seemingly unending embarrassment, were all too much to take. I had to find an effective solution.

There are several different strategies that professionals employ to curb these unacceptable temper tantrums. Determining the best strategy should not be taken lightly. Such a decision requires much introspection and depends on each individual child and the willingness of parents to use this strategy with never-failing consistency. Also to be considered are the family's values, obligations, scheduled activities and dynamics. These factors all play a role in the implementation and effectiveness of a behavior management program. For example, if a parent must take a child out into the community on a regular basis due to job requirements, that parent must feel comfortable enough with the strategy to use it consistently in public. With some children, ignoring the behavior works wonders. This was not the case with us, because Zack was never happier than when he was being ignored; in short, he would have had no incentive to alter his behavior. Also, we were encouraging constant human interaction, hoping that he would develop positive social skills as a result. For that same reason, we couldn't give him time-outs. Moreover, spanking was not an effective deterrent for him because he had an unnatural response to painful stimuli. (Instances which would hurt typical individuals rarely made any impression on him, yet the slightest loving touch often sent him over the edge.) Along with the need to curtail his inappropriate behavior, we also needed to find appropriate ways to teach him that communicating does not hurt and bonding with others is a good thing.

Our phenomenal lead psychologist, Robert, had advised us to expose Zack to non-stop early intervention therapies if we hoped to see any real signs of progress. My husband and I were wholeheartedly committed to this endeavor, so we participated in hours upon hours of grueling therapy every day. These interventions forced Zack's brain to develop new and productive neurological pathways. Every therapy session was intense and extremely difficult for Zack; therefore, he was continually on the brink of complete and total frustration. Often times I felt like I had no choice but to "torture" this son that I so loved; indeed, I had no more palatable option. He had to be pushed—and pushed hard—if there was any chance of him growing and maturing into the boy I hoped he could be. Persevering as Zack's primary "tormenter" required enormous amounts of trust and belief that what I was doing was in his best interests. Without that glimmer of potential gain, I would not have been able to continue down this path for the next three arduous years.

Endless opportunities to upset Zack lurked around every corner. When Zack was upset, he often resorted to self-stimulatory behaviors. We were committed to redirecting all of his stimming activities into more socially appropriate or "normal" alternatives.

This redirection strategy was yet another source of agitation that pushed Zack into hysterics.

Whenever Zack was asked to do something he didn't want to do (which was nearly all of the time), we were forced to endure a horrendous, screeching tantrum. These outbursts were a source of deep irritation and embarrassment for me. In an effort to eliminate his frustrating response, we implemented a technique I "fondly" labeled the "therapy hold." This hold is particularly controversial in some circles because some view it as cruel and unusual punishment. In fact, I seldom performed it in public for fear that others would not understand the purpose and necessity of the hold nor our desperate situation. This method worked for us, however, and has worked for countless others as well. I believe the therapy hold has the potential to produce marvelous results if used correctly and consistently.

Initially, Robert demonstrated this process for me, telling me that I would be performing it so often that the first one was "on the house." Let me tell you, that first one was a doozy! Robert had to restrain Zack for a very long time during a temper tantrum, complete with his excruciatingly loud, high-pitched screeching. My heart went out to them both. I began to wonder if Robert had the stamina to win this battle of the wills. The demonstration was truly beyond description. Actually, I think it would have been easier for me to perform the hold on Zack rather than watch someone else endure the tantrum. Zack was *my* responsibility, after all. It was hard for me to knowingly subject someone else to this unbearable situation.

This technique is not for everyone, especially not for the faint of heart. Nevertheless, I had come to trust in Robert's judgment implicitly, and the use of this tactic *did* prove effective in helping our family get Zack's tantrums under control. Every time he screeched, I sat down on the floor with my legs crossed, grabbed him, and held him ever so tightly while pinning his arms to his chest with one of my arms. Both of his knees were tucked in with my other arm so that he could not move at all. Zack was still screeching, mind you, and now his mouth was only inches away from my ears. I quietly repeated again and again, "You need to be calm and quiet. You need to be calm and quiet." In complete and utter desperation I would pray, tears streaming down my face, "My baby! My baby! What has happened to my baby? Lord, help me get through this! Help me get through this! I can't do this alone!"

Restraining Zack proved even more frustrating in our situation than it might otherwise have been. Although he was 33 months old when James and I began this intervention, his receptive language was that of a 12- to 18-month-old. That being the case, we were sure he didn't understand one word of this "mantra" being spoken to him. Regardless of this fact, we refused to let him go until he was both calm and quiet. Then we would release him immediately, thus providing positive reinforcement for his change of behavior. Even though he didn't fully comprehend the words "calm" and "quiet," he gradually learned to respond in a calm and quiet manner.

As I understand it, the purpose of this approach is two-fold. First, it teaches the child that he has control over his own behavior as well as the consequences that follow. Also, if the child has a strong sensory need, this tight embrace can be very soothing. Although Zack most definitely had a strong sensory need at the time, this particular restraint just made him furious. He became incredibly anxious any time he was touched, except when it was on his terms. The therapy hold took place on *my* terms, not Zack's, so it took him quite a while to adjust to the process. Ultimately, he was able to learn how to avoid the unpleasantness by eliminating his intemperate ways.

Over the course of the first month, Zack and I had an average of 20 therapy holds per day, each lasting about 15 minutes. My ears would ring even on the rare occasions when he wasn't screeching, which made me wonder if I had suffered some degree of hearing loss. The volume of his screaming really was insufferable. The second month, we decided to take Zack off of dairy products at the recommendation of several books I had read. He must have experienced withdrawal, because over the next two weeks the number of restraints nearly doubled, and the tantrums were more severe. Then, for the remainder of the month, he settled back into his previous pattern. The third month, after Zack's system was through flushing out the casein (dairy) proteins, he averaged 10 to 15 holds per day with the duration being around 10 minutes. By the fourth month, I was encouraged by the dramatic decrease in frequency and intensity of his tantrums. Approximately 10 holds a day were required, each lasting only five to 10 minutes. This trend continued until Zack was also taken off gluten, a protein substance found in wheat, oats, barley, and rye, when he was a little over three years old. This time we had to cope with an entire month of detoxification and subsequent withdrawal tantrums. But after that, things began to settle down again, and the need for therapy holds became progressively less frequent.

Then something extraordinary happened! When Zack was about three and a half years old, I was able to start reasoning with him about his behavior. The therapy hold wasn't gone for good, but we were getting closer to that goal. If he started to throw a tantrum, I would ask him, "Do you need a hug?" This put the ball in his court, giving him the opportunity to demonstrate some self-control. (Incidentally, I chose these particular words for a specific reason. An adult trying to handle an altercation involving any child at school or on the playground might use this very question. I hoped that someday Zack would be able to take these familiar words spoken by a stranger and still be able to calm himself down.) Sometimes Zack would answer no and would self-manage his negative behavior by changing it into something acceptable. When this did not work, I would continue, "Do *I* need to hug you?" This put the ball firmly in my court. This question meant that he must shape up now, or else. He would either say no using an appropriate behavior modification, or we would resort to the therapy hold.

This exercise played a significant role in helping Zack meet a crucial developmental milestone: he learned how to take control of his own behavior so that I wouldn't have to do it. Children with autism often discover that self-control and behavior management are difficult skills for them to master. Undoubtedly, Zack needed this therapy hold method to replace unacceptable behavior with appropriate self-management. In the beginning I wondered if it would ever really get through to him and make a difference, but it did work. . .eventually.

One of the most frustrating things about autism is that no skill is ever acquired quickly. As a parent, the sooner you come to terms with that fact, the better off you will be. Because I was an impatient person, this was a difficult lesson for me to learn, but I did manage to do so with the Lord's help. While God used me to teach Zack self-control, He also used Zack to teach me some measure of patience. Much to my surprise, thankfulness, another blessing of the Spirit, was also imparted to me as a result of my experience with Zack's autism.

For instance, I am very thankful that he was so young when we attempted to address these tantrums. Zack was strong for his age, and these restraints were quite a workout. Had he been older, I might not have been physically strong enough to control him for such long periods. This strenuous undertaking ultimately paid off, and I will always be grateful for that fact.

The progress we made with the help of this valuable technique provided us the opportunity to explore the world outside our house. What a wonderful gift was given to us! It allowed Zack to expand his horizons like never before. Now I had the chance to embarrass myself at Wal-Mart in a much more satisfying way. I could actually teach him all about things like produce: "This is a banana. Ba-na-na, ba-na-na. It is yellow, ye-llow, ye-llow. Bananas are for eating. Eat, eat, eat. I like bananas. They are sweet. Yum, yum, yum. And look, the lemons are yellow too! Lemons are not sweet. They are sour. They make my face look like this." (Imagine a sour lemon-face.) People certainly stared at me like I was an escapee from a mental hospital, but that was just fine with me. I often *felt* like a mental patient who had just escaped.

These "produce aisle reflections" were a step in the right direction, however. With every little step I felt a little more hope, and I would hold fast to that hope with all my strength. Allowing myself to be encouraged by tiny hints of progress prevented me from being entirely consumed by sadness and desperation. Clinging to any small hope empowered me to survive the challenges that every day held, while maintaining a bit of sanity.

Remember, when your child has a tantrum, don't have one of your own.
—Dr. J. Kuriansky [1]

Not only so, but we also rejoice in our sufferings, because we know that suffering produces perseverance; perseverance, character; and character, hope. And hope does not disappoint us, because God has poured out his love into our hearts by the Holy Spirit, whom he has given us.
(Romans 5:3-5)

1Copyright 1996 Cook Communications Ministries. God's Little Instruction Book For Women by Honor Books. Used with permission. All rights reserved.

6

String: Obsessions Redirected

Of all the disturbing expressions of autism, I think the one that bothered me most was the self-stimulatory behavior, also called "stimming." This characteristic can't help but scream out, "Hey. . .look at what that weird kid is doing. What in the world is wrong with him? Why is he doing that? Why doesn't he stop?. . . .He must have autism."

Whereas screeching and tantrums are viewed as the workings of an ill-behaved child, a youngster who incessantly wraps and then unwraps string around his finger, oddly flaps his hands, or growls like a dinosaur for hours on end may as well be wearing a neon sign flashing, "mental defect." Of course, I never wanted anyone to be thinking such a horrible thing about my precious little boy. I so desperately loved him, but I knew that these conspicuous mannerisms would be far too hard for most people to ignore.

Many experts believe that children with autism are often frightened and perplexed by their environment. They have such a difficult time processing and making sense of their external surroundings that they create a constant "white noise" or distraction which they can command. This avoidance behavior usually meets a particular sensory need as well. It can manifest in many forms, but the form of the stim in and of itself really isn't that significant. These children perceive that they can control some aspect of their world by using this sensory input that soothes them and allows them to tolerate being unavoidably trapped in a confusing and scary place. The problem with this form of survival adaptation is that it does not allow these kids to function in any kind of "normal" way within a social climate.

Often times, children with autism like to watch spinning things or shiny, glittery things. They may flick small objects just inside their peripheral vision. Many organize things obsessively or have non-functional routines that they can't deviate from under any circumstances. There are more commonly recognized stims as well, such as hitting things in a repetitive manner, walking or loping in circles, and inordinate blinking or head-shaking. Probably the most familiar stim is hand-flapping. Sometimes a child with autism will repeatedly pick up small objects like leaves or wood chips and then watch them fall to the ground as they drop them.

Every child with autism is a unique individual, and from that uniqueness emerges an individual expression of autism. No two children with autism are exactly alike with predictable behaviors and symptoms. Unlike diabetes or heart disease, for which tests are standardized and diagnoses often inherently obvious, a diagnosis of autism requires input from a multidisciplinary team of experts as well as parents. That being the case, these self-stimulatory tendencies are still far more glaring than the other, more subtle characteristics of autism.

The first stim Zack demonstrated was a constant desire to pound things with a stick. All boys like to hit things, but typical boys hit things in a "normal" way. After a while, a typical boy moves on to another activity or incorporates some sort of social routine, with the game evolving in some manner or form. Zack, on the other hand, would have struck objects with his stick for hours without deviating in the slightest—had we allowed it. Ignoring the real world and entering his very own introverted "stick world" was second nature to him. Every time we made him stop the whacking, huge tantrums followed. It was absolutely maddening! At least 20 times a day, I attempted to redirect him to an activity that was less obsessive/compulsive and more socially acceptable. I tried to encourage more "normal" activities like running, jumping on a trampoline, or playing a musical instrument. (Society deems these forms of escape appropriate.)

When my efforts to redirect him failed and the tantrums persisted, I resorted to the therapy hold. But first and foremost, I sought to find a suitable alternative to his stimming. Replacing a stim with an activity that provides a similar sensory experience is the best way to redirect the non-desired behavior. In this way, the sensory need that has been met by the stim is now being met by the new activity. The goal is to introduce the child to a socially appropriate means of achieving the calming effect he or she desires without appearing so odd.

Zack's flailing, for example, was fairly easy to extinguish once we discovered the intrinsic benefits of our small exercise trampoline. The vestibular motion he experienced on the trampoline was similar to that of the up-and-down motion of his arms. It also provided a visual sensation approximate to watching the stick go up and down. Jumping on a trampoline is a much more acceptable pastime, and Zack found it entertaining enough to make the elimination of this stim relatively painless.

Over the next two years, every time we successfully extinguished one stim, another would inevitably manifest itself. We went through the sand-falling-through- fingers phase, the picture exchange card-dropping-and-flittering phase, the walking-and- loping-in-circles phase, the hand-flapping phase and the incessant-dinosaur phase. But before I describe these stages, I have to address the most difficult stim we ever ran across. This one was absolutely insidious, because we were unable to find a decent substitute that met Zack's particular sensory need.

String! String! Why did it have to be string? I could stand *any-*

thing but string! Why string was ever allowed to co-exist in Zack's universe is beyond me. It is a horrible, vile substance; and if I never see string again, it will be too soon. Now, you may be asking, "Why all of this fuss over something harmless like string?" Well, it doesn't seem so harmless when your son insists on wrapping it and then unwrapping it around his fingers 24/7. Whenever Zack got his hands on string, it was as if he had wandered off into some sort of dream world where no one else was welcome—not even me. Without a doubt, this solitary activity both thrilled and placated him at the same time. As I watched, I couldn't help but find this extremely focused yet spaced-out demonstration profoundly unnerving. This was not good for Zack at all, and I immediately saw the need to put an end to the fixation. For all the tantrums ravaging our lives, the worst ones always came when I took his string away. Exasperated by such outbursts, I hunted for string around the house to discard every morning for months, hoping that Zack would not be able to find any. Yet somehow he always managed to track some down—every morning.

After weeks of failed redirections, we resorted to systematic desensitization therapy (or "cruel and unusual torture therapy," as it came to be known in our house). We draped a piece of string over the armoire door, just beyond Zack's reach. He would fume and fuss for about 15 minutes and finally move on to something else. When he wasn't obsessing over the string, we would lower it to his level. If he grabbed the string and started to stim, we would raise it up until it was once again just out of his reach. And then, the inevitable tantrum erupted. These events unfolded over and over for about three months until he was finally able to ignore the string completely, even when it was available to him. (*Thanks so much for coming up with that great strategy, Robert! I think Zack and I would still be searching every morning for errant string without your brilliant help.)*

Then Zack began picking up sand and watching it fall through his fingers, over and over and over again. Every time he went out to the sandbox, that was all he wanted to do. Since one of the many developmental delays Zack experienced at this time was a lack of pretend play, we took advantage of this opportunity to teach him how to play with dump trucks. This included showing him how to get his hands muddy without screeching and how to take turns with the hose. We also encouraged him to make truck noises to further develop his oral motor skills. All of this teaching and forced engagement, however, ruined the whole sandbox experience for Zack. He soon concluded that it would be easier to stim on something else, and stim on something else he did.

Since Zack was basically nonverbal when we first started working with our Birth to Three agency, one of the communication strategies they tried was the Picture Exchange Card System (PECS). This strategy uses laminated cards with pictures on them, which represent words. By presenting a specific PEC to another person, kids lacking verbal skills can learn to communicate. Initially, we had approximately 50 cards, ranging from food to family members to favorite activities. Many parents benefit a lot from these cards, and life with their special child becomes much more pleasant and manageable. Our problem was that the only thing Zack wanted to do with the cards was throw them up and watch them flitter to the ground, and throw them up again and watch them flitter to the ground, and. . . well, you get the picture. The therapists and I used these cards for the distinct purpose of teaching him vocabulary, so in the long run we ended up using a lot more than 50 cards. But Zack was never allowed to handle them himself, for obvious reasons. There was no way these PECs were going to help Zack communicate beyond the benefits of increasing his base vocabulary. Teaching him sign language was our best—in fact, our only—conceivable plan of action.

Next came one of Zack's easiest stims to redirect. He had gotten into the habit of walking or loping in circles multiple times a day, usually in the vicinity of our living room. When I caught him in the act, I always brought this behavior to his attention: "Zack, what are you doing?" Sometimes he was so engrossed in the movement that I had to physically stop him before he acknowledged my existence and listened to me. He would answer, "Rau-ow, rau-ow," while spinning his finger next to his cheek. This was his way of saying, "I'm going around and around." Then I would gently grab his hand, demonstrate how to tap my leg, and say, "Let's run, Mom." Together we ran from the living room to the kitchen, then to the foyer, and back to the living room. This accomplished two goals: 1) I was encouraging a positive social interaction; and 2) I was redirecting a very odd behavior to something more appropriate.

Running is much more socially acceptable, and Zack really enjoyed it. A few months after introducing this technique, something clicked, and he would actually catch himself going in circles. He would then self-manage and redirect his own behavior by coming over to me, tapping my leg, and giving me his approximate version of, "Let's run, Mom." He was choosing to curb his odd behavior and solicit human interaction, which is practically unheard of for someone with autism. (This redirection strategy is also terrific if you decide that you need to lose a few pounds. It works great on both counts.)

By the time we arrived at the next stage, I was able to redirect verbally without too much effort. Zack had the tendency to flap his hands when he was waiting for me or was bored. On the rare occasion when he was out of his familiar environment, surrounded by a lot of strangers or noise, he also expressed anxiety in this way. As long as I was able to give him some one-on-one attention in order to distract him or settle him down, this wasn't a monumental issue for us, compared to the next stim.

Finally, we had to deal with the incessant Dinosaur. For some reason, this stim was particularly difficult to extinguish. Zack was quite awkward socially and rather unsure of himself. In addition to this hindrance, he had to bear the burden of his unrelated speech disorder (apraxia of speech), which made intelligible articulation extremely difficult. Thus, his favorite game on the playground was Dinosaur. Now, I recognize that lots of kids love to play Dinosaur, and if he had played this game like typical children, then I would have been fine with it. Had he incorporated talking and social routines rather than obsessive/compulsive tendencies into the game, I would have been thrilled with that expression of age-appropriate interaction.

But Zack's game of Dinosaur was unquestionably disordered. He contorted his hands into extremely warped, weird-looking claw shapes and ran with a very peculiar gait. He never talked, he only growled. Completely oblivious to the signals sent out by the other kids when they had enough, Zack continued to play with great fervor. This aggravated the other children considerably, and the entire scenario was very painful for me to watch. I desperately wanted Zack to fit in, but it was obvious that his overzealous execution of the game made him fall dismally short. I had to make him stop, and I had to stop him *now*!

So I would put an end to the spectacle by attempting to explain to Zack that the other kids were all done. A screeching tantrum always ensued, as did my implementation of the therapy hold. This managed to replace the initial awkward display with an even more intriguing yet disturbing exhibition. Curious, bewildered observers couldn't help but swarm around and stare at us. I spent many tearful moments praying for an effective distraction that never came. While Zack and I suffered through the ordeal together, I tried to focus on the encouraging aspects of the situation. My child with autism had the desire to interact with the other kids, which was an incredible wonder in itself.

Unfortunately, Zack didn't yet have the skills to interact with enough normalcy to make and maintain friendships. For the next year or so, I taught him the words he must say if he was going to play Dinosaur. I insisted that he use phrases such as, "I'm going to eat you!" and "Run away! I am a big, mean dinosaur!" That way, he would practice his language skills while attempting to develop peer relationships. "Shortly" after I implemented this intervention strategy, Zack's teacher sent a note home praising his progress in the social realm. Describing how he had initiated the Dinosaur game with his peers at recess, she was thrilled because his behavior appeared so normal to her.

But I suspected that, in reality, something quite troubling was afoot. Were Zack's actions really normal, or were they only *relatively* normal on the surface? Immediately I called his teacher and asked her if Zack spoke any words at all during the course of this game. When she told me that he only growled, I explained that he was forbidden to play unless he used his words. It had taken me six months to persuade Zack to play the "talking" version of Dinosaur without a tantrum. He required absolute consistency between the home and school environments if he was ever going to master this skill. I didn't want to work on this game even one day more than was absolutely necessary. Thankfully, Zack had a wonderful teacher who was willing to work with me toward achieving common goals. As an added precautionary measure, she and I set a time limit of five minutes per Dinosaur game. To help Zack transition out of the activity without incident, we counted down each minute. This also kept the obsessive/compulsive quality of the game at bay.

Zack's adherence to our matter-of-fact rules concerning Dinosaur play greatly helped him achieve an appearance of normalcy. This, in turn, made it easier for him to make and maintain friendships. As his imitation skills emerged, he found these peer groups more rewarding as well, because he could follow their lead. Receiving more explicit direction during play time and talking through upcoming events beforehand also helped Zack transition between activities more gracefully. These strategies were all intended to help him fit in and feel like an accepted member of the group.

It wasn't an easy or quick road for any of us to travel, but we did eventually manage to pull Zack out of his own little dream world and into a healthier, happier, less frightening real world. Now comfortable with friends and other meaningful relationships, he no longer has to take refuge within himself. We have our precious little boy back. Almost two years later, I am still often reminded of where Zack used to be—lost and alone. Seeing him now—talking, engaging with others, and enjoying their company—I am utterly amazed at how far he's come. Zack's transformation is nothing short of miraculous. The prayers and dreams we shared for our beloved son have arrived at an astonishing destination, and we couldn't be more grateful.

I have held many things in my hands and lost them all; but the things I have placed in God's hands, those I always possess.
—Earline Steelburg[1]

Be joyful in hope, patient in affliction, faithful in prayer.
(Romans 12:12)

1Copyright 1996 Cook Communications Ministries. God's Little Instruction Book For Women by Honor Books. Used with permission. All rights reserved.

7

Green: Obsessions Exploited

The obsessive/compulsive element associated with autism can really wear a parent down. Our Zack was so fixated on the color green that at times I was entirely at my wit's end. He only wanted to eat off of a green plate with a green fork or spoon, and he only wanted to drink out of. . .you guessed it, a green cup. This overzealous attraction to green made eating out impossible. Few restaurants use green plates, and taking Zack to an establishment that used any other color would have inevitably resulted in distinct humiliation. So we were held captive within the confines of our home. As frustrating as this predicament was, however, at least it was private. Zack had many other, very public compulsions, so it was a blessing to work on some things without an audience. This particular issue with the color green took about three months of tantrums and therapy holds to quash.

But it didn't stop there, unfortunately. On one occasion, Zack had a complete meltdown at a bowling alley birthday party with a million pairs of eyes watching. (Okay, it was probably more like 150.) What was the reason for this outburst? Since Zack wasn't the birthday boy, he couldn't get his hands on the super-cool "Incredible Hulk" balloon. Failing to possess the Hulk was not the issue—he could have cared less about the character. This particular balloon was the only one at the party that was green, and Zack was determined to have it.

We were attending a party for our pastor's son, and the very special balloon belonged to the guest of honor. Pastor Doug was well aware that Zack was often difficult to manage, to put it mildly. Yet he was one of the few dear people who understood our desperate need as parents to have Zack invited to a party, despite his severe challenges. Doug very graciously offered us the irresistible balloon in an effort to mollify Zack, knowing full well that he would be upsetting his own child. Of course, we refused, because the real world simply does not work that way. Besides, we were not about to reward Zack's inappropriate behavior. Next, Doug tried to give Zack one of the other non-green balloons, hoping this would cheer him up. With sadness and frustration, we were forced to explain that the obsession was over the color, not the Hulk. And then, knowing that Zack was not going to recover from this incident any time soon, we felt we had to leave the party.

His fixation with the color green didn't end there, either. One of the biggest struggles we encountered was convincing Zack to dress himself. Many of his self-help skills were delayed, but this one was especially infuriating to teach him because he only wanted to wear green. He wanted his socks, underwear, shirts, pants, shoes—you name it—all to be green. Well, a kid who only wears green clothes doesn't exactly project normalcy, and we were striving for the appearance of "normal" whenever possible. Not only that, but do you know how hard it is to find green shoes and matching green socks when you need them? It is not as easy as you might think.

Every single morning for a year and a half, it was the same story. Zack never dressed himself happily. He had the physical ability to do so, but he just chose to be whiny, incredibly slow, and uncooperative. One morning I just couldn't take the fussing and inevitable battle any longer, and I snapped as I felt the blood boiling in my ears. Beyond frustrated, I yelled, "You want green? You want green? I'll give you green!" I stormed into the kitchen and grabbed a green marker. Then, I stormed right back and put green marks on the tags inside all of his clothes. Even though the marks weren't visible to casual observers, to Zack's mind the clothes were all now green and therefore acceptable. Instantly he smiled and happily and quickly dressed himself with a perfectly pleasant attitude. If only I had lost my cool sooner, I guess I could have saved myself an awful lot of grief. Because the green wasn't noticeable to anyone, including Zack, when he was wearing the clothes he soon forgot that he had to obsess about wearing green. Over time the issue just sort of faded away.

Next, Zack became obsessed with frogs—small frogs, tall frogs, polka-dotted green frogs, frogs that swim and frogs that hop, frogs that make Mom's head go POP! He was so fixated that he refused to do any activity at all unless there was a frog connection. Reading, painting, dancing, playing in the backyard, therapy drills, etc., were completely distasteful activities to him. This used to drive me absolutely crazy because the vast majority of activities do not *have* an inherent frog connection. But after my experience with the green marker, I began to wonder if there was any way I could use Zack's obsession to my advantage.

Many children have a security blanket or special stuffed animal that they would take everywhere, given the opportunity. This is quite typical and usually doesn't strike people as odd. Zack's special stuffed animal was (of course) a green frog that came to be known as Soggy Froggy. On the surface Zack's relationship with his frog may have appeared completely normal, but it was not. He did bring the toy along everywhere he went, but that was where the normalcy ended. Any sort of pretend play such as feeding, cuddling, or having Froggy talk or participate in activities was completely absent. This lack of pretend play (especially play with social influences) is common in children with autism. Most need to be taught how to play in this manner because it does not come naturally to them. Since Zack's play skills were so underdeveloped, we used his obsession with Soggy Froggy to encourage maturation in this area.

Our green friend "participated" in nearly all of our play therapy sessions for the first year and a half. We would take Soggy Froggy from Zack and make him "play" with us. Initially Zack would scream because we had taken his toy away. After several months of explaining to him that he could only have Soggy Froggy back if he made the frog play as we did, Zack got the hang of it. We would also model how to feed him, put a diaper on him, and brush his teeth. Every time Zack successfully performed a typical play routine, we would reward him with a frog sticker. The stickers not only made him ecstatic, but manipulating them also further developed his fine motor skills. This strategy motivated Zack greatly, and before too long he had a huge notebook filled with frog stickers. He also had an abundance of socially appropriate play routines. Thankfully, we had found a suitable and successful motivational tool.

Many children with autism thrive in an activity if there is an immediate reward involved. (Who doesn't?) The motivators do not need to be sophisticated; tasks that might easily bore a typical child often hold great appeal to an autistic child. For instance, I took an empty coffee can and poked a quarter-sized hole through the plastic lid. When Zack completed a task or drill, I would allow him to drop a small object into the hole. Some children may choose miniature cars, plastic bugs, or an assortment of things. As long as the child loves the object, this reward system can be very inspirational. Our family used—yep, that's right—little plastic frogs.

Another one of Zack's delayed skills was his underdeveloped interaction with books. He was more interested in turning the pages back and forth than in the actual story. This fascination with page-turning is much more typical of children one to two years of age, and Zack was three years old at this time. He was also so wrapped up in "all things frog" that for a while I could only gain and maintain his attention if I read him books about frogs. Naïvely,

I thought that once he learned to appreciate the story in the book, he would be willing to read about other things with me as well. Unfortunately, this did not turn out to be the case. Just as with all other things related to frogs, Zack's obsession with frog books was soon grossly out of control.

Since she was a teacher, my mother-in-law always had a supply of used children's books. Every visit to our house was an opportunity for her to bring us a gargantuan box of books. Of course, most of them had absolutely nothing to do with frogs. I knew deep down that these books could really help Zack expand his horizons and areas of interest if only I could get him to read them with me. Since I already had in my possession a vast quantity of frog stickers, I started hiding frog stickers on nearly every page of every book so that Zack would be willing to look at them with me. This strategy was wildly successful. He loved this "Where's Froggy?" approach, and slowly but surely he started to develop other interests. As he began to appreciate things such as airplanes, cars, dinosaurs, and other animals, fewer frog stickers were necessary. Eventually I was able to wean Zack from them altogether.

Still, when necessary, we utilized the benefits of frog therapy. For example, Soggy Froggy performed many vocabulary drills with us. Sometimes I would use him to help me hold a picture card up to my face while I said the object's name. It was easier for Zack to make eye contact if his beloved frog was right there next to my eyes. (Please don't ask me if I was jealous of the frog because I believe I'd be embarrassed by my answer.) At other times our green buddy would "answer" the drill questions to help keep Zack on track. It was considerably easier for him to do the hours upon hours of therapy when Froggy took a turn every now and then. Our pal was also instrumental in teaching Zack opposites. For example, I would put Soggy piggyback on my shoulders and ask the frog if he wanted to go *slow* or *fast*. He would have to "answer" one way or the other before we could move.

He would hop *over* the box or hide *under* the box; or we would put a cape on him, and he would fly *high* or *low*. He would be *awake* or *asleep*. (You get the picture.) Since Zack was unable to learn things on his own, it was necessary to educate him about everything, and most everything required frog assistance in one form or another.

One deficit many children with autism have is the inability to ask questions. Typical kids learn a great deal about the world around them by asking questions. In fact, most "normal" kids go through a rather annoying phase of incessant question-asking. Zack, however, never initiated any questions whatsoever. We had to teach him how to do so because he was incapable of naturally acquiring this skill.

Once again, frogs played a major role in our intervention program. The first question we started with was *what is it?* I would often grab a paper grocery bag and throw a handful of toys into it. Then I would tell Zack, "I have a surprise for you!" Before I would let him feel around inside and pull something out of the bag, I insisted that he ask (in succession as his skills developed), *what?, what is?,* and finally, *what is it?* When we first began using this strategy, only fun things like frogs, dinosaurs, and cars were present in the bag. To increase his levels of flexibility and receptive language, other more basic, less intriguing items such as pencils, socks, tape, pictures, and eating utensils were slowly added to the bag.

The next question we worked on was *who is it?* We included many stuffed animals, dinosaurs, frogs, and people in this "game." One of Zack's favorite hobbies at the time was ringing the doorbell. He didn't have the social skills necessary to go beyond pushing the button, so we had lots to teach him. My husband, my oldest son, or the therapist would sneak out the back door and around the side of the house with the various animals in tow. They would then place the animals at the front door, ring the doorbell, and hide within earshot. Zack would have to ask, *who is it?* and wait for a response before he was allowed to open the door. Then Zack took his turn outside. (Incorporating gross motor activities into therapy was always very beneficial for Zack. For the most part, it helped him stay settled, focused, and happy.) When it was Zack's turn to ring the bell, the animals would "ask," *who is it?* We taught him to answer appropriately. From there we were able to further develop the skill with more back-and-forth conversation: *How are you? I'm fine. It's nice to meet you. Please do come in, frog, etc.*

Where questions were next on our list, which were relatively simple to teach. Playing hide-and-seek with the frog worked marvelously. All we had to do was remind Zack to use his words while he was searching: "Where are you, Soggy Froggy? Where are you?" Of course, the frog took his turn hunting as well and would model even better questions that contained more abstract concepts, such as "Are you *under* the bed? Are you *inside* the dishwasher? Are you *in between* Puppy and Honey Bunny?" We took advantage of every possible opportunity to teach Zack something new or review something old. By doing so, we helped him generalize specific concepts to a variety of different contexts.

Getting Zack to ask the question, *why?* was our next endeavor. As part of our vocabulary drills, we discussed the name of an object and its specific function. For instance, we would explain to him that this particular item was an airplane, followed up with the question, "Why do we use an airplane?" And then we would answer, "To fly from one place to another." This was not inherently obvious to Zack, so we had to drill him for hours on such topics. When he had enough vocabulary and understanding of the world around him, we were able to teach Zack to ask *why?*

By encouraging him to be the "therapist" in charge of drilling us, he practiced his language *and* enjoyed the subtle educational aspects of the session far more than he would have as the indefinite student. Sometimes we would set up a pseudo-classroom environment where one of Zack's toys would have a chance to "answer" the questions. Zack loved being the one in charge so much that we were able to teach him a great many things about his surroundings using this technique. Using basically the same process, we taught Zack to ask the question, *how*?

Because it is, by nature, a much more abstract concept, instructing Zack to ask *when?* was the most challenging of all. We began our attempts by asking, "When will Dad be home?" or "When will the therapist be here?" "Soon," "later," or "tomorrow" would be the answer, but it was obvious that this concept wasn't really registering with him. I suspect that the most probable reasons were the lack of immediate feedback, along with Zack's limited ability to concentrate. Regardless, we needed a superior strategy.

The next technique was much more successful. I had already been using an egg timer to help Zack transition more gracefully from one activity to another. Five minutes before every scheduled change, I gave him minute-by-minute reminders so that he could adequately process the information and prepare himself for what was coming next. We used the egg timer to teach Zack what 5-, 10-, 15-, 30-, and 60-second intervals felt like. Then, when Zack really wanted to participate in a particular activity, I insisted that he use a *when* phrase (i.e., When hot tub?). My response included a number in seconds, and together we would set the egg timer. He would happily watch until the buzzer went off, for he found this egg timer quite fascinating. I really hit the jackpot with this amazingly simple little tool.

It always felt like a major accomplishment when I was able to find a way into Zack's brain and teach him something useful. This kind of success was truly a cause for celebration. It was rarely easy, but I often prayed for wisdom—that I would be inspired with just the right strategy for Zack. My prayers were always answered but not always immediately.

I spent many sleepless nights over the course of the first two years brainstorming about creative and innovative ways of teaching Zack a single concept. The likelihood of him understanding something new with my initial plan was poor, at best. In many cases Zack could only learn a concept after it had been presented to him in a half-dozen different scenarios. In hindsight, I think that my relentless resolve to teach him a concept no matter how long it took, or how many various methods proved necessary, really paid off. These efforts resulted in a truly comprehensive program, which helped Zack generalize remarkably well in the long run. Failure to generalize from the therapy to the real world is a symptom of autism that is often difficult to overcome. Zack's apparent slow-learning style may have been, in reality, a blessing in disguise.

As I lived through this painstakingly slow process, I wasn't able to recognize it as a blessing. Truth be known, I found the whole prolonged journey incredibly frustrating because I couldn't see the forest for the trees. I couldn't see that Zack was recovering right before my eyes because I was too focused on the everyday struggles. Time and time again, God gave me a practical opportunity to further develop my patience, whether I wanted to or not. He used Zack's autism to teach me in spite of myself. Maybe one of these days I'll learn not to resist the growth process God has in store for me. Then perhaps, I can learn to look around and appreciate the beauty of a green forest.

Give your troubles to God; He will be up all night anyway.
—Unknown[1]

He will not let your foot slip – he who watches over you will not slumber.
(Psalm 121:3)

1Copyright 1996 Cook Communications Ministries. God's Little Instruction Book For Women by Honor Books. Used with permission. All rights reserved.

8

Summers at College Heights

Summer is by far the worst time of year for a family dealing with autism. The services provided during the school year are reduced dramatically (if not cancelled entirely), and all semblance of routine flies out the window. In our case, we spent more money on extra therapy assistance during the three months of summer than we did the remaining nine months of the year. Other families may spend a lot of money in the summer too, but they have the freedom to do cool things like taking vacations to Disney World or buying a season pass to the local swimming pool. Families like ours have to fill each moment of every day with autism therapy. We were also attempting to pay attention to, or otherwise occupy, two additional children. Trust me when I say that our summers were *anything* but fun.

James and I have some dear friends who run a fabulous Christian preschool and kindergarten called College Heights. The school remains open during the summer, providing a daycare environment with a hint of academic focus. When I inquired about accommodations for Zack, they regrettably refused, citing their inability to effectively address his special needs. Children with autism require so much one-on-one attention that many settings are too understaffed to adequately handle probable disruptions. This was inarguably true in their case.

Also, Zack wasn't yet potty-trained at three years, nine months of age. Being potty-trained was a non-negotiable prerequisite for all students registered at this school. Nevertheless, we were still looking for some kind of quality summer program where we could expose Zack to a peer group. College Heights graciously agreed to let me bring all three of my kids to the school if I was willing to stay with Zack to provide the substantial support needed. Because Abbie was only 21 months old at the time, I was going to have to change her diapers anyway, so I assured them that I would be responsible for Zack's as well.

This first summer at College Heights was absolutely draining because Zack didn't have any social skills at all. He didn't know how to share or take turns, so when I tried to include him in an activity where these skills were required, he would often throw a screaming tantrum. Most of the tantrums at home were reasonably under control by this point, but Zack found out that adjusting to this new environment with new kids and new social expectations was beyond difficult. Frequently and tearfully I was forced to extinguish his socially inappropriate behaviors by implementing the therapy hold. Sadly, even though Zack was beginning to transition much of his sign language into verbal language at home, here at school he again was too overwhelmed to remember to employ his newfound language skills.

In addition to social challenges, Zack had a very strong sensory need; that is, he had to participate in gross motor activities on a nearly constant basis in order to function with any approximation of normalcy. Because of this sensory need, he found it extremely difficult to sit still during show-and-tell and story time. This particular school has a very strict policy about children learning to be quiet and settled for such activities. These are great skills for any child to master, and I whole-heartedly support their desire to teach their students to behave in this manner. Unfortunately, Zack was utterly incapable of acquiescing to those rules at this age. So, during these quiet and still times I took him into another classroom for one-on-one therapy without any distractions. Having a private moment together allowed me to escape the feeling of being on constant display. Also, this change of pace allowed him to squirm and subsequently settle down, which he obviously needed.

Dramatic drops in his blood sugar were also quite common with Zack at the time. I suspect that this was the result of his persistent demands for physical activity. Unless I had the presence of mind to give him snacks every hour, these dips in his blood sugar levels made therapy sessions rather exasperating. My time alone with Zack gave me the perfect opportunity to feed him without inciting school-wide snack frenzies.

Summer was peppered with many instances that reflected Zack's egregious, odd, and confusing behaviors. Onlooking children were understandably curious, and they couldn't help but ask a multitude of questions: "Why doesn't he talk? Why won't he color with a crayon? Why does he scream so much? Why do you have to hold him like that? Why does he always want to play Dinosaur? Why do you stay here with him when all of the other parents just drop off their kids?" I was inundated with question after question. Giving a satisfactory explanation to one group was futile because a new group would inevitably wander over and ask the same questions all over again.

It was emotionally very draining, explaining my dear child's oddities over and over again while dealing with tantrums and trying to teach him difficult social skills. There were many embarrassing moments. When the kids brought swimsuits and played water games on water days, it was particularly hair-raising. On one occasion, Zack dropped his swimsuit and peed for what seemed like 10 minutes straight—in front of God, all the kids, and everyone who happened to be around that day. For a prim and proper Christian school, you can imagine how this sort of thing would be frowned upon. Yeah, that was a fun day.

Despite this fiasco, what caused me the most angst was the realization that even the youngest children, who tended to be self-absorbed and not particularly observant, could see Zack's deficits so plainly and easily. Instantly they concluded that Zack wasn't "normal." Every probing question made this inescapable truth even more heart-breaking.

Dejected, I tried my best to explain Zack's disorder to the confused little ones: "Zack has autism. It is really hard for him to talk. This makes him very frustrated sometimes, so he screams and acts out. I hold him like this so he will learn not to scream. Can you imagine how frustrated you would be if you couldn't talk? It would be very hard, don't you think? When he colors with a crayon, it hurts his hand, so he has to keep practicing until it doesn't hurt anymore. He also has to be taught how to take turns and share because of the autism. I need you to be patient with him, and I also need you to help me teach him how to share and take turns. God wants us to love everybody, even people who are different, like Zack—especially people who are different like Zack. He needs a lot of love and help in order to learn and get better. Will you help?"

Many of these kids jumped in with open, loving hearts, and I was so grateful for their understanding natures. Of course, Zack didn't want their help: he didn't want to interact with the kids, share, or take turns. So once again I had to go through the pain of coming to terms with my son's practically non-existent social skills. My friends at the school could see that this experience was taking its toll on me and offered thoughtful words of encouragement. They told me regularly how much they appreciated my honest explanations and the opportunities I provided for their children to develop sensitivity and compassion for people with handicaps. In spite of their kind words, my job remained very difficult.

That first summer at College Heights was so very hard for me. I was on the verge of tears most of the time, and after only three hours, I would come home emotionally spent and absolutely exhausted. Because I was incapable of doing any more decent work with Zack after visiting the school, our college students helped carry the burden by picking up some of the remaining therapy hours each day. My husband, James, also handled an occasional hour or two when I just couldn't bear the thought of doing any more. It was such a relief to know that I could count on him whenever I needed him. James's therapy sessions were not as intense as mine, because he hadn't been as extensively trained as I. But Zack was compelled to engage, and this in itself was immensely beneficial.

By the grace of God, I survived the first summer at the preschool, and more importantly, Zack did too. Now it was time to get into a routine with the public school system. Thankfully, we had many opportunities to introduce Zack to social skills during the school year. Marsha, our awe-inspiring social worker, tackled critical social skills individually with Zack first. Then she encouraged the implementation of these skills in the classroom with the help of his peers. Marsha and I were kindred spirits, so we were always in agreement about the direction of her therapy with Zack. She was a pure joy to work with, and I very much appreciated having her on our team. Because Marsha had worked diligently with Zack during the school year, the next summer at College Heights was infinitely easier to live through.

Zack was potty-trained by then, so technically I should have been able to leave him at the school, but we all knew Zack hadn't made enough progress for that to become a reality. So I brought all three kids there again and stayed as I had the summer before. I still had to facilitate social interactions between Zack and the other children, but his overall demeanor was decidedly improved.

This time, the children only asked me one simple question: "Why do you stay here when all of the other parents leave?" I was greatly relieved because I could see that they were questioning *my* behavior, not Zack's. He was no longer inherently odd in their eyes but normal enough not to draw attention! We were actually making progress! I couldn't allow myself to believe it at first. Was this improbable transformation a reality? Was I caught up in a daydream? Would I wake up distraught yet again, as I had done for so long? Then I "pinched" myself and realized that I was indeed awake. With a huge smile on my face, I shared with the little ones my desire to stay and play because it looked like a lot of fun. It was still challenging work, but Zack had come so far that my burden was significantly lightened.

After practicing with a crayon for an entire school year, Zack was actually willing to do some of the seat work at College Heights. He would hold that crayon for three minutes before he decided the sensation was just too intolerable to continue. He was also able to sit quietly through show-and-tell and story time with minimal support from me. Also, his recess behavior was much more "normal." Although I had to redirect him from the "talking" Dinosaur game occasionally, he was able to do so without throwing a tantrum. By this time he had also come to understand that it was inappropriate to expose his naked self to the entire school, thank the Lord!

Our third summer went even better than the second. Now five years and nine months old, Zack had officially lost the autism diagnosis, according to the experts in Albuquerque. Plans were in place to transition him to a regular kindergarten class in the public school system that autumn. The only special service we requested from Zack's public school kindergarten was speech therapy because of his apraxia of speech disorder. Even though his speech was still considerably difficult to understand, Zack's behavior at College Heights was terrific. Now I could drop all three kids off and go on my merry little way, just like all of the other parents. Zack was able to handle the quiet activities and the seat work without incident. He played nicely with the other kids at recess, acting pleasant and polite and fitting in very nicely. It was absolutely glorious! My Zack could now handle himself in an appropriate manner without my constant intervention so I could have some much-needed time to myself. Not only was my son returning to normalcy, but my life was slowly and surely returning to normalcy as well.

Zack had made such incredible progress over the years that I was even able to drop him off at Vacation Bible School that summer. Fortunately, the camp was organized by the College Heights staff, which greatly put my mind at ease. Believe it or not, my once autistic boy was completely content with being dropped off in this foreign environment, and he did just fine. In fact, Zack was even brave enough and comfortable enough with his surroundings that he gladly and confidently stood up in front of 150 kids and recited his Bible verse into the microphone to earn his sticker for his team. Granted, given Zack's apraxia, the ladies in charge had to determine if his gobbledygook was clear enough to give him credit (which they did, bless their kind hearts). Still, what a remarkable transformation had taken place in my son! No one could deny the changes in him. He was a living miracle, right there before our very eyes.

When the odds seemed wholly against me, I survived Zack's autism. This was a miracle too—one I'm impassioned to share with others. What I would have given for a fellow autism mom willing to communicate her struggles to me! I desperately needed someone who could offer hope, provide comfort, and tell me there might be a light at the end of this formidable tunnel. Having prevailed over my son's autism, I wish to be that someone for others. Let me keep your dreams alive.

It is, in fact, possible to endure this experience while growing, maturing, and learning more about your Maker and yourself in the process. Believe it. My family is living proof. Take heart and dream on.

> *The ultimate measure of a man is not where he stands in moments of comfort and convenience, but where he stands at times of challenge and controversy.*
>
> *—Martin Luther King Jr.*[1]

> *Consider it pure joy, my brothers, whenever you face trials of many kinds, because you know that the testing of your faith develops perseverance. Perseverance must finish its work so that you may be mature and complete, not lacking anything.*
>
> *(James 1:2-4)*

---

1 Copyright 1995 Cook Communications Ministries. God's Little Instruction Book For Dad by Honor Books. Used with permission. All rights reserved.

9

Potty-Training: It Is Possible

Potty-training is one of the most exasperating aspects of parenting. Some of my girlfriends claim that their kids potty-trained themselves when they were ready, but I'm still not convinced that they are being completely honest with me. How on earth could they have managed so easily, when my experience potty-training my children was so painstakingly slow and frustrating? Even teaching Jacob and Abbie was vexing; I wasn't really satisfied with their capabilities in the restroom until they were four and a half years old. Perhaps I just don't have the "gift."

Instructing Jacob to poop only in the potty apparently wasn't clear enough. I suppose there were too many loopholes in that statement; instead, I had to provide examples of all conceivable places where pooping was unacceptable: "Don't poop in your pants. Don't poop in the sandbox. Don't poop on your bed. Don't poop on the couch. Don't poop in the bathtub. . . ." You get the picture. You should have seen the disaster area that was our kids' bathroom. For a year and a half it emanated noxious fumes reminiscent of an outhouse. Jacob's aim was such a problematic issue that I would have to constantly tell him, "Don't pee on the seat. Don't pee on the floor. Don't pee on the wall. . ." Yes, we tried numerous creative incentives, such as placing colorful cereal O's in the bowl to make the experience more interesting and motivating. We also insisted that he clean up the messes he made, hoping that would persuade him to pay better attention, but nothing seemed to work. I reminded myself on a daily basis, "This *is* temporary. Eventually he *will* be potty-trained."

It's not like we started training Jacob too early. He was at least two and a half, I'm sure, because we were starting to get questions and comments from both sets of in-laws concerning our potty-training initiatives. They were under the impression that we should have already begun the process months ago, since all of *their* children were completely trained by the age of two. Of course, they raised their babies during the era of cloth diapers, which were conducive to quick and satisfactory results. (But after two and a half years with disposable diapers, who in their right mind would desire to go down that disgusting road?) There was also the distinct possibility that our in-laws' memories were not serving them honestly. How could two people trained by the age of two have three children who each struggled with the issue until the age of four and a half? Something wasn't adding up.

Our troubles with Jacob's aim and inappropriate locations were only the beginning. We also struggled to convince him to take the time to relieve himself before the immediacy of the moment got the better of him. Finally, during the first week of first grade, an impetus to change his procrastinating ways arose from an embarrassing accident, helping us turn the corner in this area. In front of every classmate in the room, Jacob completely soaked his pants. The poor teacher had no opportunity to discreetly handle the situation. She was absolutely wonderful, though, and took the opportunity to talk to the class about sympathy and empathy. How would they feel if they were teased about such a thing? Then the entire class prayed for Jacob. (Mrs. Douglas, you are one in a million! Thank you.) Despite the fact that Jacob was one of the oldest kids in his class (nearly seven years old), a major humiliating incident like this was necessary for him to take his pressing urges to urinate more seriously.

My youngest, Abbie, started too early at 20 months of age, but it was of her own volition. We had just finished potty-training Zack, and there was an inordinate amount of potty-talk (not to be confused with potty-mouth) going on in our household. Every time Abbie soiled her diaper from that point forward, she would just rip it off, no matter where she was or what her circumstance may have been. Things got to be pretty exciting, especially with her bowel movements, so we decided to just go ahead and begin her instruction. After all, girls are supposedly easier to potty-train than boys, right? And I had definitely paid my dues. Surely I deserved one child capable of being trained by age two, or so I hoped. Well, we didn't have the aiming problem, obviously, but everything else was rather similar to our experience with Jacob. We had more than two-and-a-half years of accidents with Abbie before she had complete mastery over the process. Again, I clung to my encouraging words: "This is only temporary. Eventually she *will* be potty-trained."

Potty-training can be especially difficult for children with special needs. Because they can be so far behind developmentally and have so many other issues to address, children with autism who manage to get potty-trained usually require a much longer training period. Moreover, they are usually much older than typical children. I have a dear friend with a four-year-old boy, for instance, and she is currently at her wit's end after six months of failed attempts in the bathroom. He only has success if taken every hour on the hour, but he doesn't yet recognize or understand the signals from his body. I have another friend with a 10-year-old who has an accident every time he plays in the water.

The Lord was very gracious to us regarding Zack's potty-training. Although nearly four years of age, I do believe he was the easiest of the three. At two years and eight months chronologically speaking, Zack was only 12 to 15 months old developmentally. His receptive language was so poor that there was no reason to explain the whole toilet routine to him. At age three, he was only 18 to 22 months old developmentally, and his receptive language was still very much delayed. So again, we held off on the training. As he approached three and a half, Zack was toying with the idea of converting some of his sign language to verbal language. So, we were not going to give potty-training (or anything else, for that matter) the opportunity to impede him in any way, shape, or form. The following summer—as he was set to transition from the Birth to Three program to the public school—seemed an ideal time to try.

We started with the traditional potty-training method. Zack was given all of his favorite drinks and placed on the toilet for five to 10 minutes every half-hour. Diapers were replaced with underwear (always a delightfully fun, messy time in the life of a parent). A reward system of his beloved frog stickers was also implemented. As I knew he would, he adored the stickers and couldn't wait to get his hands on one of them. Offering something Zack so strongly desired could have served as a good incentive, but his failure to understand what was required to gain the prize only produced an additional level of frustration for him.

He didn't like being wet or messy; but again, he didn't comprehend the cause and effect of the situation. After a month of nothing but accidents, I was beginning to question whether or not he was really ready (from a developmental standpoint) for this potty-training stuff. Mustering up a great deal of faith, I yet again told myself that someday Zack *would* be successful. He just *had* to! I was unwilling to consider the alternative, but I had run out of ideas. I needed help, and thankfully, help was on its way.

Cynthia, one of the therapists, taught therapeutic dance. Sometimes she would do deep pressure, vestibular-type activities with the big, bouncy exercise ball. Zack would lie on his tummy on top of the ball, and we would either firmly push down on his shoulders and back, roll the ball over him, or make him balance on top of it. We would also wrap him up in a blanket and swing him. These types of activities had more of an occupational therapy emphasis. Moving Zack's program in this direction made a lot of sense to me because I knew all too well how much he benefited from occupational therapy. If he had just completed an especially grueling speech therapy session, he would settle down and regroup so much faster if we were able to introduce this sort of sensory "diet". I didn't need any convincing to support this strategy because the benefits were undeniable, so I was on board immediately.

Cynthia would also bring over different kinds of music for our listening pleasure. Some included nature sounds with birds and waterfalls and the like. As we listened, we interpreted the music and danced around with colorful little scarves. Even though I am a music enthusiast and a huge fan of dance, I have to admit that I felt rather silly and certainly didn't think this frolicking with scarves was any kind of *real* therapy. Zack enjoyed it, but it seemed hokey and nonproductive to me, especially when there were so many more important skills to work on instead of dance moves. Couldn't we do an activity with clear, discernable value? I didn't want to waste one single minute on ineffectual foolishness—I was desperate to make progress and make it fast! Smiling on the outside, I was inwardly filled with apprehension.

Cynthia defended her strategy, stating that Zack would learn to bond with others while participating in a social activity, which he did. She also said that he would develop better body awareness and would come to understand how his body was connected to the world around him. This struck me as complete and utter nonsense, but I could tell that Cynthia's heart was in the right place. So I decided to give it a try for a while, just to see if anything good could come of this so-called "therapy." Did Zack ever discover a body/world connection? Who knows? I do, however, know one thing for sure: I gained a priceless revelation of my own through this experience.

This therapy was unquestionably enjoyable for Zack. Yet, despite his love of scarf-dancing, he would always stop abruptly for no apparent reason. Immediately, he would go a corner and stim on something. Stimming was still fairly common when Zack was engaging in vocabulary drills, sign language drills, or other less-entertaining activities. But Zack was thoroughly engrossed with the dancing one minute, and then off in the corner the next, which was most surprising to us. Normally he would become a little too preoccupied and obsessive/compulsive when involved in such an enjoyable activity. In fact, I often made a point to limit these preferred activities to five minutes and then redirect him to something else so he would have no opportunity to fixate. Also, this strategy helped teach him how to transition between environments without fussing. Zack's curious behavior of inexplicably abandoning his much-loved dancing activity left me quite perplexed.

It was as if something was going on with Zack's body that was too distracting and confusing for him to deal with. An overwhelming sensation had to be forcing him back into his own introspective world. I would draw him back into the real world as I did multiple times each day, and inevitably, within five minutes, he would pee in his pants. Enough time must have passed in those five minutes (believe it or not) that I failed to see the correlation right away. Then, the light bulb finally illuminated over my head. Eureka! By Zack, I had it! He was stimming because his body was sending him confusing signals, and he didn't know what to do about it. That nature music with the waterfalls was really inspiring his little body to go potty. Once I made the connection between the stimming and the accidents, we took him to the toilet whenever he forewarned us with a stim. He had a successful outcome within five minutes every single time we used this method. Finally, he was able to earn those very coveted frog stickers.

After Zack adjusted to the routine, we began to talk about how his body felt when he stimmed in the corner during scarf-dancing time. "How do you feel?" we would ask. We had drilled Zack on emotions like "happy," "sad," "angry," "afraid," and "mad" as part of teaching him social skills, but of course, none of these descriptions adequately represented the urge to urinate. Although he just sat there and didn't respond, I knew his body was expressing a sensation to him. So I told him that this unfamiliar feeling was his body's way of telling him to go potty. After a couple months of reminding him to pay attention to his body, Zack was successfully trained—just in time for school in the fall. What a glorious time to be alive! My boy with autism was potty-trained! Praise the Lord! Now my dances and smiles were irrepressible and completely genuine.

Children are likely to live up to what you believe of them.
- Lady Bird Johnson [1]

You turned my wailing into dancing; you removed my sackcloth and clothed me with joy, that my heart may sing to you and not be silent. O Lord my God, I will give you thanks forever.
(Psalm 30:11-12)

1 Copyright 1995 Cook Communications Ministries. God's Little Instruction Book For Mom by Honor Books. Used with permission. All rights reserved.

10

Siblings: Little Helpers from God

I firmly believe that our other children, Jacob and Abbie, were a tremendous asset in Zack's recovery from autism. With all of them just two years apart, Zack had a built-in peer group with typical role models. I also feel the birth order of our children provided a significant benefit for Zack. At those times when he was aware of his surroundings and willing to imitate, having a precocious older brother to emulate was an immense blessing. Also, his little sister turned out to be one of my greatest inspirations. I was ever so determined to work with Zack, lest she overtake him in one area or another.

People sometimes ask why we risked having a third baby when our second had autism. The fact is, Zack had the regressive form of autism, so he didn't start exhibiting autistic traits until I was already pregnant with Abbie. I also wanted so much to know the joy of having a daughter if at all possible, for in my heart I knew our family was not yet complete.

Because Zack screamed so much during the first year, it took much begging and pleading to convince James to try one more time to get our girl. He wondered, "What if we have another child with reflux? Don't you remember the vomiting and screeching? Zack is still such a handful. What if we have another high-maintenance baby?" Admittedly, this was a legitimate concern. I reasoned that after having to deal with it once, surely the Lord wouldn't expect us to handle the challenge of another infant with reflux. Little did

I know the plans He *did* have for our family.

Well, James finally warmed up to the idea, and before long we were expecting! Thanks to the marvel of ultrasound, we had known about both boys beforehand. Since this baby was to be our last, we decided to take advantage of our final opportunity to be surprised by the gender. I was so thrilled when our daughter was born! At last, my longings and prayers had come true. Not only did I have my precious little girl, but I also had managed to avoid a lifetime of teasing from James. If our new baby had been another boy, I'm sure I never would have heard the end of it. To our relief, she was a delightful, wonderful, easy newborn with no evidence of reflux. What a blessing Abbie was to us— the perfect addition to our now complete family.

We were also incredibly blessed to have only one child with autism. I personally know several families with more than one child on the spectrum. In fact, the odds of having a second child with autism are much greater (one in 10) than the national average (one in 91). How these families survive is inconceivable to me. Each child requires so much attention and time, so how is it possible to adequately address each one's particular issues and therapy needs? I can't even begin to imagine dealing with such a responsibility! Our home barely survived this adversity with only *one* child affected.

Autism parents are often faced with very real concerns for the other children in the family. Without a doubt, brothers and sisters miss out on many of the nurturing, entertaining, and enriching opportunities afforded more typical families. Siblings of a child with autism don't get their fair share of attention and expressions of love; it simply isn't feasible when one child must have everything a parent can give and more. Feelings of guilt are common, even though it isn't the fault of the parent or the siblings that the child has autism. Although the difficult situation isn't anyone's fault, the consequence is an extremely altered family dynamic.

Because Abbie was so little at the time, I just dragged her along to all of Zack's therapy, whether she liked it or not. At least I was always nearby, even though I couldn't be focused on her most of the time. I doubt, however, that she even remembers the most trying elements of our therapy sessions. I was far more concerned about the effects of Zack's autism on Jacob. The first year and a half of interventions was so incredibly difficult that weeping was a huge part of my everyday life. I cried more tears around Jacob than I could possibly count, so he was understandably quite distraught during this period. What he needed was the security of a mom who was handling everything just fine. Yet I wasn't, and worry had overcome us both.

I knew it was unfair to expect one so small to have to deal with such a heavy burden, so I tried my best to provide activities to make Jacob feel special and loved. Unable to spend any real quality time with him myself, I could at least offer him a distraction and escape. We enrolled him in a Mom's Day Out program for a while, but unfortunately it wasn't a good match. He frequently acted out, which suggested to us that he wasn't ready for preschool yet. Jacob didn't want an escape from me; what he wanted was a mom he could depend on. Despite my desire to be that mom, I just didn't have anything left to give because my plate was already intolerably full.

In another desperate attempt to help Jacob feel special, I hired our respite provider to give him piano lessons. This way, one of the gazillion people coming to our house for Zack would also be there to do something special with him. However, Jacob was a little too young and silly to actually make that much of a positive experience. The only extra-curricular activity that really panned out for him was playing on the soccer team. He had a marvelous time running around in the fresh air with his friends and finally had a suitable outlet for his feelings. The Lord is so good! Fortunately, when I had been unable to be there for Jacob, our loving Father was there all along.

One thing I certainly regret about my relationship with Jacob during this time was my intense desire for him to be more independent and make wiser choices. Whenever he made an immature decision that required action by me, I handled it with far less grace than I care to admit. In many instances I was awfully hard on him because I desperately needed for Jacob to take care of things on his own. Although he is two years older than Zack, Jacob was still very young (only four and a half) when we began this journey. My demands on him were far from reasonable, yet I made them anyway. I felt that I had no choice in the matter but to expect Jacob to become more self-sufficient. In a more perfect world I could have been the mom Jacob desired and deserved, but our world was far from perfect. I just couldn't stretch myself any thinner.

Jacob is really a remarkable boy. He has always had such a spirit of helpfulness, and I often enlisted his help with Zack. Time after time I commissioned Jacob to redirect Zack's stimming, and time after time Jacob forced Zack to engage in some manner of play. I spat out a multitude of instructions to him every day: "Go get Zack's attention.... See if you can get him to copy your funny faces or sound effects. . . .Teach him how to use the dump trucks the right way. . .Go blow bubbles with him." Not only did Jacob obey happily, but he did so with all the skill and self-assuredness of a professional therapist. Having been exposed to hours upon hours of therapy sessions, he knew instinctively and precisely how to "play" with his brother.

Jacob would authoritatively chime, "Zack, look at me." Then Jacob would bring the toy airplane up to his face, encouraging eye contact. "This is an airplane, air-plane, air-plane. It flies in the air. Flies, flies. It makes this noise. Can you make this noise? Make this noise, Zack. This is a dump truck. It dumps the sand. Dumps, dumps." He was also very good at letting me know when Zack was not paying attention to him and required my assistance in order to make him engage. Jacob has always thrived in front of an audience, so his role as a therapist provided a perfect stage. Both boys appear to have benefited from this mentoring situation and have become close friends in the process.

Even now, years later, Jacob has such a tender, giving nature. Occasionally he shares his frustrations with me about a difficult child at school or on the playground. If I happen to be aware of any specific issues, I explain that the kid needs to be helped and accepted—just like Zack. Immediately and confidently Jacob will befriend the child, and with compassion and patience, he will start to "play" in a very therapeutic way. His spirit appears to be naturally drawn to special-needs children.

Siblings of challenged kids have a different lot in life, and there is just no getting around it. But this doesn't have to be a negative inevitability, because they often develop a beautifully insightful and considerate view of life and other people, respectively. Many seek occupations filled with opportunities to minister to those with special needs. I wouldn't be at all surprised if Jacob pursued such loving avenues of employment.

Not only does Mom's relationship with the other children take a severe hit, but so does the marital relationship. In our case, there were no ugly fights or affairs. (Quite frankly, who has that kind of emotional energy when one has a child with autism?) Yet there were definitely times when I didn't feel as connected to James as I know I should have been. Yes, we cried together and comforted each other, but every single conversation revolved around autism and Zack, as did all of our activities. For three years autism completely took over our lives. We lived, ate, and breathed autism. It was insidious, creeping into every single aspect of our so-called lives. Even during our rare date nights, as we checked out our movie options, we had no enthusiasm for anything currently showing at the theatres. Instead, we usually found ourselves at the local Barnes & Noble bookstore, searching the shelves for books about autism.

I've often heard that a woman should be a Christian first, wife second, and mother third. This list is supposed to reflect the order of priorities for a Christian woman's life. Despite my efforts to live according to these honorable ideals, my reality couldn't have been further removed from them. I was, first and foremost, a desperate mother in constant supplication, begging God for her son's autism to disappear. Second, I was an exhausted autism fanatic. *Nothing* came in third. For me, there was no room for anything else. I had absolutely nothing left to give—emotionally, physically, or otherwise to anyone or any- thing.

In spite of—or perhaps because of—this fact, God chose to cover us with an added measure of grace. He was so very good to us. As the Lord protected our marriage through this incredibly difficult time, He made our relationship stronger in the process. I cannot imagine enduring this ordeal with anyone but James. He is the one person who truly understood what I was going through and stood by me anyway. "For better or for worse" has been his pledge to me. He not only has fulfilled that promise, but he has done so with such courage, love, and integrity that I couldn't respect or love him more. From the very first time we talked together, I knew that James was my intended. Although I didn't understand my sense of assurance back then, I certainly do now.

"Your children learn more of your faith during the bad times than they do during the good times."
—Beverly LaHaye [1]

Give thanks to the LORD, for he is good. His love endures forever.
To him who alone does great wonders, His love endures forever.
(Psalm 136:1, 4)

---

1 Copyright 1995 Cook Communications Ministries. God's Little Instruction Book For Mom by Honor Books. Used with permission. All rights reserved.

11

School Productions: From Stares to Stars

"You only get one chance to make a first impression." This may be true when it comes to people, but can the same be said about school productions? My first encounter with a school production that included Zack was not a good one by any stretch of the imagination. Actually, it wasn't even Zack's program; his five-year-old brother Jacob was participating in his very first formal program at preschool. James was out of town on business, so I was on my own with all three kids. For a typical family, this scenario might be slightly more hectic than usual, but doable nonetheless. Yet, we were not a typical family.

Zack was three years old, nonverbal, and had the receptive language of a child half his age. Also, his behavior issues were still at the forefront of our intervention programs; in other words, he was completely unmanageable. Before the production even began, he insisted on crawling through the tunnel formed by the undersides of the folding chairs. Up and down he crawled, beneath every row of eager, proud parents. Many of the moms were wearing their Sunday best. Sitting in dresses and skirts, they undoubtedly wondered why I was allowing Zack to be so inappropriately positioned. He also insisted on growling like a dinosaur as he crawled from one end of each row to the other. This was embarrassing to say the least, but as long as we were still waiting for the show to begin, I could almost pretend to be distracted by one-year-old Abbie. After all, I needed to get her settled down and quiet before the performance commenced.

However, once the program began, I had to insist that Zack stop pestering everyone. Obviously, the audience was expected to sit still and be quiet. That seems like a reasonable expectation, but of course, my little ones had other intentions. Throughout the entire program Zack fussed loudly at me, not screeching (thank goodness) but whining like an extraordinarily difficult two-year-old. At home, we were in the midst of the worst therapy hold struggles, an exhibition I desperately hoped to avoid with so many attentive parents present. With the certainty of failure looming over me, I didn't want to push my luck by demanding complete obedience from Zack. Settling for relatively non-disturbing behavior was my only option. Whining would have to be okay, or I'd have no choice but to implement the hold. Yet with every whine my anxiety was spurred to new levels.

All the while, Abbie occupied herself by climbing all over me and groping for the camcorder. Her mission in life as a typical one-year-old was to touch every button within her reach. My video clip was a dismal failure—the worst in "recorded" history. The room was getting warmer by the second, and I sensed hundreds of pairs of eyes all focused on me. How come there is never a good cave around when you need one? I didn't possess the courage to look around to see if my perceptions were accurate. I felt completely incompetent as a parent yet ever so grateful that no one said anything hurtful. After this experience I never wanted to attend another school program again, but if I absolutely *had* to go for some reason, I would *never* be responsible for the children all on my own!

My husband and Abbie attended the remainder of Jacob's programs that school year while I stayed home and worked with Zack. It was not fun, but at least that way I could deal with his outbursts more effectively and privately. By the end of the school year with help from the therapy hold and dietary restrictions, Zack's tantrums were, for the most part, under control. He was talking a little, and his receptive language was catching up nicely. It was therefore somewhat easier to curb his unusual and inappropriate behaviors. Going places with him was becoming far less conspicuous and frightening.

James and I even made several attempts to take Zack to Jacob's programs. Unfortunately, his sensory needs were still quite strong at four years of age, so we spent a fair amount of time trying to persuade him to be still. Our efforts were always thwarted by Zack, as well as by Abbie, who was now a typical two-year-old. We often had to excuse ourselves and head outside, where they could bounce around and move to their heart's content without being a distraction to the other families. By this time, Zack was enrolled in his own DD (developmentally delayed) preschool, but thankfully he wasn't involved in any of their productions. Dealing with the problematic issues likely associated with such a performance was beyond the capacity of my already aching heart.

As the next year rolled around, Zack was talking even more, and his receptive language was near grade level; so we were able to reason with him about his behavior with satisfactory results. We were also able to adequately handle his sensory needs by allowing him to vigorously exercise on the trampoline, play with the big exercise ball, or ride his bicycle before attending the performance. He was attending his second year at the DD preschool, and once again did not participate in any programs of his own. Even though his sensory needs had become easier to deal with, his non-participation in performances was still a blessing. Due to the severity of his apraxia, Zack wasn't even willing to *try* to sing until he was almost six because it was so incredibly difficult for him. I was so surprised and excited the day Zack decided to sing—for years I thought that day would never come. We were in the minivan. What was our destination? Who knows? What I do know for certain was that we were listening to a Veggie Tales Silly Songs CD. With great enthusiasm and big, booming voices, Jacob and Abbie were singing along.

I had been more than passionate about not allowing Abbie to surpass Zack, if at all possible. Keeping his skill levels ahead of hers was unbelievingly challenging at times, yet I had somehow just barely managed to be successful. When it came to singing, though, I had no chance of victory. Abbie loved to sing, and Zack couldn't sing at all—at least not yet. Then, one day, completely out of the blue, Zack chimed in with his brother and sister. I couldn't believe my ears at first! Bless his heart; he is my only tone-deaf child. No question about it, Zack's voice was coming through loud and clear. It wasn't easy for him, because he made a lot of motor planning mistakes. But he was willing to try and was enjoying it, just like any typical child. Actually, I shouldn't have been all that surprised, since Zack had lost his autism diagnosis about six months earlier. Still, this unexpected expression of normalcy caught me completely off-guard. Moments like that one never cease to amaze me. My sense of gratitude moved me to tears, and such things still do, even to this day.

Last year Zack was enrolled in a mainstream kindergarten class, so we could no longer hide from his inevitable participation in school productions. Would we survive? Only time would tell. With my nerves on edge and desperately praying for peace of mind, I headed off to the first program. Much to my surprise, I bumped into Robert, our lead psychologist from our Birth to Three program, whose child was performing as well. What a lovely opportunity to visit and (hopefully) enjoy our children. Their musical featured a cowboy theme with the children dancing and singing, as well as playing pretend fiddles and harmonicas, which also contributed to the fun. My earlier conversations with Zack were so encouraging.

He appeared to enjoy the rehearsals, but how would he respond to being placed in front of a large audience? Hoping for the best, I took a deep breath and prepared myself for possible heartbreak.

I quickly realized that my worst fears were put to rest when Zack's joyful smiles could not be contained. Pouring every ounce of his being into the choreography, he was the most animated child there. Everyone watching could tell he was thoroughly enjoying it. He was incredibly cute and entertaining, and I overheard many flattering comments from nearby parents. What a beautiful blessing for my incredibly fragile heart! Afterward, the families and teachers shared a meal. Zack sat next to me, ravenously devouring broccoli with ranch dressing. Amazed, I turned to Robert and asked him, "Did you ever think you'd live to see the day when Zack would participate in a school program with such unbridled enthusiasm—and then follow it up by eating broccoli?"

"Never in a million years!" Robert replied.

Zack's transformation was nothing short of a miracle, and both of us knew we were privileged witnesses.

Next on the calendar was the Christmas production. Besides a large number of complicated songs to remember, there was a machine blowing glittering, fluffy snow-like stuff onto the children. It was quite mesmerizing to those of us in the audience, yet Zack managed to stay focused on the show. He didn't disappear into his own little stimming world as he had done when he was younger. (What a blessing to be past the stims!) As astounding as this was, nothing could compare to the next wonderful thing that happened.

The lights were dimmed very low during one of the songs. All of a sudden, there was a barrage of camera flashes. Memories of Zack's previous hysterics regarding cameras came flooding back. Although he now tolerated having his picture taken, he had never experienced so many flashes at once. "How would he handle this sensory overload?" I fretted. Panic threatened to overtake me, and my heart raced. It felt like someone had turned up the thermostat in the building. When I finally took a much-needed breath, I realized that Zack was just fine—no screeching, no tantrum, not a single negative reaction from him whatsoever. His beautiful smile never left his face. Once again we had front-row seats to watch a miracle unfold before our very eyes!

The theme for the final program was a Mickey Mouse Club Jamboree. Before the individual roles were assigned, the children took turns trying on the various costumes. According to his teacher, Zack looked quite dapper with his gorgeous blue eyes twinkling and thick, brown perfect curls peeking out from under the black top hat. Complete with boots and a tuxedo jacket with tails, Zack thrilled all of his classmates when he was chosen as the ringmaster. The special night was soon upon us. Never in my life have I seen a cuter little boy than my Zack. Even more remarkable than his adorable appearance was the fact that he could now wear a costume without a hint of green and tolerate a hat on his head. These were no small triumphs.

As the ringmaster, Zack's role was to wave a wand embellished by a long, glittery ribbon. Then he was to flick the stick as though it were a whip at the child dressed up as a lion. When I heard about his costume and the responsibilities that came with the role, I was troubled by flashbacks of Zack flailing his stick and his eternal wrapping and unwrapping of string. I could still hear the screeching that ensued when I demanded for him to stop. I feared momentarily that the past was going to come back with a vengeance.

I thought, "What do you mean he gets to flick a stick? One with a mesmerizing string on the end? Relax Mom. Just take a deep breath. Now take another, and then another. Okay, now that I have recovered my emotions, I feel sure he will do just fine. Zack will not stim on the stick, the ribbon, or anything else this program has to offer. He will enjoy this experience immensely, and no one will be the wiser about his history with autism. I can finally enjoy this experience too, as a mom should."

Thank you, oh Lord, my strength and my Redeemer, for giving my son back to me. He is my amazing little miracle, and I will never, ever take him for granted. You have brought such joy to my distraught heart that words cannot truly express my gratitude to You.

Nothing great was ever achieved without enthusiasm.
-Ralph Waldo Emerson [1]

In that day you will say: "Give thanks to the LORD, call on his name; make known among the nations what he has done, and proclaim that his name is exalted. Sing to the LORD, for he has done glorious things; let this be known to all the world. Shout aloud and sing for joy.
(Isaiah 12:4-6a)

---

1 Copyright 1996 Cook Communications Ministries. God's Little Instruction Book For Men by Honor Books. Used with permission. All rights reserved.

12

Birthdays: From Fits to Friends

Having a child with autism can often make social gatherings a living nightmare— that is, if your presence is even requested at the special occasion in the first place. I had first hoped that the cessation of invitations following Zack's diagnosis was nothing more than the result of very busy lives for every family with little ones. But I undoubtedly had the impression that my friends felt very uncomfortable around Zack. I suspect they just didn't know how to interact with him or what to expect. I could hardly blame them; half the time *I* didn't know what triggers and situations lay ahead. Walking on eggshells while holding my breath was a common occurrence when *I* spent time with Zack, and I loved him desperately.

I also could relate to the reservations of other parents: Would he hurt their kids? Would he throw a tantrum and screech? Would I, the exasperated mom, be a wreck yet again? Would I talk their ears off describing the latest and greatest autism therapy technique? Would I be too intense, insisting that my kid engage with someone on some level, despite the probable eruptions?

Regardless of the reason, the invitations rarely came. Yes, my feelings were hurt, and I felt sad that the relationships with our friends had changed. I wished so badly that my kid could fit in, but he just didn't. Because of our son's severe challenges, our dynamic with the outside world was also severely challenged. Although being excluded was an understandable result of our situation, I'm sure it was not the intention of the other parents to hurt me. Sadly, my friends could not relate to my experience because their children were not social outcasts. Their children had friends who invited them to attend their parties. They fit in, but my Zack did not.

Even hosting our own birthday parties was a challenge. When Jacob turned five, he desperately wanted to have his party at Peter Piper Pizza. We assumed this option would be less work. Hosting a party in a "clean" house was impossible, given the demands of therapy, so we welcomed the chance to let the restaurant do the clean-up instead. Zack was, for all intents and purposes, nonverbal at this point. He screeched when we tried to videotape the singing, the cake, and the presents. Every incidental touch in the climbing area brought about even more screeching. Thankfully, the entire restaurant was incredibly loud, and Zack was so well hidden by the climbing apparatus that it wasn't obvious to everyone whose child was carrying on so. I know this sounds awful, but usually when I took him out in public everyone knew this "problem child" was mine, so the unpleasantness must be "my fault." It was nice, then, to have a brief moment of anonymity upon occasion.

After this experience, we decided it would be much easier in the future to just have simple parties with a few close friends willing to come to our home and "go with the flow." Because Zack's oversensitivity to cameras was still problematic, we weren't able to get pictures or video footage for another two years. Smaller groups in a familiar environment with familiar people seemed to help him handle parties more easily. A limited number of activities, such as simply riding bikes or playing in the backyard, kept him from feeling overwhelmed by the social occasion.

Our very gracious neighbors were well aware of our circumstances. Despite the high probability of inappropriate outbursts from Zack, they consistently invited all of us to their twin boys' birthday parties. I was so grateful to them for accepting our family and our difficult son at a time when we all desperately needed to be included. These wonderful people also granted me a nice perk in the process of being so loving. Attending their parties gave me an ideal opportunity to gauge Zack's social progress from year to year. This, in turn, inspired me to come up with new, productive strategies for his continual development of social skills.

The first of these neighborhood birthday parties was three years ago. Zack was three and a half, and all social interactions were enormously difficult for him. "Musical Chairs" was first on the list of activities. I tried my best to explain the rules to Zack beforehand so that he could be prepared, but my efforts were all in vain. He was so fixated on the green chair that nothing else mattered. The fact that he had managed to remain in the game after the first couple of turns was irrelevant. He had been displaced from the only "acceptable" chair, and this spurred him to bawl uncontrollably. On the verge of tears myself, I realized that pulling him out of the game was my only option. I wanted to be discreet, but his tantrums were at their worst at this age, so incorporating the therapy hold was inevitable. I prayed, "This is so hard, Lord; carry me! Give me the strength to survive this trial! I want to give up! I want my baby to be okay! I don't want to do this therapy hold! I don't want to draw attention and curiosity to him! I just want my baby to be okay! Make him okay! Make him okay! I need him to be okay!"

"Simon Says" was next on the agenda. Zack was not yet interested in imitating his peers, so this game was also discouraging. At least this disappointment was subtle in nature, as it was for the next two activities. Singing "Happy Birthday" and opening presents made no noticeable impression on Zack. He didn't participate in any of the festivities, nor did he watch what the other children were doing. Unless I forced the issue, all interaction with others was absent.

He didn't want to jump in the big, bouncy blow-up castle because the other kids might have touched him in an unpredictable, uncontrollable manner. Smacking the piñata with the baseball bat was the only aspect of the party he really enjoyed. Of course it was fun—he *was* flailing a stick, after all. But even the piñata would have been a dismal failure had he been old enough to wear a blindfold. Fortunately, he was considered part of the younger class of kids and wasn't forced to tolerate such an "unacceptable" sensation.

Throughout most of the afternoon, Zack was quite overstimulated by all of the activity and excitement. Desiring to escape into his own little world, he made multiple attempts to sit all alone in a quiet corner where he could flap his hands. Not on my watch! My Zack was going to learn how to tolerate life if I had anything to say about it. As I redirected this persistent stim and brought him back to the social environment, I could see and feel the stares. Many who were present were not aware of the particulars of our situation, but surely they had their suspicions about his disturbing behaviors.

A few months later Zack turned four, and we hosted a small birthday party with our family and friends. I remember Zack running with his friend, Alex, who was three years older. Both managed to trip and fall into cactus. Alex reacted as any typical child would. Verging on hysteria, he screamed and writhed in pain, making his parents' needle-plucking task nearly impossible. Our Zack, who often screamed in response to a loving touch, sat quietly and perfectly still. Easily and methodically, James and I pulled out the spines. It was the one and only time in the history of Zack's autism that I was thankful for his unnatural lack of responsiveness to external stimuli.

Around this time we took a trip to Colorado to help some friends celebrate their daughter's birthday. Except for his own siblings, Zack knew none of the children. This party was the biggest I had ever seen; there must have been 50 kids and tons of parents. Bombarded with activity after activity, the celebration was deafening and dazzling. Thoroughly frightened, Zack needed to get out. For two hours he wandered aimlessly, flapping his hands. This environment was enormously trying for Zack, and I found myself torn between visiting with friends and attempting to make my precious boy stop his odd behavior. Enjoyable as visiting would have been, my beloved son took the first priority. Drawing him out of his stim was not going to be easy, however, because this event was far beyond his ability to cope. Mustering up the courage and strength I needed, I tried my best to help him without causing a scene; but once again, my efforts failed miserably.

In situations like that one, it was imperative that I intervene. Sadly, tantrums would be the inevitable result. Despite my desire to help him understand the social world, every unnerving episode made it crystal clear that we still had a lot of work to do. So when the school year began, I volunteered to assist in Zack's classroom once a week during the lunch hour. He would require both my support as well as that of his teachers in order to master effective social skills. My participation in the classroom activities provided a much-deserved break for his teachers. At the same time, I was able to model for them strategies that had been successful for me. This also provided the opportunity for us to brainstorm about solutions together when issues arose.

Much of my time at school revolved around playing games. I wanted Zack to notice the actions of others, handle his emotions more appropriately, and practice taking turns and sharing. One activity that was especially popular was playing recordings of silly songs and acting out the lyrics. We took turns picking our favorites and pointing out the superb interpretations of everyone involved. This activity helped the children become more observant, while also providing a gross motor "fix." The board game "Candy Land" was fabulous for encouraging social/emotional maturity. Even though getting the kids to take turns was relatively easy, the far greater challenge was insisting they come to terms with the game's inherent chaos and disappointments. The children and I came up with encouraging phrases, which we then practiced over and over and over.

By the time the neighborhood twins had another birthday party, Zack was no longer flapping, thank the Lord. Now four and a half years old, he once again had no interest in the "Happy Birthday" song or the presents. But I did manage, without too much persuasion, to get him to try jumping in the air-filled castle. The thought of being touched was still distasteful to him, but his desire to bounce was strong enough to overcome his apprehension. Of course, he still wished to sit only in the green chair while playing "Musical Chairs." Even so, the game etiquette he had learned at school helped him maintain a relatively pleasant attitude, despite the instances when he found himself on an "unacceptable" chair. What a proud moment for me as Zack's mom to see him make that much progress. Taking in a deep breath, I basked in our success.

When Zack lost the game, however, things deteriorated rapidly. Even I was caught off-guard. Zack was too caught up in his emotions at that moment to apply the "good loser" lesson from school. Crying inconsolably, he required a 10-minute recovery time from his meltdown. Rather than allow myself to feel defeated, I decided to focus on the positive aspect of the situation—at least now he cared about winning. Even though he continued to have the occasional trying moment, we were still making strides in the right direction.

When it was time for "Simon Says," Zack understood the rules of the game and imitated the actions of the leader. Again, I found myself relaxed, reveling in the progress he'd made. But then again, my satisfaction was overshadowed by another loss and another outburst from Zack. As was so often the case, I could sense every eye on me! At least this time I didn't feel like someone had turned up the thermostat. Having been in the trenches for almost two years, I guess my skin was tangibly thicker. Perhaps because Zack's autistic manifestations were no longer as severe or widespread, I had gained a better perspective. Volunteering in the classroom had also made a dramatic difference. Greatly encouraged, I continued to help in Zack's class for another year.

When the twins hosted their next party, Zack actually enjoyed playing the games. Although he was disappointed when he lost, he kept himself from losing control. Jumping in the castle was "awesome" to him, and he wasn't bothered in the least when the other kids bumped into him. He joined the group to sing "Happy Birthday" and even paid minor attention to the presents.

Zack also made attempts to talk to his peers. Yet, his poorly articulated comments were very difficult to comprehend, so he did not get much feedback from the other kids. Amazingly enough, Zack took it all in stride. Other than his obvious speech disorder, there were no noticeable developmental delays that would catch the eyes of the other parents. It was such a relief to no longer feel like we were the object of everyone's attention!

Another party started out with the children riding bikes. Zack was perfectly capable of riding his bike without training wheels on a smooth surface, but this was a dirt road peppered with plenty of ruts and bumps. He crashed many times and cried a bit, but one would expect this reaction from any five-year-old striving to keep up with the big kids. To my delight, he happily participated in the other birthday games. Thankfully, once again, no questioning glances were sent my way.

Another year later, we found ourselves back at the twins' house. Zack was now six and a half, and he had become an incredibly pleasant, obedient child. He enjoyed taking part in all of the games with a huge smile on his face! I was pleased to see how nicely he interacted with his peers. Although they still had some difficulty understanding him, the other children acknowledged him and responded to him as well. He was so self-assured and happy, handling himself with more grace and maturity than some of the older children!

Because all this was so far beyond the realm of our experience, I momentarily wondered if I might be hallucinating: "Am I dreaming? Is this *my* Zack? Can these visions really be taking place?" After pinching myself several times, I realized that this incredible scenario was our new reality! My son had come back to me—a more wonderful blessing I could never imagine!

Zack's world is a very different place than it was a mere few years ago. Although he is rather tough out on the soccer field, I'm quite confident that he would cry if he were to fall onto another cactus. We had wanted to comfort him with our touch for years. Now we can do so freely, without fear of him screeching. I suppose all of those years of occupational therapy gave Zack a greater understanding of the world around him, which subsequently allowed him to better interpret and handle external stimuli.

Several other victories have been won as a result of these occupational interventions. The wind used to bother Zack's ears something fierce, and he had been unable to bear loud movies or music. He used to freak out when his hands were dirty. Bright sunlight also sent him over the edge. Now these very things don't affect him negatively at all.

We spent two years desensitizing Zack to camera flashes and the camcorder, trying to help him understand that he wasn't being hurt. For that reason, flashing toys were incorporated into our therapies. When he was older, he started paying attention to our little "ham," Jacob, who enthusiastically posed for pictures. Once Zack resolved to imitate and keep up with his older brother, the situation really began to change for the better. Also, when he became aware of the fact that other kids would tease him if he didn't behave a certain way, this became a powerful motivator as well. Caving in to peer pressure didn't come right away, but over time this new behavior did emerge. Parents of teens often worry about the power their peers wield, and rightly so. But in our case, with Zack so young, we have welcomed this positive influence with open arms.

Our amazing boy has come so far that my presence is no longer necessary during play dates and parties. Sometimes Zack still needs a little encouragement to participate in a strange environment, but if he feels comfortable with just one child, he does just fine. At school, when he has the option to work on an activity alone or with a friend, he usually chooses to work by himself. Many people prefer to work on their own, so this doesn't really concern me. He doesn't mind working with others, however, when it's expected of him. He actually has friends. He is sweet, affectionate, well-behaved, and pleasant to be around. I had hoped for this day, prayed for this day, and pleaded for this day; but I don't know if I had ever truly thought this day would ever arrive. Zack's transformation is as remarkable as the universe is vast, and we are blessed beyond belief.

The mother's love is like God's love; He loves us not because we are lovable, but because it is His nature to love, and because we are His children.

—Earl Riney[1]

Have mercy on me, O God, have mercy on me, for in you my soul takes refuge. I will take refuge in the shadow of your wings until the disaster has passed. I cry out to God Most High, to God, who fulfills {his purpose} for me.

(Psalm 57:1-2)

---

1 *Copyright 1995 Cook Communications Ministries.* ***God's Little Instruction Book For Mom*** *by Honor Books. Used with permission. All rights reserved.*

13

Weather: Understanding the Elements

Many children with autism are particularly sensitive to weather conditions. During his first year of early intervention, Zack was definitely one of them. Unrelenting whines and screams emanated from our precious son nearly every time he ventured outside. Squinting always accompanied the fussing, and his annoyance and discomfort were unmistakable. Bright, sunny days were by far the worst. Our hometown is located in southern New Mexico, where we have approximately 345 sunny days per year. Snow birds flock to our city every winter to enjoy our clear, blue skies and temperate climate. As gorgeous as our days are here, the sun was not appreciated in any way by our family at this time.

I am aware that countless people (including myself) are sensitive to bright sunlight, but Zack's violent response was like none I'd ever seen. Dealing with Zack's public tantrums was difficult enough at his age, but persuading him to go outside for a mere moment was an even greater challenge to overcome. The short trip from our front door to the minivan elicited intense protests and tantrums.

Even though they may have relieved his eyes, he refused to wear sunglasses. I suppose this new sensation of darkened vision, like so many others, was just as intolerable to him as the light.

Negative reactions from Zack were common on overcast days as well. Maybe his ultra-sensitive eyes still couldn't handle exposure to even filtered sunlight. Perhaps he was irritated by the occasional breeze. (I know for a fact that the wind bothered his ears, because he would often scream and cover his ears on especially windy days. Something about this sensation really sent him over the edge.) On rainy days, especially if there were several in a row, Zack grew progressively more lethargic and uncooperative.

But Zack's overall response was never quite as severe as on stormy days. We spent these days engaging in quiet, more subdued activities. Neither of us felt up to a lot of hard work at such times, so we took it much easier, resting in the love of our relationship. We cuddled, read books, and played in a subdued manner. I used to call these "lost" days, even though they really weren't. My sense of guilt over the less than "productive" time made it difficult for me to recognize that these calm days filled with human interaction still played a very important role in Zack's recovery.

When we were knee-deep in all-day therapy, some days were definitely better than others, while some days were just so unbelievably bad that I wanted to give up, crawl into a hole, and "die already." Really trying days always seemed to take place when the windstorms in our area were just beginning, or dying out. Because daily therapy sessions were so challenging, Zack often protested about having to participate. But when something was going on with the weather, he was even more adamant than usual about not being touched and resisting therapy. Instead, he only wanted to hide under a blanket in his room with the lights off. On these days no amount of therapy holds would force him to engage, make the screeching stop, or keep him from stimming.

Our amazing psychologist, Robert, always seemed to have an infinite supply of effective solutions for our issues, yet even he was extraordinarily concerned about Zack's disturbing behavior. Watching this intense manifestation of autism was difficult enough for me to come to terms with, but seeing Robert's troubled expression was even more disconcerting. He was the one professional I had come to rely on for hope, even if it was just a tiny glimmer. But at these times, nothing in his face suggested hope—quite the opposite, in fact. I was fearful that Zack, who was just beginning to show some progress, was going to slip away from me forever. I fretted over the possibility of losing my baby completely, not even able to imagine how I would deal with such a devastating tragedy. Because I loved my adorable child more than life itself, I wanted him to understand the depths of my love and bond with his mommy as a boy should. His heart-breaking behavior was not at all what I had desired or anticipated. How could I be expected to handle the unbearable?

My faith teaches that I should be at peace in all circumstances. In my head this made perfect sense, but my heart took much longer to come around. I know that I have the assurance of heaven through the sacrifice of Christ, and this knowledge is very comforting. With this understanding comes the freedom to live according to God's will. I surrendered to this truth with my mind in the early days of our journey, but emotionally I felt so incredibly helpless and hopeless. Watching Zack's severe tantrums and complete inability to socialize on any level, I would fall apart again and again. Crying and praying, praying and crying, I asked God why my precious boy was so miserable, so unreachable, and so horribly symptomatic on these days.

At this point Zack didn't have the language necessary to understand my questions or tell me what was wrong, so I was so completely clueless and thus felt discouragingly inadequate. I desperately prayed, "Lord, I need wisdom. I need a revelation. I need a solution. Help me! Help me save my Zack from this hideous disorder. Autism is stealing the life from my beautiful boy!"

Although my father suffers from sinus headaches whenever the barometric pressure changes too rapidly, it never occurred to me that Zack might be plagued by this condition as well—until one fateful day. It was the day after Thanksgiving, and I could not get out of bed for the life of me. I had such an awful headache, like none I had ever experienced. The morning light was excruciatingly bright, and I was extremely nauseous. If anyone had dared touch me, I would surely have screamed. I was suffering my first migraine headache, and it put me out of commission for two and a half days. Who would ever have thought that the torment of a migraine would be considered a blessing? But in my case it served an amazing purpose, providing me with some desperately needed insight. Once I had recovered, it dawned on me that my experience with the migraine was suspiciously similar to Zack's reaction to stormy days.

The next time a front blew in, Zack predictably reverted to his stormy day- behaviors. Hoping to curb the awful screeching and stimming, I gave him some ibuprofen. After 20 minutes without any improvement, I thought to myself, "Maybe the medicine wasn't strong enough." It surely wouldn't have been strong enough for *my* migraine. I then gave him a dose of acetaminophen, since it can be administered in an alternating pattern with ibuprofen without risking an overdose. Believe it or not, within 10 minutes he was smiling, happy, and ready for therapy. I was so impressed by his remarkable transformation that whenever I saw Zack slipping into another migraine I gave him the two medications concurrently. Within 10 minutes, he was better. It worked like magic! I could hardly believe how easy it was to help him get back to "normal."

One more comment about the migraines: as I placed Zack on the dairy-free, gluten-free diet, the frequency of the migraines greatly diminished. When we transitioned Zack to the preschool, we had a doctor's note approving our treatment for migraine symptoms, just in case it was necessary. In the course of the two years he was at this school, he only had three migraines. Since then, he has not had a single migraine symptom. I don't know for certain that this improvement is connected to the new diet; there may be some other explanation. At any rate, I couldn't be happier.

The sun still irritates Zack's eyes, but his reaction now falls within the range of normalcy—no more screeching and carrying on as before. The same is true with his response to the wind. I can only venture a guess at the reason for these phenomena. Perhaps having the language to express "it is too bright" or "it is very windy" now helps Zack process his external environment better. Maybe these sensitivities somehow remedied themselves as the new neurological pathways were being formed. We never performed any specific drills to teach him to handle the effects of weather. Quite frankly, I can't even begin to imagine how one would go about setting up that sort of program. Again, I'm thrilled with the outcome, regardless.

Consecutive rainy days still make Zack lethargic and uncooperative, but I believe it's a result of his body reacting to an insufficient amount of sunlight. Many people don't feel like themselves after several rainy days. In fact, some residents of overcast areas must use a regular dose of light therapy to ward off depression, anxiety, and sleep disorders. James and I personally experienced the effects of sunless days while visiting Seattle. After just two days, we found ourselves under the solarium sun-lamp catching some rays. When the timer clicked off, we were disappointed, feeling the need for more "happy" time. I suspect Zack takes after us in this respect.

Many children with autism have a very difficult time getting a good night's rest. Light therapy, melatonin supplements, blood pressure-lowering drugs, and other sleep aids are often used in an attempt to remedy this condition, with varying levels of success. James and I felt extremely blessed that there was no need to medicate Zack in order for him to sleep. He gave up napping at the age of two, but when he slept at night, he slept well. We hoped that his uninterrupted REM sleep would allow his brain to build the new neurological pathways we desired for him to have. Whether or not the long nights truly helped with his recovery, we considered ourselves fortunate for the restful nights we were able to enjoy. So many parents don't have this luxury and are severely sleep deprived, which makes their day-to-day dealings with autism even more difficult.

Now that our family has overcome the challenges of Zack's autism, I'd like to be able to report that I have learned my lesson and now continually live with a sense of peace at all times, regardless of our circumstances. Truth be known, my heart still takes longer than my head to live accordingly. It is not quite as slow as it once was, perhaps. I think such lessons come our way throughout life, giving us ample opportunities to grow and mature. As we grow closer to the Lord, we learn to trust Him more completely, thus finding it easier to allow His Spirit to influence our lives. As the Holy Spirit leads us, He empowers us to fulfill God's purposes.

It is impossible for that man to despair who remembers that his Helper is omnipotent. - Anonymous*[1]

I have learned the secret of being content in any and every situation, whether well fed or hungry, whether living in plenty or in want. I can do everything through him who gives me strength. (Philippians 4:12b – 13)

1 Copyright 1996 Cook Communications Ministries. God's Little Instruction Book For Men by Honor Books. Used with permission. All rights reserved

14

Soccer: Success in the Social Realm

During my initial attempts to write this chapter, I discovered my inability to adequately describe my husband's experience as Zack's soccer coach. I truly appreciate James's involvement in this particular therapy. (Yes, it definitely was therapy, and it also was a lot of hard work—don't let him fool you.) Acknowledging the great benefits of his sacrifice, I wanted to include his experience in my book, but I found that I could not do it justice on my own. Therefore, this story wa written by both James and myself and is told from his perspective.

To all the parents who take time out of their busy lives to coach youth sports: my hat's off to you. The amount of patience, determination, and commitment required is not lost on me. One has the responsibility to teach not only the rules of the sport but also good sportsmanship, friendship, loyalty, teamwork, and leadership. I know because I coach Zack's under-six (U6) soccer team. At the start of every business week, I compare notes with a coworker/fellow U6 coach. We ask each other how our respective teams performed at their games, as well as how we were surviving the coaching experience.

Recently he expressed concern over one of the kids on his team who appears to struggle with ADHD (Attention Deficit Hyperactivity Disorder). He made observations such as, "This child is not very focused. He often doesn't pay attention. Some days his coordination is completely absent." After patiently listening and empathizing with his plight, I responded, "You know why I'm Zack's soccer coach, don't you? When Zack first started soccer, there was no way on earth I could comfortably leave him in the hands of another authority figure, no matter how trusted or respected he was. It would have been impossible for that coach to handle his autism. You think ADHD is bad? You have no idea! Imagine a kid that refuses to kick a ball that isn't green, obsessively winds his fingers in and out of the goal netting, or cries if another child touches him." This simple yet boastful conversation—men do compete over the oddest things—put everything back in perspective for my colleague. Sitting down to write this chapter has sent me back to that first season. Forced to stop and reflect, I found myself praising the Lord for all of the progress our son has made over the past few years.

Zack started playing soccer in the fall of 2004, at four years of age. From the very beginning, his autism demonstrated itself with a vengeance. I had fully expected Zack to break down for one reason or another that first day, but I was surprised by how quickly and violently the initial tantrum occurred.

The field was bursting with happy, enthusiastic children and parents. All of them were enjoying the beauty of a perfect autumn afternoon, and excitement abounded—except for Zack. For some seemingly mysterious reason, he proceeded to throw himself on the ground and scream as though he were being burned alive. His problem was not that he had been physically injured in any way; he was just consumed with hysteria over the fact that some other child had dared to kick his *green* soccer ball. If one of the typical children on the team had reacted in this manner, I would have given him (or her) a stern lecture and a timeout on the sidelines, but I didn't feel that I could impose the same consequence on Zack. After all, I knew that he could not help himself from behaving that way. Yet, I was nearly paralyzed with doubt. Forced to immediately deal with the situation while the other children and parents watched with obvious curiosity, I prayed for wisdom and strength. And this was only the first of many similar challenging moments that would follow over the course of that first year.

Upon evaluating my decision to put Zack on a soccer team, I realize that I had not fully appreciated the continuous struggles my wife endured during therapy sessions. I had witnessed her frustrating attempts to get him to interact. I had personally experienced his breakdowns in private and public. Many a cart-full of merchandise was left sitting in the checkout line at Home Depot because I had overextended Zack's tolerance for that environment. Each exasperating incident meant an immediate trip to the car so that both Zack and I could regroup. Embarrassing as these kinds of scenarios were, at least I had the freedom to depart and leave the spectacle behind me.

Soccer was a different story, however, because I could not simply collect Zack and go. In addition to being a coach for my son, I was also the coach for all the other children on the team. Of even greater importance, I was absolutely determined to see my son succeed—not merely at soccer, but at a normal life. I wanted him to be able to make friends and experience the camaraderie of teammates. But none of these dreams were to be fulfilled on this first day of soccer. Much to my dismay, instead of taking his first steps into a greater world, Zack was lying on the ground, thrashing and wailing inconsolably. All of his teammates shied away, as if they feared Zack's malady would next claim them.

Tantrums over the green ball were only a taste of what was to come. Lord help me and the rest of the team if Zack kicked the ball and it didn't go where he anticipated, if another child beat him to the ball and kicked it instead, or if another child (even one from his own team) scored when Zack wanted to make the goal. Every "unacceptable" instance resulted in an embarrassing exhibition. Dramatically throwing himself on the ground, he would whine, pout, and cry. Zack then adamantly refused to participate in any way, shape, or form.

Chaos is a typical state of affairs in the U6 soccer league. Tatianna and I affectionately refer to it as "amoeba soccer" because all of the kids swarm right around the ball, moving about in the form of an amoeba. The majority of the game is left up to chance, with no logical rhyme or reason, since these young players are too inexperienced to employ any real strategy. For a child who found it extremely difficult to handle the absence of structure and predictability, this was a particularly exasperating environment for Zack. In an attempt to escape, he would often wrap his hands up in the goal netting rather than remain in the midst of the chaos. This activity didn't appear even remotely "normal," especially when he had to be pulled off the netting and then off the field. The resulting outburst would have been much more characteristic of a child half his age.

But this was only the tip of the iceberg. During some games Zack was so distraught that slimy booger streams flowed from his nose to his knees. The gook spread to his uniform, his hands, and his arms. Meanwhile, the other players were disgusted beyond description. Admittedly, this was not a very effective means of "winning friends and influencing people"!

So, we taught Zack socially appropriate reactions to every potential circumstance that he would likely encounter on the soccer field. Both at home and during practice, Tatianna and I drilled him on appropriate responses to various situations. For example, if he kicked the ball, and it went askew: "Oh well, try again." And if the other team scored: "D'oh," à la Homer Simpson or an even more sportsmanlike, "Nice shot." We also taught him what to say if a fellow teammate scored: "Hooray for us!" or "Great job, <u>(name of child)</u>." Believe it or not, because Zack failed to recognize the positive aspects of a teammate scoring, it was necessary to teach him even this fundamental truth. Walking and talking him through these scenarios beforehand helped to counteract his uncertainty and gave him a sense of control in his environment. Unfortunately, this strategy took a great deal of time to take hold and make a difference. Meanwhile, I still had his tantrums to address.

Being responsible for the entire team, I wasn't free to drop everything and perform our trusty therapy hold on Zack every time there was an inappropriate outburst. As frequent as these conniption fits were, I would have had to spend the entire practice time restraining him. Instead, I was forced to ignore the tantrum until I was able to redirect the other kids to a more independent soccer drill. Occasionally Zack had spent enough down time during his wait that I was able to talk him through the problematic issue sufficiently. Other times he required an extra tight embrace to satisfy his deep- pressure sensory "fix."

When it came to the green soccer ball, an initial concession was made. Zack, and only Zack, would have the privilege of kicking the very special ball. This was the only way I could get him to participate in the practice. Once Zack started to enjoy soccer a little more, I slowly encouraged him to kick the green ball back and forth with a teammate. Working on sharing and taking turns helped him to become less rigid in his demands. In turn, this promoted a more reasonable demeanor and created a more enjoyable experience for Zack and all those around him. After about three months, he was captivated enough with soccer that I was able to successfully address the occasional tantrum with a time-out. At those times, he was penalized by having to sit on the bench and watch as the other kids enjoyed their sport. Not wanting to be excluded from the fun, he began to change his behavior for the better.

Months later I managed to convince Zack that the green ball was not official. If he wanted to be a big boy like his older brother Jacob and play soccer, then he had to use the ball approved by the league. Being a big boy had become very important to him, praise the Lord! (It was sure nice to have an effective strategy at our disposal.) The green ball stayed at home from that point forward, earning the title of "official backyard ball." Giving his ball a position of honor helped assuage his lingering feelings of disappointment. We had effectively dealt with one more of Zack's peculiarities.

Eventually Zack also began to care about his teammates' impressions of him, not that they would have teased him for being odd, because wonderfully gracious kids comprised our team. Even so, we made a point of beginning to talk with him about his unusual traits. Because he had no innate understanding of what children nowadays consider strange, social "faux pas" had to be spelled out for him. Desiring to fit in, Zack made a genuine effort to do things the other kids would consider normal. Reminding him of the opinions of others became another powerful tool—one that we were then able to apply to other areas of his life.

Like most children, Zack had his moments of selective hearing and lack of focus. In this area he was quite "typical." At least this was a widespread challenge for me as a coach, rather than a specific frustration limited to Zack as a result of the autism. When I sought to tackle this challenge, I was inspired to borrow a strategy from one of Zack's intervention plans. After frequently witnessing his attention dramatically improving with intense physical activity, I decided to have the distracted members of the team run laps around the practice field. Implementing this routine also promoted a better attitude and spirit of cooperation, and I'm convinced that it also helped the entire team get in better shape from a cardiovascular standpoint. Though the jury is still out as far as the other children are concerned, without a doubt it dramatically helped Zack concentrate.

By Zack's final U6 game, he had become a leader on his team. To make sure that his teammates lined up correctly before the kick off, he verbally and physically directed them into position. He no longer became upset when the other team scored, and he congratulated his own teammates when they made goals. Rather than simply trying to take the ball from his own teammates, he now called for the ball when he was "open."

Typically, a U6 player has just as great a chance of losing the ball to his own teammate as losing the ball to the other team. That being the case, one particular instance inspired Zack to do something truly amazing. After just gaining control of the ball, he became aware of his own teammates rushing toward him in an effort to complete the "amoeba formation." Fearing that their unbridled enthusiasm would impede his efforts, he yelled out, "Get away!" His outburst was so loud and authoritative that every single child on the field instantly stopped and backed away. When the other team came to its senses and charged, Zack managed to dribble the ball between all of the players and score. In the aftermath of his goal, his teammates cheered his impressive skills. They had grown to appreciate our son as a fellow soccer player and as a friend!

More remarkably, Zack reciprocated the sentiments. He had finally taken running steps into that greater world—the world I had desired for him on that very first day of soccer practice. He was experiencing the joy of friendship and the camaraderie of teammates. The Lord had certainly answered my prayers. Not only had I survived the embarrassment and frustration of coaching under incredibly trying circumstances, but my son was actually living a life filled with meaningful human interaction. That, more than anything, was worth cheering about!

Impossibilities vanish when a man and his God confront a mountain.

—Robert Schuller[1]

Jesus looked at them and said, "With man this is impossible, but with God all things are possible."

(Matthew 19:26)

---

1 Copyright 1995 Cook Communications Ministries. God's Little Instruction Book For Dad by Honor Books. Used with permission. All rights reserved.

15

Television/Movies/Computers: Engage or Eliminate

The influence of television, movies, and computers on children is a hot topic right now. With heavy bombardments of commercials, questionable viewing material and language, and the lightning speed at which these images flash before young impressionable eyes, there is certainly reason for concern. Internet access has its own risks—sexual predators and pornography, just to name a few. These stationary visual activities have also been held responsible for the rise in childhood obesity and heart disease. Many special interest groups are advocating increased awareness of the dangers of these media for children. With autism, this issue becomes even more relevant.

Many children with autism are never happier, more pleasant, or docile than when they are placed in front of a TV screen or computer game. These activities may appear harmless on the surface, but I assure you they are not. Granted, there may be no immediate physical threat, but these distractions are non-interactive. Herein lies the problem: self-stimulatory and/or obsessive compulsions can easily thrive in such an environment. Yes, there may be some basic educational or social benefits involved with these activities; however, they do not teach practicalities or present tools that help one function in the real world. Communicating in a meaningful and rewarding way with others is lost in this environment. These skills, reinforced in a variety of ways for typical children, are inherent deficits for those with autism.

In the short run, allowing an autistic child to watch TV or play on a computer may give parents a welcome respite. Yet in the long run, one most likely may be doing this child a great disservice.

When our Zack was two and a half years old, he loved TV, just not in the same way as other kids his age. With every exposure he transformed into a zombie-like creature. Now, I realize that typical kids tend to get lost in their shows too, but there was something eerily different about the way Zack watched TV. He didn't giggle when something funny happened, he wasn't sad when something sad happened, and he was never frightened during the scary parts. In fact, he didn't react to anything on the screen at all and expressed no emotion whatsoever. It was as though he wasn't *really* watching or understanding; instead, he seemed compelled to enter a near-comatose state. Clearly, television was not good for him in any way, shape, or form.

At the onset of Zack's unofficial autism diagnosis, we implemented our policy of limited viewing. He was allowed to watch 10 minutes at a time, three times a day, as a reward/down time. Because it exposed him to letters, numbers, and colors while modeling appropriate peer interactions, the one program he was allowed to watch was *Sesame Street*. About a year and a half later, we also introduced Zack to *Dora the Explorer*. We hoped that the unique format of this program, which encourages children to blurt out responses, would give him more practice speaking. Abbie, at only two years old, was far more enthusiastic and successful at saying "backpack" than Zack, who was four. As my discouraged heart tried to come to terms with this fact, I decided that I was not up to the challenge, so Dora was no longer a welcome visitor in our house.

We spent a great deal of time and effort trying to keep Zack's skills ahead of his younger sister's. Having been exposed to all of his therapy sessions, Abbie was ahead of the game. In fact, she was so advanced for her age that the two of them were neck-and- neck for a while. Was this trend going to continue indefinitely? Was my beautiful boy destined for a life lacking any potential? Constantly reminded of Zack's widespread developmental delays, I often found myself disheartened. As sad as I was, I do believe, however, that this situation created within me a desperate sense of urgency. This, in turn, inspired me to action. Never was my motivation for therapy greater than when Abbie was chomping at Zack's heels.

Outside of the 10-minute TV sessions, the remainder of Zack's waking hours was filled with one type of therapy or another. He was forced to engage with a real live human being, whether he liked it or not. Trust me, most of the time he did *not* like it. We reviewed emotions, vocabulary, and everything else he didn't know *ad nauseum*. For two years we continued to limit his TV-watching until he had the receptive language and emotional awareness to watch appropriately and with normalcy.

I remember the first time Zack cried during a sad movie. The very fact that he was moved to tears was a miracle. I also remember the first time he giggled hysterically in response to some silliness portrayed on another show. Zack had such joy on his face and in his heart! Instead of just zoning out, he was taking a real interest in the story. The world was starting to open up for him, and he was embracing—not escaping—the wonder of it all.

Of course, with every achievement came new challenges. Even though we had been successful at getting Zack to understand his emotions, we soon discovered that we had actually been a little *too* successful. Our next struggle was the need to constantly remind him that TV shows are not real. Overly consumed with the plot, he had gone from one extreme to the other. He would fly into hysterics when he witnessed something sad, becoming inconsolable for 20 minutes at a time. His oddities were once again surfacing.

Fortunately, with conversation and explanations, we helped him talk through his emotions. We helped him further develop his language skills by having him practice sentences such as, "I'm so sad" or,

"I want to cry." As time went on, we introduced an additional layer of complexity. By asking Zack to imagine and describe a more desired alternative, we allowed him to practice communication while simultaneously nurturing his creative side. We would then reward his efforts by acting out the preferred scenarios, further developing his pretend-play skills.

Zack's interest in computers began later, when he was about four and a half. As with television, we had very specific rules concerning his computer time. At the beginning, he was limited to two, 15-minute sessions a day. An educational emphasis was a must, and he had to play with Jacob or a therapist. We insisted that Zack share, take turns, practice his words, and engage with the other player for the duration of the activity; otherwise, it would be terminated immediately. As he got older and more cooperative, we gradually increased the time period to 30-minute increments.

Because we have successfully addressed these issues, we are now much less concerned about Zack watching TV and movies or playing on the computer occasionally. There is little time during the week for these types of activities anyway with all his homework, chores, soccer, basketball, and music lessons. We allow the kids to indulge somewhat over the weekend, especially if the weather is dreary. Of course, on nice days we send them outside to breathe the fresh air and get some exercise. As trying as Zack's autism was on our family, it did provide us with several unexpected blessings. In this case, we were forced to establish a limited yet reasonably healthy balance of sedentary endeavors—a result that now brings great satisfaction to my heart.

The best things you can give children, next to good habits, are good memories. —Sydney J. Harris[1]

1 Copyright 1995 Cook Communications Ministries. God's Little Instruction Book For Dad by Honor Books. Used with permission. All rights reserved.

Tatianna Dickens

The LORD works out everything for his own ends.
(Proverbs 16:4a)

16

Picking a School: A Crucial Consideration

There are many questions to consider when determining which school would be best for a child with autism. First, does the child have an overall level of compliance and behavior management that would be sufficient for the school environment? Now, I am not implying that the child will never have an incident that needs to be addressed. Even "normal" kids have their moments, as we all do. But it is extremely important to have an adequate behavioral management plan in place at home that can also be implemented successfully at school. Do you have good strategies for your child in place when challenging situations arise? Is your child a danger to himself, other students, or the teachers? Will your child be so disruptive that the teachers will be unable to effectively run the classroom? Will your child deny the teacher an opportunity to teach the other kids as well as your own?

If your answers to the last three questions are yes, then I highly recommend the continuation of your home-based program until these issues are better under control. Incorporate the therapy hold or use an alternative strategy such as ignoring the tantrums until they cease. Find an effective medication for self-injurious behavior if necessary. Design a picture schedule board to ease transitions if your child needs one. Every child on the autism spectrum is going to have unique challenges and issues requiring unique responses, so develop a plan that works for both your individual child and all authority figures dealing with him or her.

Is your child potty-trained? If not, this may be problematic for some private schools but not for others. Does your child have any dietary restrictions, and if so, is the school willing to accommodate them? Are the teachers educated about autism to your satisfaction, and if not, are they enthusiastic about learning and willing to work with you? In our experience, some qualified teachers were difficult to work with because they projected the impression that their opinions concerning our child were superior and therefore indisputable. This scenario may prove moot if your strategies already work, but for those that don't, take heed! Chaos is the most likely outcome. Without a teacher focused on using a teamwork approach, I fear that your success will be limited at best.

Often times the best teachers know nothing about autism initially but are willing to learn and be trained. They may end up being the perfect match for both you and your child. Implementing complementary goals and strategies both at school and home is crucial for success because children with autism thrive on consistency and repetition. If they're exposed to conflicting approaches and therapies, the probability of regression and/or negative behavioral repercussions is significant.

One of my friends has a son who experienced a failure in consistency of methodology within the classroom, and it quickly evolved into a disaster. According to the Individualized Education Plan (IEP), her son was only to be spoken to with pro-active, positive words such as, "Now we are going to sit at the table. We are going to be nice. Hugging is better than hitting." When he sought attention by behaving inappropriately, the teachers were supposed to engage him more intently and frequently. He was also to be directed to perform helpful chores such as sweeping or carrying boxes so that he could receive a desired sensory input and feel a sense of purpose in the classroom. The teachers were supposed to forgo the use of the PECS (picture exchange card system) for communication purposes and rather use verbal instructions since his receptive and expressive language skills were delayed but adequate.

Instead of following the specifics laid out and agreed to at the IEP meeting, the teachers used the PECS. They also spoke negatively to him in a reactive manner: "Don't do that, _____ . Stop doing that, _____. Stop it, _____." They failed to engage him for the entire 30-minute lunch period leading up to his usual acting-out time. They also failed to redirect him with a beneficial sensory chore. As time went on, my friend's child got increasingly more out of hand in the classroom. He craved better quality engagement time from the teachers but didn't know how to ask for it. Because of his echolalia, he came home from school, muttering to himself, over and over, "Don't do that, _____. Stop doing that, ______. Stop it, _____." Her son's persistent negative comments made it crystal clear to my friend and all of his therapists that the IEP wasn't being implemented in a satisfactory way.

She found another school that better met her son's special needs. The teachers at this new school were unfamiliar with autism but took all of my friend's suggestions to heart. They also allowed autism consultants to visit the classroom to model appropriate strategies for them. Her son almost immediately rebounded in this new, productive environment and continues to make great progress at this school.

I highly recommend that every parent of a preschool-aged child with autism visit as many of the classrooms and teachers in the schools located in your district as possible, both public and private. Bring your child along as well, and see how he or she reacts in each setting. Observe how the teachers interact with your child and vice versa. Did they get down to the level of your child's face? Did they try their best to engage your child, even if your child didn't cooperate? Did the teachers have personalities well-suited for your child? What is the child-to-teacher ratio? Children with autism usually require a lot of attention most of the time; so usually, the lower the ratio, the better. Can you volunteer in the classroom or visit on a regular basis? This is a great way to make sure everybody is on the same page. If the school or teachers resist your occasional presence in the classroom, be wary. Most likely, they enjoy doing things their own way and are too inflexible to work with you.

Does this school have an all-day option available when your child is ready to attend all day? After the first year and a half of being Zack's primary therapist, I discovered that it was such a blessing to find a suitable full-day preschool program. Having the opportunity to recover and regroup made it so much easier to brainstorm about the therapy sessions that continued after school and on the weekends. Yes, the non-stop therapy was still in full force at this point, but at least I could muster more energy and enthusiasm for all the work involved because my burden was now shared with others to a large degree.

Parents also need to ask pointed questions when considering placement of their children in schools geared for autism. If the classroom is specifically designed for children with autism, does it provide access to least-restrictive environments with typical peers as their social skills develop? Does the school offer partial inclusion into another classroom or Head Start program? Assimilating children with autism into typical societal environments should be encouraged as soon as possible. A good indicator for this transition is the onset of peer imitation. If one moves too slowly in this respect, additional quirky or disturbing attributes may surface.

When Zack began imitating his peers, he was in a designated autism classroom. Biting and hand-licking were the two modeled oddities he picked up from the other children. Thankfully, we were able to discuss with him the inappropriate nature of these habits as we worked toward the elimination of them. We were also fortunate that he had access to a Head Start program, which provided him with more typical role models to emulate. This class was so ideal for Zack that we were willing to drive him to another town every morning for two years in order for him to attend.

Another favorable consideration for this school was their well-equipped sensory room. Is there a sensory room in the school you are considering? If not, are there sufficient opportunities for your child to participate in such activities in the classroom between especially challenging sessions? This sensory diet is often greatly beneficial or even necessary for children with autism to process what they have recently been taught, and it may also help them settle down when transitioning to something new. When Zack's intervention program began, he required a sensory "fix" every 20 minutes. Using any and all effective motivations at our disposal, we gradually pushed him to increase the time intervals. By the time he entered the preschool a year and a half later, he managed well for about an hour without participating in a sensory activity.

Moreover, when you're weighing your designated autism school options, the quality and quantity of therapy offered in the classroom should be a major determining factor. Do they have therapy centers or activities in their classrooms that will encourage your child to grow and develop? Do they have physical, occupational, and speech therapists? How many hours of therapy would be offered to your child? Do they have a social worker or guidance counselor that you trust and respect—someone you can talk to about your child's strengths and weaknesses? Do they have an aide who can provide a more structured recess environment? I cannot even begin to express how important this final question is. Many children with autism struggle to conform to a social free-for-all like recess. I think you would be hard-pressed to find even one of these children equipped with the social skills necessary to survive this period of time without severe behavioral consequences at worst, or nonsensical stimming at best.

Even when Zack lost his autism diagnosis and advanced to a regular kindergarten class, the lack of structure at recess and before school highlighted his social inadequacies. When we transitioned him from the autism preschool to our local public school, everything was new to him—the playground, the kids, the teachers, and the rooms. Surely he felt overwhelmed, but who wouldn't?

After James dropped him off every morning, Zack would just stand there by the wire fence all alone on the playground, waiting for the one child he knew and felt comfortable around. If she didn't make it to school that day or was running late, he continued to wait. He would never leave the comfort of the fence nor seek out the company of another friend. Not only did this look incredibly odd, but it was absolutely heartbreaking for James to watch. We had worked so hard with Zack on his social skills, and we desperately wanted him to fit in so that he could have friends and be happy.

Because some people tend to freak out when they hear the dreaded "A" word, we had hoped it wouldn't be necessary to divulge Zack's previous autism diagnosis to his new teacher, but we just couldn't allow this playground scenario to continue. Within two weeks' time, I scheduled a meeting with the teacher, the speech therapist, and the principal to share Zack's history along with our concerns. After promising to offer verbal support at home, I asked them to gently encourage Zack to play with the kids before school. Because of his speech impediment, I also requested that they make sure Zack wasn't teased by the other children. At the time, I believe that they viewed me as an overprotective, slightly "crazy" mom who wasn't going to relent until some policy was in place. We appeared to be in agreement as far as encouraging Zack to make friends was concerned, but with a new teacher on duty every two days they failed to follow through on my teasing concerns.

Then we had to deal with the infamous "pine cone incident." One day Zack was sent to the principal's office for throwing pine cones at some boys. Upon further investigation we found out that these boys had been teasing him and calling him "Baby" because he was crying. Now I'm not saying that lashing out with pine cones was the best way for Zack to handle himself or the situation. However, if someone in a position of authority had been just a little mindful of what was going on, his behavior never would have escalated to this point in the first place. After this incident, the school decided to make more of an effort to ensure that Zack wasn't being teased. They paired him up with some of the more considerate children on the playground, and 10 days later he was interacting with his peers in a completely appropriate, typical way. He only needed an ounce of support for success. Yet in order for his special needs to be taken seriously, some extra persuasion from me was necessary.

Zack gained so much ground in the social realm that before the school year came to an end, he was telling James, "Dad, I want to go into the playground all by myself." He no longer wanted to be escorted from the curb. Along the way, he met a classmate who was also walking alone. Zack initiated the conversation, bragging about his "big boy" status. James' heart broke once more but in a much more rewarding way this time. It was the kind of heartbreak parents of typical children experience all the time. Although the tears were welling up within him, James could revel in the bittersweet yet appropriately independent words of his once nonverbal, friendless son.

My initial fears about a "freak-out" reaction in the classroom were justified, I'm sad to say. During the school meeting I disclosed how Zack used to scream when touched on someone else's terms. I shared this information, not in an effort to frighten or intimidate the teacher, but rather to reveal just how far my amazing little boy had come. Instead, however, what the teacher heard was, "He screams when you touch him." Subsequently, over the course of the next two weeks, she continually reported her attempts to limit her physical contact with Zack. She also mentioned that he was acting especially spacey and unfocused—characteristics she had failed to notice prior to our meeting. It was as though she needed to reconcile Zack's behavior with her own preconceived notions of autism, which was precisely the situation I was hoping to avoid.

Before too much time had passed, she gradually realized that Zack didn't have to fit her profile for autism. Eventually she grew to care deeply for our charming little guy. Everyone who spends any real time with Zack can't help but fall for him with his gorgeous blue eyes, curly brown hair, and sweet, loving disposition. But I digress. . .such is the privilege of an adoring mom. We were fortunate that we had a teacher soft-hearted enough to overcome her previous assumptions. Such like-minded people need to be the ones interacting with your child.

If you are a member of a support group, listen carefully to the parents who have gone before you regarding the selection of the right school for your child. Draw on their experience and listen to their advice. They can share some keen insights about the strengths and drawbacks of particular schools and teachers. Ask many questions and take good notes. Don't be afraid to advocate for your child because no one else is going to care about your child with the same degree of passion. I'm sorry, but this is a reality. Educate yourself so that you can be the best, most-informed champion for your precious baby. Do your best to fight for the specific needs of your individual child.

Also, if you are a person of faith, ask your heavenly Father for guidance and wisdom, patience and perseverance, and everything else that you need. He is strong in the midst of our weaknesses. He will help you make the right decisions and carry you through this incredibly agonizing experience.

Accept No Autism!

The only thing children wear out faster than shoes are parents and teachers. —Unknown [1]

If any of you lacks wisdom, he should ask God, who gives generously to all without finding fault, and it will be given to him. (James 1:5)

---

1 *Copyright 1995 Cook Communications Ministries.* ***God's Little Instruction Book For Mom*** *by Honor Books. Used with permission. All rights reserved.*

17

IEP Meetings: Learning to Advocate

Learning how to advocate for your special needs child can be very intimidating, especially if you are unfamiliar with the workings of your particular school district. Under the Individuals with Disabilities Act (IDEA), the programs and services your child requires will be agreed upon during the Individualized Education Program (IEP) meeting. Once the IEP paperwork is signed, it is legally binding, so be as persuasive and forceful as possible without creating an atmosphere of animosity. Your child is depending on you to understand this process and advocate in his or her best interests.

We found that *The Complete IEP Guide: How to Advocate for Your Special Ed Child, Second Edition* by attorney Lawrence M. Siegel to be our most valuable resource. Not only is this book written in plain English and easily understood by all laymen, but it also offers guidance on assessments, eligibility, specific goal- and objective-setting, access to least-restrictive (mainstream) environments, planning of supportive arguments and rebuttals, due process options, and many other topics as well.

The group attending the IEP meeting is likely to consist of the school's principal or vice-principal, the head or representative from the special education department, the therapists expected to provide services, the lead teacher, a social worker (optional), as well as you and your representatives. You have every right to invite those capable of lending support to your convictions. If you have private therapists, consultants, or experts, ask them to accompany you as you plead your case. I strongly recommend that you write down every name, every position of authority held, and every dissenting opinion presented. In my case these meetings were such a blur afterward that I often found it difficult to recall the name of each person involved and my specific impressions of our discourse.

Prepare your notes beforehand so that you can adequately and competently support your position. Try to anticipate likely responses from your school district, and bring convincing rebuttals on paper to the meeting. At Zack's first IEP, James and I requested two hours a day of speech therapy, but we were unprepared for the speech pathologists' reply: "Two hours of speech therapy would be too stressful for Zack." If we had been thinking more clearly, we could have explained that all of his therapy was stressful for him because his brain was being forced to develop new neurological pathways. Stressful or not, two hours a day of speech therapy was exactly what he needed. Thrown off-guard, we let the comment go undisputed.

If at all possible, make sure that your spouse is present at the meeting. Most likely you both have different strengths to offer to the process. For instance, I had much more knowledge about autism in general, as well as working with Zack specifically. But half-way through each meeting my emotions would begin to get the better of me, especially when I felt as though our advocacy was failing. I often fell into a state of irrepressible sobbing as I hit that breaking point. James, on the other hand, is very even-tempered. He possesses wonderful communication skills and far more emotional stability than I. Knowing full well that I could not continue on after reaching this point, he would take over, allowing me the chance to regroup. Although my tears were heartbreaking for him to watch, James does acknowledge that they likely appeared to be a powerful weapon in our arsenal. If there was just one school member on our team with an ounce of compassion, perhaps he or she would be inspired to work harder to further the accomplishment of our goals.

Arrange for a babysitter, especially if you have more than one child. I wish we had followed this good advice. During most of our IEP meetings, all of our three children were present. This was very distracting to say the least, and usually James was responsible for keeping them occupied. At our second IEP meeting Abbie had just turned two, so she was enthralled with the dry-erase board and markers. She was very good at pulling off the caps of the markers, drawing teeny-tiny little circles, and placing the caps back on the markers. I vividly remember the awe-filled expression of surprise on the occupational therapist's face as she showed off her fine motor skills. On the other hand, our Zack, who had just turned four, was still screaming every time he was prompted to hold a writing utensil. Seeing Abbie surpass her brother in this area did not provide the peace I needed to survive the meeting. If we had employed a caregiver, I would have been spared this discouraging reality taking center stage of the meeting. Thus, avoid such distractions whenever possible so you can focus on the task at hand.

When the meeting comes to an end, take your time reading through the paperwork. Make sure that you leave with your own hard copy. Most likely, an official document will be sent to you with all the agreed-upon alterations. Before you sign, diligently compare these two sets of paperwork to make sure that no additional modifications were made without your input and consultation. Both subtle and more obvious changes within the agreement can greatly affect the quality of education your child receives, so be on the lookout for unapproved variations.

I highly recommend talking with other parents in your area who have already been through this experience. Get feedback about the managerial personalities and processes that are unique in your particular school district. Ask about their experiences with the administrators and teachers. Are they knowledgeable, compassionate, and easy to work with, etc.? Do they make parents feel guilty about the magnitude of services requested by claiming that other children will suffer if the district agrees to your petitions?

By law, the district administrators cannot legally blame budgetary restraints for services declined, yet this excuse is widely presented across the country. Unfortunately, financial considerations do play a role in the decisions made. The more persistent the parents, however, the more services are provided. Unpleasant as this fact is to consider, it is a reality nonetheless, so persevere. Run the good race. Your little one is counting on you to finish in good standing.

Since no two children with autism are exactly alike, no two will exhibit identical manifestations. Nor will all issues be resolved using identical strategies. IDEA recognizes that each program will be different, based on the needs and temperament of the individual child. Your school district is required to provide an appropriate education for your child but not necessarily the very best possible education. Be ready, willing, and able to describe and defend the clearly appropriate environment for your child.

Of course, if you feel that the end result of the IEP is unsatisfactory, you will have to decide if pursuing mediation and/or legal recourse is worthwhile and in your best interests. James and I, for instance, desperately wanted more speech therapy than was offered and provided by our school district. Because of Zack's apraxia diagnosis, theoretically we could have fought for two hours of speech therapy per day in half-hour increments, which is supported and recommended by current research material. Unfortunately, the controversy surrounding the diagnosis of apraxia as a legitimate condition in general, and to Zack specifically, would have been the most difficult argument for us to win in court. Moreover, we would have had to hire legal counsel to represent Zack. (Although James is an attorney, he is unable to practice law outside the jurisdiction of the district attorney's office.) Going through litigation would undoubtedly have been more expensive than pursuing our own avenues of speech therapy.

We also had to consider the possibility of having to maintain a good relationship with the school district for the next 15 years (including preschool) and perhaps more, if Zack needed to be held back for a year or two. Did we really want to alienate those helping our son by threatening a lawsuit at the onset of our relationship? James and I spent much time in prayer together concerning this issue, seeking God's wisdom in our decisions and learning to trust in His sovereignty (something that we have had to do repeatedly throughout this experience).

Although James and I were dissatisfied with our failed efforts to obtain enough speech therapy for Zack, the school district was willing to make concessions on other important issues. They agreed to allow teachers to use verbal reminders and instructions rather than a picture schedule board to ease transitions between activities in class. They allowed Zack to attend an all-day preschool class specifically designed for autism and staffed with a wonderful, well-trained teacher. Even though this school was in another town, he was granted access to their state-of-the-art sensory room and Head Start program. He was scheduled to have one-on-one speech therapy twice a week for 15 minutes and group speech therapy three times a week for half an hour. Occupational therapy was offered twice a week for half an hour, and even hippo (horse) therapy was arranged occasionally. One-on-one and group social skills classes were also provided by his gifted social worker. We didn't receive everything we desired for Zack, but we did walk away with quite a bit of assistance for him.

I believe the most rewarding victory from our IEP meeting was arranging for unofficial yet purposeful discussions of new goals with the teacher every month. By achieving this coup, we could avoid the stress of monthly IEP meetings and still be able to re-evaluate Zack's current skill levels. Then we could modify his programs, behavior management methods, and academic strategies accordingly. His enthusiastic, agreeable teacher and I would brainstorm about our goals and objectives in order to work more effectively as a team. As James and I encouraged Zack to generalize the same skills in his home environment, we provided him with opportunities to be more flexible and therefore more successful in life.

We also agreed that I would volunteer once a week during the lunch hour to give the teacher and her aide a break, during which time I would model a therapy session with Zack. This "break" subtly provided them with valuable insight concerning ways to get the most out of our son. Visiting the classroom on a regular basis also allowed me to make sure everything was being handled according to plan. After being an integral part of Zack's intervention program for the first year and a half, I was very afraid that my son would regress without my uninterrupted involvement. If I could offer advice to his teachers that would foster success, I was more than happy to do so. Never did I leave Zack's recovery hopes solely in the hands of the school, teachers, or therapists. Always proactive, I was passionately involved in his recovery efforts. But I did not do so alone; I leaned on my never-failing source of strength.. Without the gracious help from my Lord and Savior, I'm confident that I would not have had the stamina required to give Zack everything he needed to cross that finish line.

You may give without loving, but you cannot love without giving.
—Glen Wheeler[1]

---

1 *Copyright 1996 Cook Communications Ministries.* **God's Little Instruction Book For Women** *by Honor Books. Used with permission. All rights reserved.*

Tatianna Dickens

Whatever your hand finds to do, do it with all your might.
(Ecclesiastes 9:10a)

18

Tools: Inexpensive and Expensive

A multitude of tools are available that have the potential to help a child with autism. Some of them can be extremely expensive, such as designing and orchestrating a home-based, all-inclusive occupational (OT)/sensory room with every conceivable therapy device imaginable. When Zack went to the preschool class at our local Birth to Three program, he had access to a huge OT room. This state-of-the-art room featured a big, hanging contraption capable of being transformed into various therapeutic arrangements such as a flat swing, a bucking bronco body, a bar to hang from, a rope to climb, a push/pull apparatus, and several other pieces of equipment. (I believe it also had applications as a medieval torturing device!) Some tools are far less expensive, can be enjoyed by every family member, and can more easily be integrated into a household. Most likely, a few of them are already present in your home, like blankets and pillows. Completely free of charge, your hands and feet may also be employed as effective therapy tools.

As previously mentioned, one of the best items we ever purchased was a small exercise trampoline. Zack greatly benefited from jumping on it after he was redirected from his stims with the stick. As part of his sensory "diet," he jumped between especially challenging and intense therapy sessions. Jacob and Abbie also loved this tool, which inherently promoted social skills such as sharing and taking turns. When Soggy Froggy spent some time on the trampoline, we were able to teach Zack the concepts of up and down. Our green assistant also hid under and behind the trampoline, which provided more opportunities for learning. After observing Zack's improvement in various areas as a result of using this toy, one of my friends acquired a family-sized trampoline for her special boy. Ecstatic over her son's subsequent progress, she considers this tool one of her most worthwhile purchases.

Many children with autism love to spin around—not only as they walk, but also in more "typical" ways. They may greatly enjoy riding on a merry-go-round or spinning in someone's arms. Experts believe this vestibular movement helps to reset their brains after particularly demanding therapy sessions. Without a doubt, something about this process helped Zack, and he thoroughly enjoyed it. If he could enlist the aid of a willing grown- up, he would spin. Incorporating this motivation, we taught Zack how to say "fast" and "slow." Actually, I left all of the "spin therapy" up to our much younger college student/respite provider, Jennifer. She was infinitely better equipped to handle the assignment without getting dizzy and nauseous. What a blessing she was to us!

Often times children with autism enjoy rolling around inside carpet-lined barrels. Our Birth to Three agency had such a barrel in their OT room, but it never appealed to Zack. I was sure that this activity would have made *me* queasy; perhaps my little guy experienced a similar reaction.

Now let's move on to tools that don't elicit distasteful physical responses. One of my favorite therapy toys was a marble run, which was by far our most effective instrument in teaching Zack flexibility. Consisting of interchangeable plastic wedges of different sizes, shapes, and colors that snap together, it can be arranged however one wants. All of the pieces are designed with a slope or drop of some sort as well as a slot or runner upon which the marble moves. Zack was absolutely fascinated with this contraption as he watched the marble traverse through its predictable route. If the therapist and I decided to reconfigure the set-up, though, Zack's reaction was also predictable, but not in a good way. When we first introduced this therapy, every time we changed something, he would screech and throw either himself, the marble run, or both onto the floor. Deviating from the routine was extremely difficult for Zack. He insisted on having things a certain way in order for him to function with any semblance of a good attitude. Blatantly refusing to use any words to express his displeasure—not even "no," which he actually *could* say—he somehow arrived at the conclusion that tantrums were his best course of action.

Fortunately, we didn't have to use the therapy hold to help Zack recover from this unpredictable, as well as extremely frustrating, situation. The therapist and I would just ignore him and continue to have a blast playing with this ever-so-cool toy. After about three months, Zack finally decided that he was unnecessarily missing out on the fun and eventually learned to tolerate the changes without incident. Then we would work as a team, taking turns picking and determining the location of each new piece. All of my kids still enjoy making marble runs to this day, and I do too. I find them to be a soothing, mesmerizing, socially appropriate stimming activity. Also, they have a built-in positive reinforcement component, making the hours upon hours of therapy seemingly less tedious.

Many young children with autism discover that dropping little objects through a small hole in a coffee can lid is absolutely delightful fun. Some like a loud "plunk" when the item hits the metal bottom; others prefer just the opposite, so one needs to consider each individual child's nature and adjust accordingly. When we first started vocabulary drills with Zack, for every correct sign he gave in response to our Picture Exchange Card (PEC) we would allow him to push a little plastic frog through the hole. No longer were his gazes vacuous and disturbing. Fascinated by the resulting clanking sound, my beautiful boy once again had clear sparkles in his blue eyes. He was back, but could I sustain his interest and the quality of our connection? Attempting to prolong this moment, I would say, "Ouch, that hurts!" on the frog's behalf. More often than not, Zack would giggle, and if I was really blessed, he would look into my eyes with a glimpse of expectation, waiting for the next PEC to take its place beside my face.

Several other games have the potential to encourage more eye contact in a child with autism. Roughhousing was always one of Zack's favorite activities, even before his diagnosis. Thriving on the gross motor movement and deep pressure involved, he vigorously engaged in this activity often between therapy sessions, and it greatly helped him settle down and refocus. As he began transitioning his sign language to verbal language, we insisted that he use some of his new words before he was allowed to roughhouse, or we would incorporate the words directly into the roughhousing activity. For instance, as Zack balanced on our hands or feet, he would have to say "up," "down," "please," "forward," "backward," "more," etc. As speaking became more second nature to Zack, we would work toward increasing his mean length utterance (the number of words he strung together).

"Tickle Monster" was another popular eye contact game in our home. Using our best monster voices we would call out, "I am the tickle monster, and I am going to get you!" Zack was required to look us in the eyes before we would commence the chase and tickle fest. Again, he loved the strenuous running and giggling, so he was motivated to give us a glance. As his verbal language skills progressed, he attempted some of the monster's words, and soon he was portraying the monster. Occasionally I would "forget" to gaze at Zack as I ought. Well aware of the rules, he reminded me with a "Where eye?" I, of course, obliged immediately in response to his verbal prompt.

Several games can increase the duration of eye contact, a goal common to intervention programs. For many children with autism, what little eye contact they generate is fleeting. The first strategy involves two adults who are capable of swinging the child onto a bed. As one holds the child's hands, the other holds the feet. The latter gets the honor of receiving the eye contact. As the child swings, the adults count to three in increments matching the cadence of the swing. If the child can maintain the eye contact through the one. . .two. . .three, then he or she gets to fly through the air and onto the bed. If the child looks away, the counting begins again. The second strategy is very similar but only requires one adult, who builds a big, soft, fluffy pile of pillows. The child stands adjacent to the pile while holding hands with the adult. (It is necessary for the adult to be on his or her knees so that the same eye level is achieved.) Once again, the adult counts to three with constant eye contact, then free-falls with the child into the pillows. The adult follows up by tickling the child.

To address the sensory needs of children with autism, the dollar and mega-mart stores' inexpensive toy sections are a wonderful resource. Lots of squishy, slimy (and otherwise) tactile, manipulative-type toys fill the shelves. Such items can be used to soothe these special needs children when they are experiencing a sensory overload. By slowly building up a tolerance, these toys can even help sensory-avoiding children overcome their disagreeable reactions.

Also, whether toys are used as rewards or motivators, or as promoters of positive behaviors like sharing and taking turns, their popularity can be utilized for an even greater good. Zack overcame his fear of camera flashes while playing with a cheap, flashing toy gun. Once he realized that the cool gun lights resembled the camera flashes, great progress was made. Cheap shaving cream, Play-Doh®, Silly Putty®, bird seed, and corn starch-water mixtures provided Zack with much-needed sensory "fixes" throughout the course of his extremely demanding days. All my children enjoy playing with earthworms in soil, an incredibly intense sensory experience that I still find difficult to tolerate.

For you more creative types, there are a lot of good books out there too. For silly projects to do at home, try *Purple Cow to the Rescue*, by Ann Cole, Carolyn Haas, and Betty Weinberger, along with *The Ultimate Book of Kid Concoctions* and *The Ultimate Book of Holiday Kid Concoctions* by John E. and Danita Thomas. Just beware of ingredients and food items that may cause negative or allergic reactions in your children. Early intervention products are also available in catalogues such as Beyond Play (1-877-428-1244), Mind Ware (1-800-999-0398, www.mindwareonline.com), and Super Duper Publications (1-800-277-8737).

My all-time favorite therapy tool was our hot tub. Actually, we made this big purchase right before we received Zack's diagnosis. In retrospect, this was probably a huge blessing because I can't imagine how we would have been comfortable spending that kind of money after his diagnosis. Even though the hot tub would have been well worth the money, it would have been harder to justify in our minds. If you can afford one, I highly recommend that you consider making this expenditure.

Zack and I spent many hours in our hot tub during the summer breaks, blowing bubbles to strengthen his oral motor skills and setting up play routines that required him to use his few words. He loved to ride around on my back while the water jets pushed us around in a circle. But before we spun around, I would prompt Zack with, "Ready, set. . ." and he would have to complete the phrase with a "go." To mix things up a bit, I would count, "One, two. . ." and he would have to continue with a "three." I used every conceivable opportunity to insist that he use his verbal language skills. Jacob also participated and served as an encouraging role model; moreover, he forced Zack to take turns. Even though it was extremely difficult for Zack to verbalize, for the most part he was agreeable due to the favorable sensory environment of the hot tub.

This tool was therapeutic for me as well—that is, when I wasn't in the midst of doing therapy with Zack. The hot tub also gave us parents an opportunity to reconnect after the kids went to bed without the cost of paying a babysitter. As the jets worked their magic, I would unload, unwind, and regroup a bit. I realize that it was a big purchase, but I'm sure that I would have had to hire even more extra help without the benefits of the hot tub at my disposal. When survival is your most immediate concern, you claim respite wherever and whenever you can—even when it means a trip to the river.

You are never so high as when you are on your knees.
—Jean Hodges[1]

Come, all you who are thirsty, come to the waters.
(Isaiah 55:1a)

1 Copyright 1996 Cook Communications Ministries. God's Little Instruction Book For Women by Honor Books. Used with permission. All rights reserved.

19

Sign Language: Our First Huge Step

When Zack was first evaluated by our local Birth to Three program, he was, for all intents and purposes, nonverbal. Even though he had a handful of short words and phrases in his vocabulary, he often forgot to use them. When he did remember to use the few words he had at his disposal, his articulation was so poor that he was rarely intelligible to casual listeners. The experts determined Zack's oral motor skills to be weak and severely delayed. Immediately we began therapies to physically strengthen his mouth, but even when progress was made in this area, he still had great difficulty with verbalization. James and I made many frustrated attempts to get our son to "cooperate," but Zack was physically unable to comply with our requests. At this point we were unaware of Zack's apraxia of speech, a motor planning disorder that makes the coordination of tongue movements extremely difficult. Even so, as our stress over his lack of speech became more and more evident, we began our search for a suitable communication alternative for Zack. Since all he wanted to do with the laminated picture cards (PECS) was toss them up and watch them flitter, it was apparent that this method couldn't be employed as intended.

Thus, sign language appeared to be the most reasonable option for our family. It is inexpensive to apply, unlike the controversial facilitated communication methods that rely solely on computer technology. Also, there is some scientific evidence that sign language helps to build neurological pathways between the left and right sides of the brain, especially when the hands cross over from one side of the body to the other while communicating a phrase. Excited by the prospect of creating any promising neurological pathways and aware of Zack's strong gross motor need, James and I believed that sign language could teach him how to communicate *and* soothe him with movement in the process. We thought that if Zack never did progress to the point of verbal communication, perhaps he could gain educational opportunities through a school for the deaf. Sign language also had the potential to help Zack further develop his fine motor coordination, which was also delayed. All of these considerations led us to our final decision to pursue the sign language route.

If a child with autism does not have an additional speech disorder like Zack, however, I would not recommend sign language as the only course of action. There is nothing inherently wrong with signing, but why create a crutch where one is not needed? Now, if you like the idea of building neurological pathways across the lobes of the brain (as I did), may I suggest that you insist on concurrent verbal language from your child? This way, you can still be striving for normalcy.

Our first attempts at teaching Zack to sign were beyond challenging. He had no concept of communication whatsoever, so we were really starting from ground zero. I sat on the floor with Zack and performed the following drill:

1) I held up one of the PECS to the side of my face;
2) I said the name of the object it represented three times very slowly so he'd have enough time to process the information;
3) I dropped the card; and
4) I modeled the appropriate sign.

Throughout this entire process I was trying desperately to keep him focused and attentive. At the same time, I was attempting to keep the PECS out of his reach so he would not stim. Then I would raise the PEC once more and ask, "Zack, what is this?" hoping that he would be able to answer me with the correct sign.

We started with animal PECS because knowledge of animal names is one of the earliest developmental milestones achieved by typical children. Unfortunately, Zack could have cared less about any animals other than frogs, so our attempts were all in vain. With each passing day we were becoming more and more discouraged. So we decided to work on something much more practical, useful, and motivating, such as favorite foods and drinks. Implementing this strategy was still not easy; however, once mastered, it was one of our first big success stories with Zack.

Our Birth to Three agency loaned us a couple of sign language books. One of them wasn't very big, and we soon outgrew it. The other book had very specific instructions about sentence structure, which was above and beyond what we needed. I bought the Random House Webster's *American Sign Language Dictionary* by Elaine Costello Ph.D. because it contained over 4,500 signs. I highly recommend this resource because it has so very many vocabulary words. Some of the hand movements were too difficult for Zack to master, so we modified them to close-enough approximations. Our main goal was to teach him the importance and joy of communication, rather than expecting him to learn impeccable sign language. This concession best suited our family, yet we still had a huge challenge ahead.

Even with the food words and phrases, Zack struggled greatly to understand the purpose of signing. What was required of him exactly? He certainly was in no mood to cooperate, at least initially, since he was already so used to screeching and throwing himself on the floor every time he wanted or needed something from the kitchen. These temper tantrums were second nature to him. Just imagine how the tantrums escalated when I insisted that he perform a sign before he could receive his treat. Even though Zack isn't blind and deaf, our experience often reminded me of the Helen Keller story.

Sometimes I managed to figure out what he wanted by tracking Zack's eye movements. If I was really fortunate, he would point at the item he wanted. Once I determined the desired object, I would then close the door to the pantry or refrigerator and model the sign while saying the corresponding name three times slowly. Zack was not given the item until he attempted the sign. I would even try to place my hands upon his hands to "walk" him through the process. This technique, known as "hand over hand," can be quite effective if your child tolerates directed touching. Unfortunately for me our little guy didn't understand the hand-over-hand method at first, so he would protest by acting out in a horrendous fashion. Reacting as though I had just poured sulfuric acid all over his body, he would often screech and shake my touch off his hands. He even hit me upon occasion. How dare I touch him when he was upset? How dare I refuse him sustenance? Why is Mom being so mean?

We spent hours on the kitchen floor implementing the therapy hold during those first few months, trying to curb this behavior. When Zack recovered from his fit, we tried to sign again. More often than not, however, we were back on the floor doing the therapy hold. Both of us were crying by this point, and I doubt that we could have been more miserable.

Once again I encouraged Zack to sign because I just knew I had to get through to my precious little boy somehow. Zack *had to* understand that there was a better way to ask for his basic needs and wants. He just *had* to! Simply living with the old kitchen tantrums was not a possibility I was willing to consider, so I was going to stick with this plan for as long as it was necessary. As awful as this endeavor was, at least I felt as though I was suffering for a very worthwhile cause—something that would make all of our lives infinitely better in the long run—*if* we could pull it off.

Occasionally after two or three therapy holds, Zack would finally comply and mimic the sign. Squealing with delight, I'd pick him up and spin him around, telling him how proud I was of my big boy. He loved this positive reinforcement, so this response was highly motivating for him. I would give Zack his treat right away and then model the appropriate sign over and over again while he ate. I would also be telling him, "Good boy, that's right... cookie, cookie, cookie!" Once the concept of signing took hold, I re-introduced the animal cards as well as many others. To teach him verbs like "jumping," "running," and "eating," I acted out the movements while showing him the corresponding signs.

As he slowly but surely began to understand that sign language was a form of communication, we continued to further expand his vocabulary and mean length sign. For instance, once he knew the signs for "more," "milk," and "please," I would insist that he start using them in increasingly longer combinations until he was signing them all together. I would model the signs and say the words at the same time: "More....milk...please." I had to do this very slowly because Zack took such a long time to process all language being spoken to him.

Sometimes (especially in the beginning) I would have to watch and wait expectantly for up to seven or eight seconds before Zack could put everything together and respond in the appropriate manner. Yes, it was slow—painstakingly slow—but he was getting it! He was *actually* getting it! As we practiced more and more, during every conceivable opportunity the signing became more natural. Eventually Zack progressed so much that it was no longer necessary for me to prompt every attempt at communication! Initiating conversation is beyond huge for a child with autism! Even more amazing were the times he invented new signs in order to more effectively express himself!

The more signs Zack mastered, the more my desire grew for him to communicate verbally; he understood the basic purpose of communication now. I wanted to keep pushing him toward normalcy whenever possible, because a child who hears yet relies solely on sign language to communicate is obviously not considered typical. When I shared my desire to transition Zack from sign to speech with our initial speech therapist, I was perplexed by his discouraging response: "Until Zack has a base vocabulary of 300 words, all attempts to convert his signs to speech will be a waste of time and energy." Somewhere in our therapist's training or background, he had come across this "magic number." Essentially, he was telling me my efforts would be ridiculous and preposterous! How could he possibly know that? How could he take this seemingly obscure number and impute this restriction on my son with such unwavering confidence? I was bound and determined to prove his theory false, one way or another.

So, as I continued to teach Zack more sign language, I tried my absolute best to encourage vocalizations as well. I even tried to bribe him with frog stickers and candy, but unfortunately nothing worked. From the beginning, I had kept a detailed list of every sign initiated by Zack. (This was my standard for his true language acquisition.) Wouldn't you know it—he had mastered 307 signs when he first attempted vocal approximations. I was completely and utterly bewildered; the therapist knew what he was talking about after all. Now I had to confess my initial disbelief and extend to him an apology. Eating crow is good for everyone upon occasion; at least, that is what I like to tell myself. Actually, it wasn't at all difficult for me to 'fess up. My boy could now communicate, and that mattered far more than any blow to my pride ever could.

There is no greater love than the love that holds on where there seems nothing left to hold on to. —G. W. C. Thomas[1]

Love never fails [never fades out or becomes obsolete or comes to an end.]
(1 Cor. 13:8a AB)

1 Copyright 1996 Cook Communications Ministries. God's Little Instruction Book For Women by Honor Books. Used with permission. All rights reserved.

20

Apraxia: Motor Planning Mayhem

When Zack was about three and a half, he decided to attempt speaking. James and I were thrilled that he was finally willing to try to communicate with his mouth, which he had refused to do up to this point. However, his efforts to coordinate simultaneous vocalizations along with his 300 hand signs were far from successful. Clearly, Zack was struggling more than he ought. No matter how hard he tried, most of what came out of his mouth was complete gibberish. Even when he could produce the correct sounds, their arrangement was often mixed up, and he frequently dropped the beginnings and endings of words. Although his more-practiced words had developed consistent errors over a period of time, his new word mistakes followed no set pattern. The order of the sounds he produced was unpredictably wrong.

Already acutely aware of Zack's poor oral motor skills, we had been addressing that issue with specific exercises since his first evaluation. Despite his good progress up to this point, I'm sure he still had some lingering deficits in this area. Yet, these limitations were not considered severe enough to cause Zack's current struggles with speech. We were rather sure there was a much bigger problem at hand.

Many children with autism also have a separate, unrelated speech disorder of one form or another. Suspecting this was the case with Zack, we had to figure out what exactly we were dealing with. Our amazing therapist Chelsea, who had previously worked at a renowned autism clinic in Maryland, conducted a battery of tests with Zack. She determined that he had developmental apraxia of speech (DAS), a neurological malfunction between the brain and the tongue that impairs an individual's ability to coordinate the tongue in the proper sequences. It is also known as articulatory apraxia, developmental articulatory dyspraxia, childhood verbal apraxia, developmental dyspraxia of speech, and developmental verbal dyspraxia, to name a few. (Much controversy surrounds DAS, including its definition, cause, clinical symptoms, treatment, and even its existence as a distinct diagnosis.)[1]

Those professionals who believe this disorder stems from a lack of oral motor coordination use the term "DAS," while those who believe the problem is language-based—the child experiences difficulty placing the different parts of speech together correctly and effectively—prefer the term "developmental verbal dyspraxia." The variant names are associated with the theoretical causes of the disorder, not the defining characteristics. Since Zack had major issues with both of these aspects of communication, the specific term for his speech disorder was irrelevant. To us, it simply meant that we had one more obstacle to overcome.

Several different theories suggest explanations for DAS. One blames subtle auditory deficits that limit the child's ability to identify and process speech sounds found in conversational speech, even when hearing tests appear to be within normal limits. Another blames a general problem with learning a mature language system. Yet others say an inability to sequence specific speech sounds, syllables, and speech melody components is responsible for the disorder. In Zack's case, I whole-heartedly subscribe to this final theory since it seems to best describe our son's issues with speech. According to these experts, DAS can be attributed to problems in the child's

---

1 *Developmental Apraxia of Speech: Information for Parents* by Kathy J. Jakielski, Thomas P. Marquardt, and Barbara L. Davis (Program in Communication Sciences and Disorder, The University of Texas at Austin, Austin, TX 78712

organization and sequencing of speech components (sounds, syllables, and melody). Furthermore, even though children with DAS have mentally stored the above-mentioned skills, they do not have the ability to consistently and accurately arrange them into words and sentences. For more information on DAS, visit Apraxia-Kids at http://csd.utexas.edu/ .

Most professionals who believe that apraxia is a legitimate condition/diagnosis also agree that frequent and intensive speech therapy is the best course of action. Some recommend as much as two hours of daily speech therapy held in four, half-hour increments. Of all the various types of interventions I watched, researched, and performed with Zack, the speech therapy sessions intimidated me the most. This was the one area where I felt completely inept and in need of much more specific understanding, training, and direction. I often hoped that my inadequacies wouldn't result in failure, for Zack's sake.

Nevertheless, I plowed through it and did my best, just like I had done with all of the other therapies. Thankfully, I also received some practical assistance from Zack's preschool, the college students we had hired, and the New Mexico State University Speech and Hearing Center. Even so, we fell short of the recommended two hours per day. Because professional speech therapy costs $200 per hour and was not covered by our insurance, it was simply impossible for us to fit that expense into our already tight budget. I would have had to give up 20 hours of help from our college students for every hour of speech therapy with a professional! At this age, Zack needed the hours of one-on-one therapy more than anything else. I couldn't allow my own feelings of incompetence to jeopardize the many valuable hours we received from our students.

We started by drilling single syllables very slowly—so slowly, in fact, that some of them actually became almost two syllables. Zack needed time to understand what we were saying to him, as well as time to coordinate his tongue movements correctly. We would practice, "aaaa. . .ttt, aaaa. . .ttt, aaaa. . .ttt," followed by, "aaaa. . .kkk, aaaa. . .kkk, aaaa. . .kkk, then, "aaaa. . .ppp, aaaa. . .ppp, aaaa. . .ppp," and so on. This technique helped him to learn how to distinguish the differences between the sounds. These variations were so subtle that Zack had to use an enormous amount of concentration to master them. My heart sank as I watched my son blink and twitch his head every time he processed the information; however, there was a hint of hope. Giving Zack time to sort through the stimuli and sufficiently practice did eventually bring about success.

To help him further, we showed him how to feel the differences between the sounds by making him touch his own lips and throat. Also, to keep motivation high and boredom at bay, we invited Zack's Soggy Froggy to participate in these drills. Sometimes our green friend was the "teacher"; at other times he was the "student" who allowed Zack to instruct him during the drills.

Then we moved on to short words that were only one syllable, such as "Mom." With the same sound present at the beginning and the end, one might think this word would be easy to motor plan, but it was incredibly difficult for Zack. Calling me "Om" for months on end, I thought he would never master the initial "m" sound. In fact, close to a year of painstaking drills were required before he got it right. I remember distinctly because my birthday was approaching, and I so desperately longed to be "Mom" to Zack. Even as I slept, I often dreamed about Zack calling me "Mom." These were, without a doubt, some of the happiest dreams I have ever had.

Seemingly insignificant things can mean the world to a parent of a child with autism. As I awoke from my perfect dream, I would hope against hope: "Could today be the day? Will he say "Mom"? I wasn't *really* dreaming, was I?" When Zack entered the room and called out "Om" for the ten-millionth time, tears would again dampen my pillow, and I would lament, "Not today. Not today." I know I should have been ecstatic that Zack was initiating language with me in the first place because some children with autism never do, yet my tears still flowed. I didn't know then that my dream would live to see another day.

As I waited, we continued to drill many one-syllable words—those that had the same initial sound but a different ending (sad/sack/sat), and others that had the same final sound but a different beginning (bat/fat/hat). Once Zack could distinguish the subtle differences between the words and say them correctly, we moved on to two-syllable words. Initial, middle, and final sounds were mixed around and drilled over and over. Because these words required Zack to perform much more complicated combinations, they were even more challenging. When he made a mistake, it was usually because he was trying to talk too fast. To slow him down, I would tap the syllables out on the floor and remind him to be more careful.

This technique was ideal for floor time, but I was correcting Zack every time he made a mistake, whether we were in the middle of a speech therapy session or not. So, when we were out and about, I would tap my leg instead. Unfortunately, Zack's frequent mistakes soon left my leg feeling tender and bruised from all the tapping; therefore, we developed our own technique. Slowly tapping my fingers together, I would practice with him until I was sure he had it right. Then, we would say it together five times as I counted down on my fingers. Our routine was so consistently structured that it quickly became second nature to us both.

Sometimes Zack was completely incapable of motor planning a word despite our efforts to slow down and tap, so we incorporated a different strategy. Breaking down the word into each sound or syllable, we addressed one aspect of the word at a time. Then we combined the sections in progression. For instance, Abbie's name was especially difficult for Zack to motor plan. She was "B" for several months before we were able to get the "A" in front of the "b."

Jennifer, one of our college students, was an absolute godsend. She knew how emotionally difficult it was for me to be "Om" to Zack. Working with phenomenal dedication and love, she diligently and patiently taught Zack to say both "Abbie" and "Mom" as well as many other words. Without her help and devotion, I really doubt Zack would have made the progress he did. But in my heart, Jennifer will always be remembered for making one of my greatest dreams come true. Thank you for being such a blessing to a desperate "Mom" and her family!

A mother understands what a child does not say.
—Jewish proverb[1]

Immediately [Zechariah's] mouth was opened and his tongue was loosed, and he began to speak, praising God.
(Luke 1:64 [This verse is Zack's favorite]).

1 Copyright 1995 Cook Communications Ministries. God's Little Instruction Book For Mom by Honor Books. Used with permission. All rights reserved.

21

Oral Motor: Tongue Trials

One of the very first goals we laid out for Zack was strengthening his oral motor skills. He wasn't yet three years old, but he was already severely delayed for his age. Anxious for him to make real strides in his speech, we knew he would need to develop a greater physical mastery over his mouth. So we implemented many exercises—some of which were fun—such as blowing bubbles into the air or hot tub. Hour upon hour, I still managed to find this activity not only tolerable but amusing; therefore, it was a regular part of our intervention plan. Some of the therapies were much more infuriating for me to implement, like persuading Zack to drink through increasingly narrower, more challenging straws. He was extremely stubborn, but some of those straws were beyond difficult. (Even I would have been annoyed had I been forced to drink out of them.)

Some experts recommend that the child undergo shoulder and neck exercises such as stretching and rolling before attempting the oral motor portion of the therapy. Since Zack never had poor muscle tone anywhere else but his mouth, we personally never found this to be very beneficial. We did, however, find some of the cheek and lip exercises to be worthwhile, especially the "I Can Pop Your Balloon Cheeks" game. Zack would take a deep breath and puff out his cheeks. Then I would gently tap them with my fingers as he tried to keep his cheeks inflated. With each of my "failures," he would begin to smile and loosen his lips. He had to work really hard to regain his composure and his balloon-like appearance before I made more earnest attempts.

Another popular game was "warrior." As he screamed out war cries through his pursed lips, he also learned to hop and skip, two of the many developmental milestones we were hoping he'd reach. Making siren and motorcycle noises with matchbox cars also strengthened his lip muscles. In addition, these types of activities gave us the opportunity to teach him age-appropriate pretend play techniques.

Some of our oral motor therapies also involved food. Having Zack manipulate miniature marshmallows from side to side in his mouth or up and down on the tip of his tongue was relatively easy to encourage. Another tongue exercise involved the smearing of peanut butter all around the outer rim of his lips. He was supposed to lick his face clean, but this slimy sensation was rarely tolerated by Zack, so we made little progress on this front. Chelsea, one of our college students, suggested spreading peanut butter on T-shaped "chewy tubes" in order to strengthen his jaw muscles. To obtain the best results, Zack was supposed to chomp down on the thick, resistant portion of the tube over and over (a minimum of ten times per side, six times a day). My job was holding the T-shaped handle and ensuring its proper location between his molars. The redundancy of the drill didn't appeal to Zack as much as playing tug-of-war, so we modified it accordingly. I pretended to lose all of the contests, and he agreed to be a gracious winner. With tug-of-war sessions lasting several minutes at a time, his jaws soon became incredibly strong. By the time we discontinued this particular therapy, I could actually lift him off the ground and swing him from side to side with the chewy tube he was holding in his mouth. He absolutely adored the game and was sad to see it go, but neither my arms nor the worn-out chewy tubes were up to the challenge.

Some of the exercises were infinitely more monotonous. Practicing different letter sounds such as b, b, b and p, p, p was one of our least favorite drills; unfortunately, this was only the beginning. After mastering the simpler goals, we graduated to more complex movements and combinations such as pa-ka, pa-ka, pa-ka; ta-ga, ta-ga, ta-ga; and la-soo, la-soo, la-soo. We also attempted lip smacks and tongue clicks. These exercises required a great deal of motor planning. For the first two-and-a-half years Zack struggled tremendously, making very few strides in this area. He would get so frustrated, as would I. At this point we didn't know that Zack had apraxia. Regardless, these goals were so unrealistic that we shelved them until a more suitable time.

Some of the easier exercises were beyond tedious for both Zack and me. Trying my best to foster cooperation, I often resorted to candy bribes. (Yes, the sweets also helped me me stay somewhat energized, motivated, and willing to cooperate.) Before Zack's initial evaluation, James and I hadn't given him much candy at all. In fact, we prided ourselves for being good, conscientious parents who limited his candy consumption.

Much to our surprise, several of the experts at our Birth to Three agency actually recommended that we give Zack all the candy he wanted. This seemed absurd to us and against all our better judgment. We definitely did not want to go in this direction. What kind of junk food were we going to be putting into his already miserable little body? What would be the long-term ramifications of encouraging him to make such poor food choices? Our team was insistent, completely convinced that allowing Zack to indulge with the candy would present many opportunities for oral-motor therapy. Eventually we decided to go along with the expert opinions—at least for a little while to see if any good would come out of it.

For example, lollipops encourage sucking, thus building the muscle walls in the cheeks. The carbonation in sodas was supposed to give Zack a greater awareness of sensations in his mouth. We were told to encourage him to take a big sip and hold it in his mouth with his lips closed while he felt the bubbles work their magic on his tongue. I'll concede that his muscle tone was weak enough to make this task extraordinarily difficult. In theory, I could understand the purpose of this therapy. Candy and gum can be hard to chew, requiring substantial jaw strength for consumption. Insisting that Zack enjoy these treats with his mouth closed allowed us to address yet another monumental challenge. Also, his tongue would develop better maneuvering skills as he cleaned his teeth afterward.

Unfortunately, Zack never noticed that the candy was stuck in between his teeth in the first place. Hyperactivity and tooth decay were the only tangible results of using the gooey candy. Already having enough issues to deal with, we gave up on this particular tool fairly quickly. We did acquiesce regarding the gum, soda, and suckers, however. The gum motivated Zack to chew with his mouth closed, and the other two did seem to help him develop better muscle tone around his lips.

Years of oral motor and speech therapy drills have slowly but surely brought Zack to a point where most casual listeners can understand him 90% of the time (if, and only if, he is concentrating on what he is saying). He still struggles with pragmatics, sentence structure, word order, and verb conjugation; but we continue to work on it. Like his articulation, these skills are developing with time.

Acutely aware of what is expected during therapy sessions, Zack is extremely focused and determined, which brings about his phenomenal rates of accuracy. Unfortunately, Zack often falls victim to a common speech therapy pitfall. In everyday conversation he tends not to concentrate to the same degree and is subsequently more sloppy and unintelligible. Hence, he will continue to participate in speech drills until he remembers to think about how he is saying things. Our autism journey has come to an end, yet I still long for the day when our therapy expenses are gone for good.

At least our fears about Zack and his eating junk food have been laid to rest. Like most of us, he appreciates the occasional sweet. Very curious about the benefits of good food, he usually asks for healthy snacks. Also, he is very good at reminding others that he can't eat wheat (gluten) because it makes him cry. James and I are now confident that Zack will make responsible food choices over the course of his lifetime. I suppose if this remarkable dream can come true, our hopes for therapy-free living can come true as well. Until then, I suppose more patience is in store for our future, at least for a little while longer.

Everyone has patience. Successful people learn to use it.
—Unknown [1]

The end of the matter is better than its beginning, and patience is better than pride.
(Ecclesiastes 7:8)

1 Copyright 1996 Cook Communications Ministries. God's Little Instruction Book For Women by Honor Books. Used with permission. All rights reserved.

22

Depths of Despair: From Agony to Intimacy

When James and I were first confronted with the possibility that Zack had autism, we were heartbroken. After we received the official diagnosis, we were beyond devastated. Being forced to give up all of the hopes and dreams we had for our precious little boy was the most agonizing trial we have ever encountered. An all-consuming sorrow filled our once joyful hearts. Many nights we cried out to the Lord, "Take this burden of autism away from our sweet son and our desperate family! This is a burden far too great to bear!"

My heart aching with grief, I often felt as though a huge weight was attempting to suffocate me. There were definitely days, especially early on, when I questioned my ability to survive this experience. To be honest, some days I had no desire to endure this situation even one moment longer.

I had dealt with this magnitude of depression once before. As an 18-year-old college student who was not yet a believer, I viewed my life as one of emptiness and insignificance. Assaulted by struggles on every side and facing a future that felt devoid of meaning, purpose, or direction, I thought to myself, "Surely there must be more to life than this." But none of the things that I pursued made my life feel worthwhile. I tried to be a good person and do good things; but the more I strived, the more I realized I was incapable of true goodness. There were definitely areas in my life about which I experienced much shame, and my conscience was not going to allow me to ignore them any longer. Overwrought, I knew something *had* to be done about my guilty predicament, but what? How could I pay for the actions of my past when I couldn't even live in the present without failures? So tortured by my guilt, I considered taking my own life.

I had grown up in a church-going family, and I had heard the accounts of Christ many times. He was the Son of God. He died on the cross. He rose again. . .I got it. For years I thought His life was a very sad story with a very happy ending, but I just didn't understand the big picture. I didn't know *why* He did those things or realize then that He had done it *for me*, out of love *for me*, to pay the penalty for *my* sins so that I wouldn't be punished when I stood before my heavenly Father. I didn't understand at the time that Jesus gave me *His* righteousness and the Father would see me as worthy only if I were covered with the righteousness of His own perfect Son. It slowly dawned on me that it wasn't up to me to live a perfect life. I did not and could not earn this righteousness myself; instead, I had to exchange my unworthiness for the holiness of God's Son, who sacrificed Himself for us.

As I came to understand the *reason* for Christ's actions, I made the conscious decision to trust in His purity and worthiness as my only acceptable substitute. This transformation of my heart and mind occurred at the most opportune time, in the midst of my darkest moment. He pulled me out of my depression and gave me a reason to live. From that moment on, my life has had purpose. I may not have known exactly what that purpose was, but I have always felt loved and forgiven and accepted by my Lord. I thought at the time that my suicidal tendencies were behind me.

That is, until the depression related to living with autism struck my life. Knowing full well that I now belonged to God, suicide was not a valid option. Yet I did daydream about my life being infinitely easier in a multitude of scenarios; my own death was certainly one of them. Some days were just so incredibly hard that my only desire was to be freed from this torture—dealing with the tantrums, the screeching, the stimming, and the vomiting; persevering through the constant therapy sessions and their painstakingly slow results; tossing and turning on those sleepless nights; enduring the isolation; living paycheck to paycheck; feeling as though I were failing the rest of my family; and starting every day with exhaustion, sobs, and desperate, fervent prayers. Some days I just wanted to crawl under a rock and die. Yes, it was *that* bad. Despite my troubled spirit, I was convinced to the very depths of my being that a greater purpose could and would be served through this adversity. Regardless, it was still a staggering ordeal—one that wreaked havoc in our lives for more than three years.

During those early months of therapy, the nature and frequency of Zack's tantrums caused James and I to fear that we would be forced to institutionalize him. Were we ever going to control these outbursts? Would we be successful in our efforts before he became a danger to himself or others? I will never forget the day we recognized that we were comfortable with the prospect of Zack remaining at home indefinitely. Finally learning how to control himself adequately, he had become calm enough to assuage our fears. We could now handle him well enough to relinquish our concerns about the necessity of admitting him to a psychiatric ward.

I remember that this was an exceptional day for us. Most parents are free to assess things differently, looking forward to their children growing and maturing toward independence. Yet James and I were ecstatic to know that we would be spared the anguish of committing our son to an unhappy life in a group home or hospital. It's amazing how one's perspective can be altered when faced with a child afflicted by autism.

Unable to fathom the possibility of surviving Zack's diagnosis without the support of the other, James and I purchased two additional life insurance policies. That way, if something were to happen to one of us, at least the other wouldn't be burdened with financial difficulties in addition to struggling with Zack. We also asked our friends Paul and Michelle if they were still willing to be the legal guardians of our kids if something were to happen to both of us. They too have a special needs child but not one with the extreme challenges accompanying autism. Offering them an option to change their minds was very difficult for us, but given the circumstances, we knew it was the right thing to do. Nevertheless, the need to present this question forced us to see how incredibly vulnerable we were as a family. We had to ask ourselves, "What if our dearest friends said no? If they did turn us down, how could we come to terms with our adorable Zack being rejected in this manner?" We loved him so completely, and we desperately wanted everyone to love him as we did. If Paul and Michelle chose not to take on this responsibility, then who could we possibly depend on to love and care for him if we were unable to?

That was the dilemma: our Zack wasn't exactly easy to love, and asking someone to take on the burden of caring for your child with autism is too much—even for such dear and special people. We wouldn't wish autism on our worst enemy, and here we were, asking our closest friends if they would consider such a responsibility? Being a phenomenal couple, Paul and Michelle took all of 30 seconds before they lovingly answered "yes." (Of course, they were glad to hear about the life insurance policies, and who could blame them? Therapy is expensive, and they would have had three more mouths to feed. I would have had monetary concerns too, had I been faced with that possibility.) Their gracious response meant the world to me, more than they could possibly ever know. And I thought we had a close relationship *before* Zack was diagnosed with autism! How blessed we felt to have friends so full of love for our family, even for our very special boy. God's provision was evident, which was a tremendous comfort in our time of need.

One of the things that saddened me the most about Zack's autism was the likelihood of him lacking the capacity to pursue a fulfilling spiritual life. My walk with the Lord has carried me through times of trouble. He has also filled a void in me that I was incapable of filling on my own. He is the sustainer of my life, and I desperately wanted my little boy to develop a similar relationship with his Savior. Because of his estimated IQ of 50 and dismal language skills, I didn't hold out much hope that Zack would ever be able to experience the faith I yearned to share with him. With my aching heart full of anxiety over the matter, I would often be brought to tears while listening to the sermons at church.

It was during this time that I decided to work in the nursery every Sunday and provide therapy for Zack. This way, he could have access to a peer group, and I could help the nursery staff by handling the tantrums when they occurred. Also, I was there when it was necessary to redirect Zack's stimming. While ministering to my son, I also had a legitimate excuse to do something other than attend the service. I simply didn't possess the control over my emotions to feel comfortable in the sanctuary at that point. I worked in the nursery every single Sunday for a year and a half without fail. For anyone who has ever worked in a church nursery, you can appreciate the length of this stint. Yet, it was easier for me to be a basket case in the privacy of the nursery than to be exposed for the emotional wreck I really was in the sanctuary. Please don't misunderstand me; everyone extended us sincere sympathy. But I was just so sick and tired of wearing my emotions on my sleeve. Though compassionate, their heartfelt glances pierced me to the very deepest parts of my soul. Being reminded of my agony time and time again was excruciating. I longed to take a step back, breathe, and be free of my fragile emotions for a spell.

Now seven years old with an IQ in the normal range, Zack is asking and answering questions about God and Jesus on a regular basis—a far cry from where he once was. The Lord is so very good to us. He has taken our sorrow and given us joy in return. We will be forever grateful for the miracle that is our son. With Zack's diagnosis behind us, I am finally able to reflect on sermons without experiencing overflowing emotions. . . well, most of the time, anyway. Every now and then one comes along that is so powerful I can't help but remember those difficult days as if they were yesterday. This sermon, in particular, recently tugged at my heartstrings. [Borrowed and paraphrased with permission from Pastor Doug Coyle, Grace Covenant Church, (PCA)]:

Psalm 88

O Lord, the God who saves me, day and night I cry out before you. May my prayer come before you; turn your ear to my cry. For my soul is full of trouble and my life draws near the grave. I am counted among those who go down to the pit; I am like a man without strength.

I am set apart with the dead, like the slain who lie in the grave, whom you remember no more, who are cut off from your care. You have put me in the lowest pit, in the darkest depths. Your wrath lies heavily upon me; you have overwhelmed me with all your waves.

You have taken from me my closest friends and have made me repulsive to them. I am confined and cannot escape; my eyes are dim with grief. I call to you, O Lord, every day; I spread out my hands to you. Do you show your wonders to the dead? Do those who are dead rise up and praise you? Is your love declared in the grave, your faithfulness in Destruction? Are your wonders known in the place of

> *darkness, or you righteous deeds in the land of oblivion? But I cry to you for help, O Lord; in the morning my prayer comes before you.*
> *Why, O Lord, do you reject me and hide your face from me? From my youth I have been afflicted and close to death; I have suffered your terrors and am in despair.*
> *Your wrath has swept over me; your terrors have destroyed me. All day long they surround me like a flood; they have completely engulfed me. You have taken my companions and loved ones from me; the darkness is my closest friend.*

Psalm 88 is a song which depicts the cry of a deeply troubled soul—of ultimate despair and inward turmoil. The struggle of the soul is always the greatest of all struggles. It encompasses internal struggles with one's self as well as with God. Questions arise such as, "What is the meaning of this, God? Where are You?" The confusion and helplessness are devastating. The psalmist agonizes because he suffers in utter loneliness and isolation; he is completely without companionship. His despair is not merely the result of his suffering, but that he must endure *alone.* All he can hear is the sound of his own voice fading into thin air.

The writer goes on and on in deep despair, and then merely concludes. No answer is forthcoming. No word of hope is offered. This psalm does not end with an encouraging, "Yes, life is rough, but you need to look on the bright side." There is no bright side here. Other psalms of lament usually have a note of optimism somewhere, but this one portrays only gloom from beginning to end.

You might be saying to yourself, "Well, I'm glad I'm not dealing with that kind of despair." If that's your current situation, thank God for His kind providence, but you can still learn from the psalmist. What if your spouse, a child, or a friend is going through a time of deep discouragement? Listen and learn for their sake. What will you do when devastation *does* come to you? Desperation and hopelessness may one day cross your path. Listen now, and cling to your newfound understanding when darkness threatens.

This psalm brings us to our knees with a concept most find difficult to accept. We must face the reality of the fallen world in which we live—a world that is scarred by the consequences of sin. Second, this psalm shows us no way out whatsoever. What are your present circumstances? Are you struggling with the devastation of disease or some other seemingly insurmountable challenge? The fact is there may *not* be a way out for you. This hardship may be within God's providence or His sovereign will for your life.

There simply may not be an escape for you from this particular predicament. The psalmist teaches about despair with word-pictures: He describes the emotions as an engulfing wave. He portrays the one who suffers as in a dark pit with no way out, surrounded by nothing but bleakness. He grieves to find himself in a place where he would prefer to die rather than go on fighting.

Is that how you feel? Are you in the dark night of the soul? Not just a tough time, not just in a crunch, but the dark night of the soul? The starkest Scriptures are the most credible witnesses of God's presence that His presence is always with us, even in the worst of times. There is something in the worst of times that can be experienced, something of God, which one *will not* and *cannot* experience at any other time! Why is this true? When I have suffered the most, when the pain cannot be any worse, when the sense of being abandoned is the strongest, when the feelings of worthlessness cannot be more acute, why at *that moment* do I relate to God in a way that is so unlike my experience of Him at any other moment?

The gospel provides the answer, and it teaches us how to rightly understand Psalm 88. This psalm is not yours; rather, it belongs to Jesus Christ. No matter how great our despair seems, all of the elements of this psalm are only fully realized in Jesus and in Jesus alone.

It is not a prediction of Christ's sufferings, but it does articulate for us the angst Jesus would experience to an even greater degree than this psalmist could ever imagine.

Jesus cried out to God the Father in the Garden. He was extremely troubled as sorrow weighed heavily on His soul. Jesus was abandoned by His companions and betrayed by one of His own. He saw His disciples slink away and His mother separated from Him. And as He hung upon that cross, the mighty wrath of God was handed over to Him. The wrath our sins deserve was endured not by us, but by Him. Then there was darkness. In the gospel according to Matthew, he records that darkness was literally Christ's last companion.

The psalm, as we read it, is left open ended. Christ had not yet come. But the questions raised by the psalmist have been transformed for us by the work of Christ. Christ answered this prayer by putting this prayer upon His own lips. Jesus identified with us in the depths of the fall, the depths of woe. God Himself laid our despair on His own son, Jesus Christ. This is why I can say, "When I suffer the greatest in this life, when I am in the deepest, darkest hour, it is *then* that I most know God. *It is then that we can taste to an infinitesimal degree the sufferings our Savior endured for us!*" Whatever our despair, His was far deeper. Whatever our pain and loneliness, His was far greater.

The fact that we despair and ask questions is a sign God has *not* abandoned us. God is big enough; He can handle everything we ask of Him or say to Him. He knows how He has made us—as personal beings with a capacity to suffer and a capacity to question. Struggle with Him if you must, but I pray that as you reflect on Christ's fulfillment of this psalm, you will be able to find solace and rest.

Because of Christ you can do that right now. Your difficulties, your disease, or your despair will not necessarily disappear. But you can choose to stop and rest in the arms of the one Who entered the pit, fell beneath the waves, took upon Himself the wrath we deserved, and entered the darkness of death. We can rest peacefully in

His arms because He too was a man of sorrows. No gut-wrenching experience nor depths of despair can compare to what Christ endured on the cross.

And because He did endure this sorrow, never will our lives be truly hopeless. He cried out for deliverance on the cross, and *there was no answer from heaven*. That cross is where he paid our penalty! There was no deliverance: Christ had to drink that cup, *alone;* for the sake of His people. Because Christ sacrificed Himself for us, utter darkness and eternal abandonment will never be our lot. We can have hope— a hope that springs eternal.

Living with autism is not an easy road to travel. But the Lord understands the pain involved, and He wants to walk beside us and carry us when we can no longer walk. He desires to use this time of anguish and distress to draw us ever closer to His heart. Share your fears, your lost dreams, and your broken heart with Him. Cry. Vent. Get angry. Most importantly, give this trial over to Him. Rely on His might, for He has the strength to heal, comfort, and satisfy all the longings of your heart. Trust in Him. Let Him into your heart and you will find the intimacy you desire and the strength you need to survive the most heart-wrenching of predicaments.

Never despair of a child. The one you weep the most for at the mercy seat may fill your heart with the sweetest joys. —T. L. Cuyler[1]

Let us fix our eyes on Jesus, the author and perfecter of our faith, who for the joy set before him endured the cross. Consider him who endured such opposition from sinful men, so that you will not grow weary and lose heart.
(Hebrews 12:2a, 3)

---

1 Copyright 1995 Cook Communications Ministries. God's Little Instruction Book For Mom by Honor Books. Used with permission. All rights reserved.

23

"Somebody Just Kill Me!": Encouraging Moments

Don't let the title fool you; I promise you won't need a box of tissues. Rather, in this chapter I share encouraging moments from Zack's journey into normalcy. It is a compilation of the amazing little episodes that gave us hope and kept us going through the especially rough patches. These moments meant the world to us; without them I'm not sure how we would have managed. Although I've related details about special times in the previous chapters, I had a few more memories worthy of a chapter in their own right. I'm saving the best example for last, so you probably won't understand the title of this chapter right away. Of course, if your impatience rivals mine, you can enlighten yourself by skipping ahead to the end.

One of our most tender moments took place when Zack had finally adjusted to his new kindergarten class. His beautiful blue eyes and amazing brown curls couldn't help but entice all the little girls to take notice and swarm around him. Perhaps the excessive attention bothered him, or maybe he was simply trying to decide which girl to pursue. Whatever the cause, he was quite reserved initially; however, after a few weeks he determined to set his sights on Brianna. She was very cute and sweet yet somewhat shy. In no time at all Zack had charmed his way into her heart. Each morning thereafter they walked hand in hand into the classroom. This was a giant step forward for a boy who used to scream at the gentlest touch!

Another momentous (as well as silly) example occurred on the soccer field at the beginning of the second season. James and Zack had been practicing a little routine all summer long as they worked on soccer drills in the backyard. Whenever Zack would score, James would tell him to pull the bottom of his jersey up over his head. Showing off his cute little Adonis stomach, Zack would then raise his arms in the air with index fingers extended. That fall, during one of the more impressive "studly" games, Zack scored twice. Completely caught up in the moment and without any prompting whatsoever, each goal was followed by the above-mentioned antics. James and I were absolutely thrilled by Zack's exuberance and zest for life. What a long way he had come from the days when wrapping and unwrapping his fingers in the goal netting was the only excitement that the game held for him. It was also incredibly uplifting to overhear the accolades expressed by the parents of both teams. Finally we were able to have fun in public with our adorable little son. An entire world was opening up to our family!

Last spring break we vacationed at Disneyland, thanks to my generous in-laws. Being a kid at heart myself, I had been looking forward to this excursion as much as my kids—maybe even more so. I eagerly anticipated the opportunity to share this experience with my children, despite warnings from people not to have unreasonably high expectations. What if our youngsters found the roller coasters too scary? Would I end up riding kiddy rides all week? Indeed, this was the case with Abbie, who was only four and a half at the time, so all of us grown-ups took turns with her in Mickey's Toontown. Having anticipated the likelihood of this, even I wasn't too disappointed to find myself there upon occasion.

It was a completely different story with the boys. Relieving all my fears, Jacob and Zack absolutely loved roller coasters. Huge smiles lit up their faces as their hands shot up into the air on the downhill slide of these rides. Watching their unbridled enthusiasm for an activity I so thoroughly enjoyed brought great delight to my heart. My boy, who used to scream at camera flashes and loud noises and refuse to move except on his own terms, handled Space Mountain like a pro! With his curly hair blown back from his face à la Kramer in *Seinfeld*, Zack and I sped across to the photo station. The picture said it all: nothing could contain his zeal for life. This experience may well be my fondest memory of Zack's transformation.

Even riding the shuttle bus to and from the theme park was fun. On every expedition Jacob was his usual outgoing self, talking the ears off his "captive" audience. This was not the least bit surprising to any of us. What *was* surprising was seeing Zack follow his brother's example. Initiating conversations with total strangers and explaining in great detail the events of the day, he would tell them all about his favorite rides. Even more astonishing, he was asking these same strangers about their day at the park. Did they have fun? What was their favorite part of the park? Astounded, I remembered that this was the little guy the experts believed would never have the capacity to socialize in "normal" ways!

One of our nicest experiences with Zack was being able to take him to a movie without him covering his ears and yelling, "Too loud! Too loud!" Getting the chance to take our special child to the theatre without incident was something we had been looking forward to for years. We had tried unsuccessfully several times during those first two years of therapy. Every failure made it clear that an awful lot of sensory issues still needed to be addressed before Zack would be able to handle this environment for the duration of a movie. I'm not sure what we did specifically, but three years of various sensory-related therapies adequately prepared him for the movie theatre experience.

Recently our family saw *Spider-Man 3*. James and I had a running bet over how many times we would have to shush Jacob during the movie because he has been our incessant talker since he was two and a half. Despite our best efforts, we haven't had much success convincing him to be quiet for any real length of time. Much to our surprise, we had to shush Zack twice as often as Jacob! It was hard to believe that our new little motor-mouth once relied completely on sign language to communicate.

Almost two years into Zack's intervention program, I had a similar experience at church. Although he had been initiating conversation with signs for quite a while, he had just started converting his signs into actual words. We were thrilled that Zack finally understood the importance of verbal communication. Unfortunately, he didn't yet comprehend the social parameters observed during a church service. Even though he was expected to be as quiet as a mouse (a church mouse, if you prefer), he was determined to practice his newfound words. Thankful that my once nonverbal boy was now talking, the last thing I wanted to do was ask him to be silent. Discouraging him went against every fiber of my being, and many times I just couldn't bring myself to do it.

But this wasn't our only issue. Because I sang on the worship team, I couldn't very well sit in the back row and run up and down the aisle between songs. So our family always chose seats near the front and hoped for the best. Not one soul said anything disparaging. (Have I mentioned yet that I adore our church body?) However, there did seem to be a buffer zone around us in which no one dared to sit, lest they be distracted. Who could blame them? I certainly would have done the same thing if I was in their place. Everyone was gracious enough not to say anything insensitive; in return, I did not take it personally that we sat in relative solitude.

This seating arrangement did lead to one particularly infuriating moment, however. James was working in the nursery, so he was absent from the sanctuary. I happened to be the only singer on the worship team this particular Sunday. My boys, six and four years old, were sitting near the front as always. They were also sitting all by themselves as I sang, which they had never done before. So when the altercation broke out, I had a ringside view but no way of refereeing.

Jacob and Zack found a photograph in my Bible, and they immediately began to fight over who could hold it. Trapped on the stage with a microphone connected to my mouth, there was nothing I could do. Nobody was sitting close enough to my boys to reprimand them. Even if they had been, I imagine no one would have felt comfortable enough with Zack's autism to do anything. Most of them had witnessed the magnitude of his tantrums by this point and probably feared that if they got involved, things would only go from bad to worse. So the dispute continued for what felt to me like an eternity: "Mine, mine, mine! Give, give, give!" As frustrating as the situation was at that moment, Zack *was* using his words. A part of me couldn't help but rejoice in the fact that my autistic son was demonstrating such "normal" behavior!

Still, it really was quite mortifying to stand up there and helplessly watch the scene my boys were making. Feeling like a bad mom whose undisciplined rascals were hopelessly out of control, I actually considered rushing over to quiet them rather than continue singing. Despite the distraction, we managed to survive this embarrassment and move forward. You may be thinking that this would have been the perfect place for my "Somebody just kill me" line, but you would be mistaken. That particular instance was not embarrassing, awkward, or public.

Instead, it occurred on a family road trip in our minivan. We were taking a trip to see my in-laws. This expedition takes three and a half hours if one is blessed with no construction, potty breaks, or heavy traffic. We managed to avoid these delays on this trip, thank goodness. What we did not manage to avoid was Jacob singing the New Mexico version of *The Twelve Days of Christmas* over and over and over. Calling birds and French hens were replaced with rattlesnakes, howling coyotes, and the like. Actually, it is a rather clever song and a nice change of pace from the original. Even so, every time Jacob slipped up, he went back to the very beginning and tried again. Just a little more than six at the time, he inevitably made many mistakes. Yet he was bound and determined to get it right, much to our chagrin. Three hours and 25 minutes into the trip, Jacob was still singing this song.

By this point I had developed a migraine, and James was exhausted from the long drive. We had begun our journey immediately after he returned from a challenging day at work, and now it was approaching 10 p.m. Four-year-old Zack was very tired, but Jacob's unending serenade had kept him from falling asleep. All of a sudden, completely out of the blue, Zack belted out (with perfect articulation, no less), "Somebody just kill me!" I think we had all been thinking something like that for the last three hours, but only our boy with autism had the nerve to say it out loud. We laughed so hard that I almost peed in my pants and James nearly drove off the road. At this point in Zack's intervention program, we were still drilling him on almost every phrase in the English language. Trust me, we never practiced the "Somebody just kill me" line. That statement, profound and flawlessly delivered, was all Zack's, and coming up with it as he did was absolutely perfect and normal in every respect.

The most wasted of all days is that on which one has not laughed.
- E.E. Cummings [1]

A cheerful heart is good medicine.
(Proverbs 17:22a)

---

1 Copyright 1996 Cook Communications Ministries. God's Little Instruction Book For Women by Honor Books. Used with permission. All rights reserved.

24

How to Help: For Family and Friends

James and I survived our autism journey with enormous support and love from our family, friends, and church body. Although we live a great distance from our relatives, they still found ways to contribute to Zack's recovery. Even so, we found ourselves especially dependent on local friends and brothers and sisters in Christ.

If you are a concerned family member or friend who wishes to help a loved one endure their experience with autism, I have some suggestions for you. Some of these ideas are fairly easy to carry out, while others require far more involvement and commitment on your part. Any level of help will likely be greatly appreciated. My guess is that most families probably feel as though they are barely able to keep their heads above the water. We certainly did.

Listen Patiently

Parents of children with autism need countless opportunities to vent their frustrations over their dire predicament. Autism is not an easy diagnosis to accept when one desperately loves a child. Depression is common, as well as uncontrollable, spontaneous crying. Feelings of hopelessness and despair are all too familiar. Expect most, if not all, of your loved one's conversations to revolve around autism. Striving toward recovery is an all-consuming endeavor. You must understand this and be supportive, regardless. Helping our precious boy overcome his autism was a hideous trial to live through, and we definitely needed to feel loved more than ever as we climbed this mountain. Having access to a friendly ear helped to ease our load tremendously.

Take the initiative! Call your loved ones and tell them that you care and they are not alone. Most importantly, communicate your willingness to listen to anything and everything they may need to share, no matter how awful. Some days are absolutely excruciating. Being able to talk about the horrors of therapy and a life overwhelmed by autism can be extremely cathartic. Feeling as though one's friends are tired of hearing about their pain produces even more loneliness, isolation, and sadness.

Provide Meals

Our church body brought us dinners for six months, and it truly was a lifesaver. If you feel uncomfortable with the special child's restrictive diet, perhaps you could bring a special treat for the other members of the family. Even this gesture would be a tremendous help. I routinely made three different meals for dinner: one for Zack, one for Jacob and Abbie, and one for James and me. When the church meals only suited us grown-ups, they were still greatly appreciated.

Therapy is so expensive that even one free meal can be a huge blessing. The struggling family may be able to redirect the money otherwise spent on a meal to finance one more hour of therapy with a college student. Providing meals may not seem like a big deal to you, but trust me, it *is* an enormous help! What an easy way to express your love to a grieving, stressed-out family. I know we felt extremely loved when we were ministered to in this manner.

Help with Financial Burdens

Offer to lend a hand with therapy costs or unexpected expenses. Every tiny bit of financial aid helps. Even 20 bucks every now and then can help an overwhelmed parent get a little extra assistance. If someone else can be paid to perform one or two hours of therapy, perhaps the parent can grab a greatly needed nap or run an errand. Moreover, many autism parents live paycheck to paycheck as we did. We wanted our Zack to get as much therapy as possible, and I'm sure we were not alone in this respect. Autism families experience flat tires and broken appliances just like everyone else, but they may not have the money to cover such surprises. Your generosity could really help them out of a bind.

This was the greatest source of help offered to us by our extended family. Yes, they babysat our kids, allowing us to escape our predicament for a few hours whenever they came to town. However, their visits were sporadic due to their work commitments and the many miles between us. James's family very generously helped us to pay for Jacob's private school. My parents sent money whenever we ran into unexpected financial strains. Knowing that we could count on our loving family during this trial really put our hearts at ease, at least from a financial standpoint. Our hearts were still very troubled over Zack, but at least we didn't have the additional burden of worrying over money.

Provide Therapy Yourself

This ministry is going to require a lot from you should you choose to do it, but it will mean the world to your struggling loved one. Offer to do an hour of therapy yourself. You don't have to be a professional psychologist, speech therapist, occupational therapist, physical therapist, or early childhood developmental specialist. If you are, donating a free hour of therapy in your field of expertise would be a phenomenal blessing. If you are a layman, you can still help by getting involved. Learn about autism in general and the individual child in particular. Learn the specifics of his or her therapy regimen. Consistency is crucial in order for most children with autism to make real gains. You may be able to get training and education from an autism consultant, if the family is already employing one. There is a good chance the parents have become experts in their own right, so they may be well-informed and capable enough of training you themselves.

By carrying some of this burden, you could have an extraordinary effect on both the family psyche and the special child. Also, you may discover in the process that you are a natural. If so, you could further develop your gift and minister to families in a way you never imagined. Do you have a mature high school or college student of your own? Is he or she looking for a ministry or a meaningful purpose in life? Consider sending them in this direction. Perhaps they will stumble upon a rewarding career path. We never had the luxury of a volunteer therapist, but I'm certain this would have been a dream come true for our family.

Babysit

Offer to babysit. Even if you only feel comfortable babysitting at night once the kid(s) are in bed, the parents would be given a chance to escape the house and regroup for a few hours. If this suggestion still sounds too daunting, watch the siblings. They enjoy feeling special too, and the frazzled parents would still enjoy a calmer household for a spell. Also, you may provide them with an opportunity to run an errand or go to a doctor's appointment with only one child to corral. Having an ounce of sanity every now and then can really lift an autism family's spirits. James and I always looked forward to our extended family coming to visit. We enjoyed their company, of course, but we also knew that we would be blessed with a date night. Even if we did end up in the bookstore reading about autism, we were still out of the house and together.

Again, if your mature high school or college student is looking for a ministry, encourage them to offer a free night of babysitting to an autism family every month. Some prep work may be required because children with autism often do not adjust well to strangers or strange situations. In addition, many children with autism are reckless daredevils and/or escape artists. These types of concerns may need to be addressed beforehand.

Continue to Extend Invitations

Siblings can't help but notice the continual focus and attention given to the child with autism. Often times they perceive this intervention program as preferential treatment; it is easy for them to equate the non-stop therapy with love. Subsequently, they may feel neglected when they receive but a minute fraction of their parents' time. You can do much to alleviate the effects of this unfair yet necessary situation by continuing to invite the siblings over for play dates.

Invite the child with autism over as well, if at all possible. It is hard enough for parents to come to terms with their child's diagnosis without the added heartbreak of becoming social outcasts. When our invitations all but ceased, I was extremely lonely. The few invitations we did receive made us feel extraordinarily loved and accepted.

Please be gracious and understanding when disturbing behavioral issues arise. And, yes, they will arise. Remember that these families are dealing with such scenarios on a nearly constant basis. Offer kind words and encouragement. Embrace the entire family despite their special challenges; they are doing the best they can under extremely trying and desperate circumstances.

Take Interest in Their Special Kid

Whenever feasible, make an effort to treat the child with autism as you would any other child. Go out of your way to express an interest in their special kid. Let your friends know that you care deeply. Ask them to help facilitate a comfortable interaction with their child; the parents will know what to do. For instance, they may ask you to crouch or sit down so you two can be at the same eye level. They may divulge specific negative triggers to avoid, or they may suggest a specific activity like roughhousing, which is often popular. They may even ask you to wait until the circumstances are optimal to maximize quality time with their child. If you notice even the slightest little measure of progress after your visit, share this observation with whole-hearted enthusiasm. We autism parents live for moments like these because they keep us motivated and ward off depression.

Words cannot adequately express how life-sustaining such an offering is to a family dealing with this crisis. We desperately wanted our Zack to be loved and accepted and included just like everyone else's kids. More than four years later, these feelings are still very much alive. Our baby has worked so hard and come so far that the possibility of rejection by anyone for any reason is absolutely unbearable. I have poured my heart and soul into this child. Everyone *has* to love him! They just *have* to! In my mind, there is no other alternative.

Teach Your Children Love

Teach your own children how to love someone with autism. Autism is a disability, just like Down's syndrome, cerebral palsy, and other conditions that restrict one to the use of a wheelchair or prosthetic. Yet there is only one distinct difference: Autism does not manifest itself with an obvious physical handicap or attribute as these other disabilities do. Children with autism look just like everybody else. In fact, I have yet to meet an autistic child that wasn't drop-dead gorgeous. I have joked with other autism parents that the genetic predisposition for autism must be located on the "cute gene." No, I am not allowing my overly sensitive mommy impressions to speak for me here. Children with autism really are amazingly beautiful.

But at the same time, children with autism are undoubtedly

quite odd on some occasions. Cruel comments have a tendency to surface among their peers if parents are not sufficiently proactive. Most parents teach their children to be sensitive and compassionate toward people with more evident handicaps. I ask that you would extend the same courtesy for the handicap of autism. Teach your children to be tolerant, not judgmental. Teach them to use kind and loving words. Even though harmful words may not directly hurt the child with autism, they still have the potential to pierce the heart of an already emotionally distraught parent.

Clean

Offer to help clean your loved one's house or hire a maid service to do so. I have never been a huge neat freak, but I do like my home to have some appearance of order. With three small kids, there probably isn't a legitimate chance of it actually being spotless. To be honest, I don't recall the last time my house was truly clean. For that matter, I can't remember the last time my house even took on the illusion of cleanliness. Therapy can be very messy, especially when it takes all of your time. If you and your child are participating in a comprehensive intervention program, a tidy house is an impractical goal.

Allowing an endless stream of people into my house when I rarely had the time or opportunity to tidy up took some real flexibility on my part. I would have loved to have had a cleaner house, especially since Abbie was crawling around on the floor during most of that first year of therapy.

Every time our extended family made their way to Las Cruces, they cleaned for us. It was such a blessing that I really wished they could have visited more often. (Ha, ha!)

Pray

Last but certainly not least, pray. Pray for the child—that the therapy would be perfectly designed according to the individual child's specific needs. Pray that the strategies would be effective to the highest possible degree. Pray that the therapists, teachers, and schools would be the best possible match for the child.

Pray for the parents—that they will have the wisdom necessary to make the best decisions for their child. Pray that they would have limitless energy and the fortitude to press on, especially on those particularly horrific days. Pray for their emotional well-being. Pray for their finances. Pray that they would not grow weary. Pray for the perseverance of their spiritual lives. Pray that their marital relationship will not only survive this attack but grow stronger in the process.

Pray for the siblings—that they would not be permanently adversely affected by their world being turned upside down. Pray that the family would have an extra measure of God's all-sufficient grace every day. Pray and pray, and then pray some more. It helps more than you may think. I know some of our very dear friends have faithfully prayed for us for a very long time. I could never adequately thank them for bestowing upon us such selfless love. I will appreciate them and their sacrifice forever.

The most effective thing we can do for our children and families is pray for them. —Anthony Evans[1]

"A new command I give you: Love one another. As I have loved you, so you must love one another. By this all men will know that you are my disciples, if you love one another."
(John 13:34-35)

---

1 *Copyright 1995 Cook Communications Ministries.* ***God's Little Instruction Book For Dad*** *by Honor Books. Used with permission. All rights reserved.*

25

Lessons Learned: Growth and Maturity

Having a child with autism forced me to learn more than I ever thought humanly possible. Researching everything from gastrointestinal issues to dietary interventions, general characteristics to specific strategies, and negative behavior triggers to effective solutions consumed my mind for three years. This phase of my life consisted of occupational therapy, sensory diets, remedies for stimming, sign language, speech therapy for apraxia, and early childhood development goals. I have experienced the depths of despair but have found hope through action. Enormous blessings have been bestowed upon me. No longer am I forced to play the part of primary therapist; I now have the privilege to act as Mom to all three of my precious children.

I have discovered that kids with autism have the potential to recover if the parents are willing to press on for years on end. Enlightened by our own experience, I am absolutely convinced that parents play the most critical role in the life of a child with autism. Be that as it may, expecting grieving parents to face this trial alone is beyond cruel. Adequate training, substantial support, and loving encouragement need to be offered by the community to sufficiently foster a child's chance of success.

I have learned what it truly means to be loved unconditionally— to be given mercies upon mercies. My family and son have been prayed for faithfully for years. Incredibly loving people saw our suffering and stepped up to help us by providing meals and financial support through extremely trying times. Our family and friends did their best to help, even though they could not fully understand our pain. They cared when we could give nothing in return. This is true love indeed.

I have learned that when God's love lives within us, even we sinners can love unconditionally. I love all of my children very much, including Zack. When my son was screeching at every turn and entirely unpleasant to be around, I became completely overwhelmed by the love I felt for him. Even as a young girl, I looked forward to being a great, loving mom. Yet, I was still stunned by the intensity of my love for Zack, who by most people's standards wasn't acting lovable at all.

Before I had children, I had trusted God to never give me a special needs child. Despite my desire to be more comfortable around people with handicaps, I remained inescapably awkward: "Should I make eye contact? I don't want to stare. I don't want to hurt anyone's feelings by not addressing them appropriately." Even though I wished for those with struggles to feel comfortable and accepted by me, I knew that I was sadly lacking in this area. For a long time I had admired those drawn to helping people with disabilities because they could so genuinely and effortlessly look past the challenges and express such love and compassion. I never felt that I had it within me to be like those people I had admired so much.

What I discovered was quite the opposite. My love for Zack was so powerful and passionate—so vehement. Dare I say extreme? One of my fellow autism moms described it so eloquently. She said she loves her son so much that her body aches from the very core. Yet there are times she just can't bear to be around him because her love hurts so much that it is excruciating. And she used to work with people with handicaps before she had children! Unlike me, she always felt that she could easily handle having a special needs child, but she was soon surprised by how different she felt as a mom rather than an employee. Having a son with autism was far more devastating than she could have ever anticipated.

Great opportunities for personal growth and introspection surface when one has a child on the autism spectrum. In fact, I can't imagine how one could fail to mature in some respect when facing this ordeal.

Learning how to advocate for Zack effectively without fear of being judged was just one more lesson I had to learn. Trusting my instincts as a mom *and* an autism expert, I no longer blindly accept the status quo. Now, if the experts want to do things their way, they have to run it by me first. I don't give up when I am fighting for something really important, yet I know how to pick my battles. Experience has taught me that appreciating good teachers and providing support to them can be much more effective than dealing with a school bureaucracy. Finding the best school environment and suitable therapists for my son are also two more skills I've been able to master.

I have learned about patience. Don't get me wrong; I freely acknowledge my own failures in this area. In fact, I've often thought my perfect bumper sticker would read: "You think I'm impatient now? You should have seen me *before* I had kids." With autism, the progress is so painstakingly slow that developing patience is an inevitable, necessary element of life. Granted, I'm still not the world's most patient person, but I'd like to think the Lord has helped me grow in this area to some degree.

My priorities have changed as well. I used to be far too preoccupied with my own appearance, as well as my own accomplishments. Taking great pride in the accomplishments of my children was second nature to me because I saw their success as a reflection of my awe-inspiring parenting skills. How self-absorbed and immature I was to believe that I had any tangible control over anything in my life, including the potential of my children.

Now I understand that my sole responsibility is to live my life and raise my kids in a way that is pleasing to God. This is where my ordained power begins and ends because God is always in control. Only His sovereign grace spares me from limitless evils and hardships in this life. All of our gifts come from Him, and our purpose is to use these gifts for His glory—not our own. Not only have I been greatly humbled by autism, but I have also been given a mission to help others in similar circumstances. My life is so busy as a result of our experience with this disorder that I rarely have the time or opportunity to obsess about fickle matters such as my fleeting outward appearance.

I have also learned that my husband is truly a gift from God. In fact, I would never have survived this ordeal without his support, encouragement, faithfulness, and love. Whenever I needed to escape from my life for a few hours and get out of the house, James would work with Zack so that I wouldn't feel guilty about needing to regroup. He was always there for me when I needed him. Families often do not survive with a child who has autism; in fact, the stress pushes the divorce rate to over 85%. Yet my wonderful husband always stood by me and our family. Even when times were at their worst, when I was a complete mess and emotional wreck, he was a rock and a stronghold for me. Holding me ever so tightly when I despaired, he shared my tears and understood my pain when I felt so alone, overwhelmed, and sad. He never argued with me about how or why the therapy should be implemented. James was the exemplary model of patience, coaching the soccer team and teaching Zack essential social skills. What a monumental challenge to overcome! Before Zack's autism, I had appreciated James for the man he *was*; now I marvel over the man he has *become*.

I have also learned how important it is not to judge a mom with a difficult child. Of course, there are spoiled brats in the world in dire need of some discipline; I'm not disputing that fact. But when I see a mom struggling for sanity because of her child, I never jump to any conclusions. How could I assume to understand this poor stranger's situation? Instead, I offer a helping hand or encouraging words. Gracious interactions can mean the world to an autism mom; I know because I've been there. Having seen the looks and heard the disparaging comments, I understand all too well the pain that comes from unwarranted conclusions others make.

In the midst of overcoming our own difficult circumstance, I gradually realized the importance of investing in the lives of others. There is no doubt in my mind that my ministry to the world is helping young children with this debilitating disorder. God allowed autism to afflict our family so that I could share our experience and offer hope to the hopeless. As a result of reaching out to other hurting families, I have developed incredibly close friendships. My feelings of loneliness and isolation have been replaced by fulfilling, rewarding relationships. Life is far richer due to the special bond we share.

Little things now take on much greater meaning. Every developmental milestone attained is celebrated. I am constantly amazed at the splendor of God's work and the beauty of His creation. I notice everything, even the curious, life-loving spirit He has imparted to my children. My thoughts are filled with gratitude and joy over the smallest pleasures in life.

Moreover, I have learned that the Lord reaches out to outcasts. Even though I spent three years attempting to make my little boy "normal," the Lord doesn't require normalcy from anyone. It is the weak, the downtrodden, the sick, the needy, and the desperate people whom He cares for the most. Strong people see themselves as having no need for a Savior; however, the weak cannot deny their neediness. Only when one experiences the depths of despair can he or she have even the slightest understanding of the suffering of our Lord and Savior Jesus Christ. Paying the penalty for our sins upon the cross was unimaginably worse and immeasurable compared to our own suffering—even the grief of autism. I may have cried enough to last two lifetimes, but I have never sweated blood in dreaded anticipation of what my future held.

Most importantly, what I learned was complete and utter reliance on my Lord. I spent every waking moment for years so exhausted, so emotionally fragile, so exasperated, so busy, and so discouraged. The only way I was able to keep my head above water was by giving it all up to Him. I knew that Zack's autism came with a purpose, and that purpose was to glorify God. I also knew that God had the power to cure my son immediately if He so chose, and believe me, I prayed for this outcome often. God's answer was no, not now—not for a very long time. First He had to teach me that I could not rely on my own strength even one tiny little bit.

Before Zack's autism diagnosis, I had considered myself a rather competent, capable person with the perseverance and strength sufficient to overcome most of life's obstacles. But I was very mistaken. I am weak and incapable, and I freely admit it. My works are dirty rags in His sight, and the only good I can do is the good that God does through me. God is powerful and strong, and He can do amazing things with our weakness. But we must first be willing to humble ourselves, acknowledge our inadequacies, and beg for His mercy and His grace. God, not me, performed a miracle on my son. He used me to perform His miracle. I have no doubt that His strength, and His strength alone, granted me the ability to do all that I did. God deserves all the credit, and I deserve none. This is how it should be.

The following depiction was written by Emily Perl Kingsley, Sesame Street scriptwriter. She so tenderly shares what it is like to be a parent of a special needs child. I read her beautiful words often, never without tears:

Welcome To Holland

By Emily Perl Kingsley

I am often asked to describe the experience of raising a child with a disability—to try to help people who have not shared that unique experience to understand it, to imagine how it would feel. It's like this. . . .

When you're going to have a baby, it's like planning a fabulous vacation trip—to Italy. You buy a bunch of guide books and make your wonderful plans. The Coliseum. The Michelangelo David. The gondolas in Venice. You may learn some handy phrases in Italian. It's all very exciting.

After months of eager anticipation, the day finally arrives. You pack your bags and off you go. Several hours later, the plane lands. The flight attendant comes in and says, "Welcome to Holland."

"Holland?!?" you say. "What do you mean, Holland?? I signed up for Italy! I'm supposed to be in Italy. All my life I've dreamed of going to Italy."

But there's been a change in the flight plan. They've landed in Holland and there you must stay.

The important thing is that they haven't taken you to a horrible, disgusting, filthy place full of pestilence, famine and disease. It's just a different place.

So you must go out and buy new guide books. And you must learn a whole new language. And you will meet a whole new group of people you would never have met.

It's just a different place. It's slower-paced than Italy, less flashy than Italy. But after you've been there for a while and you catch your breath, you look around. . .and you begin to notice that Holland has windmills. . .and Holland has tulips. Holland even has Rembrandts.

But everyone you know is busy coming and going from Italy. . .and they're all bragging about what a wonderful time they had there. And for the rest of your life, you will say, "Yes, that's where I was supposed to go. That's what I had planned."

And the pain of that will never, ever, ever, ever go away. . .because the loss of that dream is a very, very significant loss.

But. . .if you spend your life mourning the fact that you didn't get to Italy, you may never be free to enjoy the very special, the very lovely things . . .about Holland.

Shout with joy to God, all the earth! Sing the glory of His name; make His praise glorious! Say to God, "How awesome are your deeds! So great is your power." Come and see what God has done, how awesome his works in man's behalf!

(Psalm 66:1-3a, 5)

26

Food: Happier Bodies Make Happier Therapy Subjects

As a young woman I often dreamed about being a mom. This was especially true during the years I supported my husband through law school. How nice it would be to do something that really mattered. I knew there would be difficult times upon occasion; there always are in life. But I was confident that the joy of being part of a family would help me overcome any struggle. I entertained thoughts of picnics and play dates and all of the love we would share. Never in these daydreams did I aspire to be a mom who was anxious—even fanatical—over the diets of her children. Yes, I exercised and ate reasonably well, but I wasn't overly consumed with my own food choices. I can appreciate the occasional green chili cheeseburger and fries as much as the next person. Nevertheless, I have turned into a mom who is an obsessive/compulsive label reader and an extremist about the diets of her children, but I have done so out of sheer necessity.

Almost all children with autism have moderate to severe gastrointestinal problems. Many have issues with yeast overgrowth in their abdominal cavity. This condition typically manifests itself with bloating and is accompanied by extremely foul-smelling diarrhea with a strange peanut butter-like consistency. I'm sorry about the graphic description. But if you are a parent dealing with autism, chances are you know that your child's digestive tract is completely out of sorts. You also know that these issues need to be addressed and resolved. Can you imagine trying to function in life with an improperly running gastrointestinal system?

If your doctor tells you that the American Medical Association doesn't have a test for yeast overgrowth, then you should find a new doctor who is willing to test for it. A simple urine test kit is available and covered by most insurance policies with a reasonable co-pay. If you lack a cooperative doctor, you can also order this test from the company GENEVA. Then you can send it by Federal Express to a laboratory for analysis. Sometimes a yeast overgrowth can be treated with megadoses of acidophilus and other pro-biotic digestion aids alone. Otherwise, an antifungal such as Diflucan can be administered, but beware. I have known several kids who have had an adverse reaction to this medication. Hand swelling and pain are common side effects that can trigger odd stims such as finger-licking and sucking. Fortunately, in Zack's case we were able to successfully treat his yeast overgrowth issues with pro-biotic supplements. Be on the lookout for dairy products in some brands of acidophilus; if your child is ultra-sensitive to casein proteins, problematic exposures may result.

I cannot overstress how important it is to find a doctor who is willing to work with you as you attempt to address your child's medical issues. We have a wonderful pediatrician who is extremely supportive and compassionate, especially toward special needs children. Every referral for specialized evaluation we've requested has been granted. The specialists haven't always worked out to our satisfaction, but our primary care physician has never let us down.

Many children with autism have significant allergies and sensitivities to a variety of foods. Some have high levels of heavy metals in their system that may interfere with brain function or may possibly affect the body's ability to absorb beneficial nutrients. Traditional doctors often regard autism-specific tests as a worthless waste of time and resources. Although we managed to figure out Zack's gastrointestinal issues without much help from experts, we have many friends who highly recommend Defeat Autism Now! (DAN!) as a resource. This agency is comprised of a diverse group of specialists, all of whom are committed to treating the child's particular medical concerns.

Just because the American Medical Association (AMA) fails to recognize certain conditions or symptoms this doesn't mean they don't exist. After reading several books on autism, we sought the advice of a traditional pediatric gastroenterologist. Unfortunately, we were told time and time again that there were no approved tests for this condition or for that one. The expert was both unable and unwilling to address our concerns. Up until this point, James and I had always whole-heartedly trusted the AMA and their recommendations, but we were very disappointed and frustrated by our less than helpful experience.

The DAN! doctors, though expensive, are apparently much more cooperative, thorough, and multidisciplinary in their methods. They are extremely helpful in determining comprehensive food allergies and sensitivities. One of my friends gave her son soy milk and potato milk when she switched him to the dairy-free diet, but she was perplexed by his explosive diarrhea and horrendous rash. After all, this dietary restriction was supposed to help, not hurt. Traditional allergy testing provided no valuable insights, but the non-traditional DAN! experts discovered that her child had an extreme allergy to both soy and potatoes.

I have been told by some parents that one drawback to working with DAN! is their tendency to try every possible biomedical intervention all at once. Such therapies include heavy metal chelation (which has been helpful to some but quite dangerous or useless to others), antifungal medications, pro-biotics, anti-seizure medications, melatonin or other sleeping aids, anti-anxiety medications, anti-depressants, and vitamin B12 shots (which can cause pain and swelling in the hands and persistent oral fixations). These interventions can be extremely costly and time-consuming, and all of them have the potential to produce negative side effects in someone with autism. If too many remedies are tried simultaneously, it becomes so much more difficult to pinpoint a problematic reaction.

As a parent, it is very easy to put all one's eggs into the biomedical intervention basket. One can expend significant financial resources and waste a lot of precious time pursuing a magic cure instead of diving full force into an intense behavioral modification program, the only proven methodology offering a chance at success.

In addition to continuous one-on-one intervention, there are several steps a parent can take to further support a child's therapy experience. Some experts believe that children with autism cannot completely break down certain proteins, specifically gluten (found in wheat, oats, rye, and barley) and casein (found in dairy products). These undigested proteins are very similar in chemical structure to opiates. Proponents of this theory suggest that these proteins leave the stomach and enter the body through a condition called "leaky gut syndrome." They then travel to the brain and attach themselves to the opioid receptors, causing an opiate-like drug "high." These receptors are primarily located in the speech and self-control portions of the brain. Not only does the brain experience a temporary "fix," but it also responds in an addictive fashion, like that of a drug abuser.

Many children with autism babble incessantly to themselves in a spacey, unnatural giggling sort of way after consuming gluten. Zack never babbled because of his grossly underdeveloped oral motor skills, but he was definitely in a spaced-out frame of mind most of the time. Most autism experts recommend a gluten-free, casein-free (gf/cf) diet; implementing these restrictions increases the potential for cooperation, focus, and the most productive therapy sessions.

They do not suggest that this diet is a cure for autism; rather, it helps children with autism benefit more from the interventions. Unfortunately, the AMA is lagging way behind private sector organizations in their efforts to research autism. Also, this organization fails to endorse the gf/cf diet on the merits of others' research, even though there are no detrimental side effects from this diet.

I discovered these dietary interventions shortly after Zack's diagnosis. Of course, wouldn't you know it, by this time he had almost completely self-limited his food choices to milk, cheese, yogurt, crackers, bread, and Cheerios®, all of which contain casein or gluten. He was overly insistent that these foods, *and only these foods*, comprise his diet. Zack seemed to crave these treats with a passion, basically eating only gluten/casein foods for the entire year leading up to his diagnosis.

At this time we were experiencing the worst of the therapy hold sessions, with his incessant tantrums and screeching. Nothing seemed to be helping him. Would I ever get through to my precious little boy? Would he ever be okay? When I read that my child could be getting "high" as a result of his diet, this *really* got my attention! Desperate, I knew I had to at least try out this theory. Maybe my precious son would be less spacey and more focused if I eliminated these foods from his diet. Perhaps if we were fortunate, the outbursts would stop too.

The prospect of completely altering Zack's food options when all he ever seemed to do was throw a tantrum and screech was extremely daunting to me. So I decided to start slowly by only removing the dairy products. Switching his milk to vitamin D- fortified sweet vanilla soy milk was easy; he loved the taste and put up no argument. In fact, it was so sweet that I was able to sneak a couple of small spoons of puréed fruits and vegetables into every cup. This way I was able to get some crucial vitamins into his system.

Removing cheese and yogurt from the menu was much more

of a challenge. Almost immediately I noticed a reaction in Zack that I can only describe as withdrawal. And I thought the tantrums were bad *before* I took him off dairy products! Trust me, I hadn't seen anything yet! The tantrums almost doubled in frequency and intensity. As we struggled through the outbursts, I kept telling myself that there must be something to this dairy-free eating: "Look at this dramatic effect. Stick it out. Stick it out. You'll be glad you did in the end." This rehabilitation process lasted about two weeks. Then, I started to notice more cooperation from Zack, enough that I actually found myself daring to be encouraged from time to time.

One might reasonably assume that our success with the dairy-free diet would have inspired me to jump right on the gluten-free bandwagon too. Yet, this gluten-free diet frightened me more, because aside from an occasional egg, a bite of apple, and a spoonful of mashed potatoes, Zack would only eat food containing gluten. I couldn't imagine what he would eat if I insisted on gluten-free products. Having already experienced one of his three-day fasts when I made attempts to introduce a vegetable into one of his meals, I didn't have much enthusiasm for more of the same. Since I was having moderate success with Zack on the dairy-free diet alone, I stayed on this course for about six months. Then Zack hit a plateau, and his previous level of compliance with the difficult therapy sessions began deteriorating. I felt as though I had no choice but to initiate the gluten-free diet as well.

At first Zack ate a lot of eggs, apples, and mashed potatoes. As a baby, he had GERD and vomited every meal for the first nine months. Even after he outgrew this condition, he had a hair-trigger gag reflex whenever he swallowed anything pulpy, scratchy, slimy—or that had a weird texture. . .or was a mixture of textures. . .or was a color other than white or tan. . . .Everything we managed to get into his stomach despite his hysterical protests just came right back up again. This was bad, but not as bad as this second round of withdrawal symptoms. Again, we experienced Zack's intense, frequent tantrums and ear-piercing screeching. As with the dairy-free diet, a new level of cooperation and focus emerged once the gluten was flushed from his system.

I placed our oldest boy, Jacob, on the gluten-free diet as well about a year later after reading an article in a parenting magazine stating that a child over the age of seven with a distended (bloated, toddler-like) stomach is most likely suffering from a gluten sensitivity. This description fit Jacob perfectly. Since I already had one child on the diet, I figured another one really wouldn't be that much extra work. After being on the gluten-free diet for a while, Jacob not only lost the balloon-like appearance in his stomach area, but his acting out in class also practically disappeared overnight. His hyperactive tendencies and lack of focus also improved dramatically. Just when I was beginning to wonder if he was borderline ADHD, I observed the wonderful effects of this new diet. Jacob's teachers all commented on his markedly improved behavior; it was as though he were a different child.

On the rare special occasions when we do allow Jacob to have gluten, the non-stop bouncing and hyper-silliness come roaring back, along with an immediate stomach- ache. In my humble opinion, all hyperactive, unfocused children should be placed on this gluten-free diet for a while. No harm can come of it, and it may make a world of difference. Jacob definitely benefited from this restriction, and Zack did too, but we weren't quite out of the woods yet.

Even though his focus and cooperation were much improved, Zack still insisted that his food be either white or tan. We very slowly began to color his mashed potatoes with puréed vegetables, hoping that he would learn to accept a little bit of color. This did work as long as we didn't get too overzealous: the change couldn't be too obvious. He was so fond of green that we added green food coloring to his chicken nuggets, just so he would get used to eating something green. Zack wouldn't eat any green vegetables, mind you, but we had to start somewhere. After a while we moved on to other colors.

Of course, those chicken nuggets were no longer an option for us when we transitioned to the gluten-free diet. When we set out on this journey, our hometown did not have the gluten-free options currently available. Now, I find it such a blessing to have access to bread, chicken nuggets, muffins, and snack foods that I don't have to prepare myself. Our gluten-free life is ever so much easier now. I highly recommend anything and everything that can make the autism experience less of a burden. So many aspects of this trial are unbelievably difficult. As a family, I know we needed an enormous measure of grace—just to survive. Adjusting to a gf/cf diet is a challenge in and of itself; at least it was for us.

Exploring the health food stores in our area was first on my list. I purchased numerous cookbooks and all of the various flour substitutes and attempted many of the recipes, with very few success stories. I really enjoy cooking and fancy myself a halfway decent cook, yet I still failed. Zack didn't like the food, and actually I couldn't really blame him. Most of my experiments tasted awful. So very dry and crumbly, the food lacked the light, spongy quality inherent to pastries, pasta, and bread. I soon discovered the magic ingredient in all wheat-based treats: gluten. Gluten makes textures perfectly delectable. How were we ever going to live without it?

Many children with autism cannot tolerate even the smallest exposure to gluten. I have known several parents who had presumed their child was gluten-free, only to discover that their little one was severely reacting to trace amounts. This protein is hidden in foods you might not even realize. Modified food starch and barley malt extract are just two common examples. Even rice and corn cereals usually have incidental amounts of wheat flour used to stave off sticking and settling.

Upon hearing this, I searched the health food stores for 100% gluten-free cereal. Pleased with my discoveries, I took them home and shared them with Zack. He promptly refused to take even one little bite. Again, I could hardly blame him. These cereals smelled like the big vitamins I used to feed our horses as a child, and they didn't taste the way they were supposed to, either. Before insisting that we adopt this unusual breakfast option, I decided it would be best to test Zack's tolerance for the name-brand cereals; fortunately, he seemed to handle these low levels of gluten without incident. Since the flakes were tan and shared a similar texture, cereal was now a fairly easy substitute for Zack's favorite gluten-based crackers.

In an effort to further expand Zack's food options, we worked with a nutritionist. She suggested that our family play games with our food. Her reasoning was that if we made a mess and had fun, these activities would eventually translate into a greater willingness to try new kinds of food. This strategy works great with typical picky eaters. Unfortunately, my kid was nothing close to typical when it came to food. We worked extremely hard for an entire year before Zack could even tolerate the sensation of messy hands for more than 30 seconds.

Our nutritionist also proposed that I put a tiny amount of new food on Zack's plate at every meal. So I did, at every meal; and he was hysterical, at every meal. He wasn't even asked to eat the food, merely to tolerate its presence on his plate. Yet, he still reacted just as severely. Of course, the same was true when his plate, fork, and cup weren't green. Frustrated with the lack of progress, I could just imagine the nutritionist rolling her eyes and saying, "Surely this isn't working because this mom isn't actually doing what I am asking her to do." But I was, and I was just as discouraged by our lack of progress.

By the time we began the second year of this program, the tantrums and screeching had morphed into whining. If I was lucky and Zack was using his words, I'd hear an accompanying "OOOH, YUCK!" After about six months of this, I told him that if he complained, he would have to eat the new food on his plate, whether he vomited or not. Complaining about his food was second nature to Zack, so he did it all the time. Having worked so hard to make him his special food, I just couldn't listen to one more "OOOH, YUCK!" With this new policy in place, he ended up trying lots of new things, but cleaning up Zack's vomit was a daily experience. Finally, by the end of the second year, he had learned to tolerate strange food on his plate. He may not have eaten it, but he had stopped complaining.

Halfway through our third year with dietary issues, something miraculous happened. Out of the blue, five-year-old Zack tried 25 new foods, all on his own. Even more amazing, his disposition was pleasant. The most astounding surprise was that he actually ended up liking about half of these new treats, which included fruits and vegetables! I don't know why he underwent his transformation just then. Maybe he decided to emulate our oldest son, who was the best eater I had ever seen. Perhaps his throat matured and was therefore able to handle more unusual textures. I'm sure Ranch dressing played an important role; for that matter, so did beans. Finally understanding the not-so-subtle nuances of little boy-humor, Zack ate beans purely for their gas-producing properties. Even though it didn't seem like it at the time, I'd imagine that all of the food therapy games also contributed to our success. Maybe our persistence was most responsible. What I do know for sure? We are incredibly blessed that after all the time and effort invested in this undertaking, many remarkable developments ensued.

Because I had been so in tune with what my kids were eating whenever they acted up, I wondered if perhaps there were other problematic foods affecting them. I began keeping a journal of what they ate and the positive and negative effects that followed over the next two days. This journal ended up being a wonderful resource for me—one that made living with my kids a much more pleasant experience. All three of my children are very sensitive to red dye #40, which is often present in over-the-counter medications, ketchup, barbecue sauces, yogurt, processed meats, sweet drinks, sodas, popsicles, chips, cereals, candy, crackers, and nearly every artificial kid snack on the market. Within 20 minutes of exposure to red dye #40, they bawl uncontrollably.

Some children with autism are very sensitive to some artificial sweeteners, sugar, and even fructose. (On the other hand, my oldest child becomes hyper when he eats sugar but handles artificial sweeteners without incident.)

Many children with autism are sensitive to artificial preservatives like nitrates, commonly found in processed meat. Zack has this particular sensitivity, although it appears that the nitrates have to build up in his system over the course of three to four days for issues to arise. A little bit every now and then seems to be okay for him.

When Zack sneaks gluten, he cries over every single little ridiculous thing the following day. This reaction always takes 24 hours to surface with him, but it is also very common for reactions to be postponed for up to 48 hours in children with autism. Very detailed note-taking over a lengthy period of time is often required to determine which food item or chemical additive is responsible for the negative effect(s).

My journal also helped me to realize that Zack had a phenomenal day whenever he ate bell peppers the day before. Maybe this vegetable supplies a vital nutrient deficiency for him. One of our biggest challenges was to get Zack to eat bell peppers just often enough to get the benefit, but not so often that he got burned out and decided he never wanted to eat them again.

Furthermore, we noticed that his occasional sneaking of cheese or yogurt have seemed to do him no harm. Perhaps the microorganisms present in these dairy products sufficiently break down the proteins so that Zack's system is able to digest them. His stomach may have healed somewhat over the years on this casein-free/ gluten-free diet, but I'm not sure. I do know he still can't handle gluten, yet I'll happily settle for cheese and yogurt rejoining his list of approved foods.

One of the earliest concerns I had when we started Zack on the gluten-free diet was what would happen when he is asked to make his own food choices. If he gets an addictive chemical "high" from eating gluten, one slip-up could be devastating. Thankfully, my worries have been put to rest. For years I have been telling him that I don't like for him to have gluten because it makes him cry the whole next day, and I don't want him to feel crummy. Apparently, these words have made enough of an impact on him; even at seven years of age, he is determined to make good choices when it comes to food.

Some of the other sensitivities were much harder for me to figure out. The problem was that I was only thinking about what went *into* their bodies, not what went *onto* their bodies. Children get exposed to a myriad of externally applied products that contain red dye #40, for example. It is a common ingredient in sunscreen, baby lotion, shampoo, bath soap, and bubblegum-flavored toothpaste—as well as Play-Doh®, markers, and other art supplies. After many bawling sessions later, I finally discovered the problem.

The trickiest discovery I ever made occurred last summer, when our part of the country had twice the rain it usually does. Mosquitoes were out in full force. Every time my kids would go to the park or soccer field, they would get eaten alive. From morning till night I listened to them whining about their itching woes. The children's bug repellent spray was grossly inadequate in protecting them, and with West Nile virus also prevalent in our area, I just couldn't tolerate the mosquito bites one moment longer. Spraying them all over with Deep Woods Off® worked like a charm. They didn't have a new mosquito bite for 10 whole days, which was absolutely fabulous.

Unfortunately, the same could not be said about their behavior. In fact, all three of my kids scurried around in a crazed, hyperactive *Lord of the Flies* fashion for the entire 10 days. Because they failed to listen to anything I said to them at home and ignored their teachers as well, I realized that something was very amiss in the Dickens family. I knew that my children hadn't been eating any of the trigger foods or chemicals, and they hadn't been exposed to red #40 in their sunscreen. Our only new variable was the bug repellent, so I stopped the spraying and had them take an hour-long soak in the bathtub. Two days later, they were back to their usual, more-controllable—albeit still spirited—selves. I later discovered that there are several effective all-natural bug repellents available to consumers. We have had great success with Avon® Skin So Soft Replenishing Body Lotion and the boys tolerate Quantum® Buzz Away. They both have a strong odor though, so if your child is especially sensitive to smells, you may want to try one of the other alternatives. As with your dietary interventions, experiment until you can determine what is ideal for your family. Take good notes and trust your instincts. Your diligence will make life easier in the long run.

A food is not necessarily essential just because your child hates it.
—Katherine Whitehouse[1]

But solid food is for the mature, who by constant use have trained themselves to distinguish good from evil.
(Hebrews 5:14)

---

1 Copyright 1995 Cook Communications Ministries. God's Little Instruction Book For Mom by Honor Books. Used with permission. All rights reserved.

27

Recipes: Gluten-Free/Casein-Free Family Favorites

Already worn out from a day of screeching tantrums and therapy, it was now time to make dinner. The meals from our church family were such a blessing to James and me, but most contained dairy and gluten, so I still had to prepare something my boys could eat without negative side effects. But what? I was at a complete loss. I had experimented with many recipes, but most of them had been flops. Since delving into this gluten- free/casein-free (gfcf) diet left me feeling uninspired, I thought I'd share some of our most popular never-fail recipes to lighten your load. They are relatively easy and always a hit at our house.

I have seen many children react very negatively to trace amounts of gluten and casein. They act completely spacey, talk to themselves, giggle for no reason, exhibit otherwise unexplained gastrointestinal (GI) issues, cry, or throw a tantrum for no apparent reason, and/or have absolutely no capacity for cooperation or focus. Of course, I recognize that these are common, everyday characteristics of autism. However, there are children making great strides with the gf/cf diet and therapy interventions who still have the potential to suddenly and dramatically regress due to incidental exposures.

You may also want to check for other additives that your child may have issues with, such as yeast extract, nitrates, monosodium glutamate (MSG) or other preservatives, sugar, corn syrup, and red dye, just to name a few. Before using any of these recipes, I also recommend allergy testing if you have not already done so. One of my friends has a boy on a strict gluten-free/casein-free diet who is also very allergic to soy, pinto beans, and bananas. When she first implemented the gf/cf diet, she didn't understand why her son had so many lingering GI issues. Allergy testing made her particular situation much more clear and manageable. Some of my recipes don't work for her family because of these additional allergies. This may be the case for you as well, so try to rule out all foods that may be problematic for your child.*

You may find that over a period of time your autistic child can tolerate small or incidental levels of gluten or casein proteins without adverse effects. This was true in our case. Some autistic children never have GI or food sensitivity issues, but most do. I whole-heartedly believe that families should stick to the strictest diet possible that is appropriate for their special child. I never would want to encourage anyone to ignore the positive benefits that a gf/cf diet has to offer.

**Disclaimer: Just because our children can tolerate the ingredients in these particular recipes does not necessarily mean that they are safe or ideal for your family. I highly recommend that you read the labels on your preferred brands to ensure they do not contain modified food starch or whey if you are following the gf/cf diet strictly. Present in many processed and pre-made foods and mixes, these two food additives can produce harmful reactions in especially sensitive children with autism. My brands are mentioned, but feel free to modify the recipe with alternative brands in your area. Only please, please be diligent in reading your labels. I know how time-consuming and annoying this process can be, but it can make a big difference to your child. Paying attention to labels is not only important but well worth the headache.*

Mexican Sandwiches

Servings: 6

I use these sandwiches for my boys' lunches all the time when I run out of gluten-free bread. Providing protein, fiber, and good carbohydrates, they are a great change of pace from traditional sandwiches.

1 box Old El Paso™ Tostada Shells (12 count)
1 or 2, 16 ounce cans Rosarita™ Traditional Refried Beans
Half pound ground beef, browned and drained (half pound))
Half pound grated soy cheese

1. Spread refried beans on one tostada shell until completely covered (layer can be thin or thick, according to your personal preference). **2.** Next, sprinkle ground beef on the beans, and top with the soy cheese. **3.** Cover with another tostada shell and microwave for about 35 seconds.

Best Gluten-Free Pancakes

Servings: 9 kid-sized pancakes

I don't follow the recipe on the pancake mix bag. Instead I have modified it to add more protein and vitamins. My kids like them so much that they are willing to forgo the syrup. Since I try to limit sugar consumption, I appreciate this fact very much. I use Pamela's™ Wheat-Free & Gluten-Free Ultimate Baking & Pancake Mix, but this product does contain cultured buttermilk, so you may need to find an alternative to this mix if your child is sensitive to this ingredient. Namaste Foods™ [(866)258-9493] has a pancake mix with no eggs, no dairy, no corn, no soy, and no potatoes. These ingredients are common allergens, so this may be a very good option for you.

3/4 cup pancake mix
3 large eggs or egg substitute equivalent
¼ cup sliced almonds or almond meal (depending on the texture your child prefers)
2 (3.5-ounce packs) Gerber™ puréed fruit (Apricots with

mixed fruit and plain bananas are the ones my kids like the best.)

Mix every ingredient together in large bowl, and make this recipe just as you would regular pancakes. *Note: The consistency of gluten-free pancake batter is thicker than traditional pancake batter, so don't be surprised.*

Best Gluten-free French Toast

Servings: one

1 slice Food for Life™ yeast-free brown rice bread (which is especially good for children with yeast overgrowth issues)
1 egg
2 tablespoons rice milk
1 tablespoon pure maple syrup
Oil for frying

1. Mix egg with rice milk. **2.** Soak bread for two minutes and cook in light oil as one would with traditional French toast. **3.** Sweeten with maple syrup.

Chicken Nuggets

Servings: 2 to 3

These are so good that even I will eat them, and I'm not a big fan of chicken nuggets.

2 large boneless skinless chicken breasts, cut into strips or nuggets
1 egg or egg substitute equivalent
¼ cup rice milk
½ cup rice flour
½ cup quinoa flour
Salt (to taste)
Oil for frying

1. Mix egg and rice milk well. **2.** Mix flours and salt well.

3. Heat the oil. Dip chicken in egg mixture, then flour mixture.
4. Fry until golden brown. Double-dip the chicken for extra batter.

Pizza

Servings: makes one large pizza

This recipe has quite a few ingredients, but I have found that if I'm in a pinch and have run out of some of the flours, I can substitute with the same amount of Pamela's™ Ultimate Baking & Pancake Mix. My kids never notice nor complain. I use a Kitchen-Aid™ mixer, but this isn't necessary.

¾ cup warm water
1 teaspoon sugar
1 ½ teaspoons gf/cf yeast
½ cup white rice flour
½ cup brown rice flour
¼ cup potato starch flour
¼ cup tapioca flour
1 ½ teaspoons xanthan gum
1 teaspoon unflavored gelatin powder
1 teaspoon salt
2 tablespoons olive oil
2 eggs or egg substitute equivalent
1 teaspoon cider vinegar
Pizza toppings (chef's preference)
Soy cheese

1. Preheat oven to 425°. If you have a baking stone, preheat as well. **2.** In mixing bowl combine water, sugar, and yeast. Set aside for at least 5 minutes. **3.** In large measuring bowl add flours, xanthan gum, gelatin powder, salt, olive oil, eggs, and cider vinegar. Add to the yeast mixture. **4.** Mix with an electric mixer on high for 2 minutes. Spread mixture flat over baking stone or lightly greased cookie/baking sheet using a spatula. (Be patient, the dough takes some time to stretch without sticking to the spatula). **5.** Bake crust for 10 minutes until golden brown. Remove crust from the oven, add pizza toppings, and bake for another 10 minutes until the (soy) cheese is melted. *Note: This recipe comes from* The Good Food Cookbook for Gluten-free and Casein-free Diets © *2001 Laurel A. Hoekman, with a few minor changes. This cookbook is a great resource, and my next recipe was inspired in part by their tomato bread.*

Cheesy Squash Muffins

Servings: 12 muffins

I use 2 tablespoons of grated Parmesan cheese in this recipe because Zack can tolerate it, but grated soy cheese is also an acceptable substitute. Again, there are many ingredients in this recipe, but the final product is well worth the hard work. My boys love these muffins so much that they will scarf down the entire dozen straight from the oven if I don't insist that they ration them a bit. Because of their popularity in our house, I always double it. My boys prefer them cut in half with a dab of margarine. I believe the muffins would freeze well, but mine have never been around long enough to consider freezing. I modified the tomato bread recipe from The Good Food Cookbook for Gluten-free and Casein-free Diets *because my kids don't care for chives or tomato juice.*

1 cup warm water
1 teaspoon sugar
1 tablespoon gf/cf yeast
¾ cup brown rice flour or Pamela's Wheat-free & Gluten-free Ultimate Baking &
Pancake Mix (Pamela's Products™)
½ cup potato starch flour
¾ cup white rice flour or tapioca flour

1 teaspoon xanthan gum
1 teaspoon unflavored gelatin powder
1 teaspoon salt
1 ½ tablespoons honey
2 teaspoons basil
1 teaspoon oregano
2 tablespoons grated Parmesan cheese
¼ teaspoon garlic powder
2 large eggs or egg substitute equivalent
2 tablespoons canola oil
1 teaspoon cider vinegar
¼ cup applesauce
1 (3.5-ounce pack) Gerber pureed squash

1. Preheat oven to 400° . **2.** In the mixing bowl combine water, sugar, and yeast. Set aside for at least 5 minutes. **3.** In a large bowl combine the following: flours, xanthan gum, gelatin powder, salt, honey, basil, oregano, cheese, garlic powder, eggs, canola oil, cider vinegar, applesauce, and squash. **4.** Stir in flours and other ingredients slowly to the yeast mixture. Once thoroughly blended, beat the mixture on high for 2 minutes. **5.** Spray the inside of the muffin papers with oil spray. Fill muffin papers about ¾ of the way to the top. Bake for about 23 minutes, depending on your oven; they should rise while baking..

————————————

Super-Fast Tortilla Pizza Sandwiches

Servings: one

These are really great for lunches too, especially if you are in a rush.

1 Food for Life™ Brown Rice Tortillas
2 handfuls grated soy cheese
2 handfuls pizza toppings, whatever you prefer (we usually use Hormel™ nitrate-free pepperoni and chopped bell peppers)

1. Lie tortilla flat on microwave-safe plate. Sprinkle grated soy cheese on the tortilla, place the other toppings over the cheese, and then add another layer of soy cheese. **2.** Microwave flat for about 40 seconds, just long enough to melt the cheese and warm the tortilla. (The tortilla folds better when warm.) **3.** While still warm, fold in half, cut down the middle, and immediately place in a sandwich bag so the tortilla doesn't begin to curl apart on its own. The layers of soy cheese should hold everything together very nicely.

Even with these terrific recipes, our family still needed helpful strategies for surviving the gf/cf life. Every week I make a big batch of rice, mashed potatoes, and beans so that we always have them on hand. Then, after I prepare our meat, a piece of fruit, and a vegetable, we already have several side dishes from which to choose. Giving our kids some control over what they eat when so many of their options are limited makes them so much happier. Also, this strategy greatly diminishes my need to think about having some gf/cf dish for the boys at every single meal—an enormous blessing in its own right.

We also eventually found good gf/cf companies that distribute products we particularly enjoy. Namaste Foods™ has excellent brownies, pancake mix, spice cake, and blondies. Pamela's™ Chocolate Cake Mix is just as wonderful as the aforementioned pancake mix. Nana's™ Lemon and Chocolate Cookies are delicious and contain no eggs (for those with an egg allergy). For more information, contact them at (800) 836-7534. EnviroKidz™ cereal and snack bars are good and can be ordered online at www.naturespath.com . Food for Life™ tortillas and breads are tasty as well. Ener-G food, Inc.™ [(800)331-5222] carries rice bread, tapioca bread, fantastic bagels, and sweets like brownies and doughnuts. De Boles™ Gluten-free Rice Penne retains its shape nicely and is now sold at Wal-Mart. Glutino™ brand breakfast bars and cookies are some of our favorites as well. They can be reached at (800) 363-DIET, info@glutino.com and www.glutino.com .

As good as these sweets are, I still continue to try to limit our sugar intake as much as possible for the sake of my oldest child, who seems the most affected by sugar. If you are a parent who decides not to pursue allergy testing or the gf/cf route, might I at least suggest a diet with a total of 50 grams of sugar or less per day if you have a hyperactive child with autism? Most experts recommend this low-sugar diet for all kids with hyperactivity, whether they have autism or not. Sugar and corn syrup are hidden in many unexpected products, so be on the lookout. Read your labels carefully, or you may be unwittingly revving your child up.

Here is a list of good snack choices you might want to try, if your child will tolerate them: celery, carrots, raisins and other dried fruits, grapes, apples, pears, rice cakes, crispy rice bars, rice crackers, eggs, tortilla chips, dry cereal, peanut butter, and popcorn. Applegate Farms™ deli meats and hot dogs contain no nitrates. Oscar Mayer™ and Hormel™ also have nitrate-free lunch meat options, both of which are now available at Wal-Mart.

Before I had a child with autism, I considered all artificial sweeteners suspect, if not flat-out dangerous. Just to play it safe, I never consumed any until I was through having children. I figured that all-natural sugar was the better choice—not that I ingested a lot, mind you. Even so, God gave me a child with special needs. In retrospect, my preconceived notions about artificial sweeteners were kind of silly; but now that I know how my kids respond to sugar, they seem even more ludicrous to me.

We have actually noticed that our family has a greater tolerance for artificial sweeteners than sugar and corn syrup. This may not be the case for you and your family, so consider your personal options carefully. I add Sweet 'N Low™ (saccharine) to hot grits to make them more appetizing. In order to get my kids to drink more water, I also add it to decaffeinated iced tea. At the same time, they receive the added benefits from protective antioxidants. Another strategy our family employs in order to encourage greater water consumption is Sam's Choice™ Clear American flavored waters, diluted 1:1 with tap water. This water is sweetened with aspartame; but it has no caffeine, sodium, artificial coloring, or calories. Diluting the water makes it taste less like super- sweet soda, which I really appreciate. My carbonated concoction is still sweet enough for them to enjoy. Also, our money goes farther. Their teeth are spared the rotting effects of sugar, and they are even exposed to fluoride-laced tap water. Be on the lookout for fluoride sensitivities, however, because they sometimes occur with autism. Still, I realize so many issues have to be considered that it can boggle the mind.

I hope these suggestions make your life on the gf/cf diet easier or at least a little more manageable. At times it can feel like a big inconvenience, but when you see results—and I do believe you will—hopefully you will be motivated to persevere and continue on for the sake of your child.

Ask your child what he wants for dinner only if he's buying.
—Fran Lebowitz[1]

She gets up while it is still dark; she provides food for her family.
(Proverbs 31:15a)

1 Copyright 1995 Cook Communications Ministries. God's Little Instruction Book For Mom by Honor Books. Used with permission. All rights reserved.

28
What is Autism?

Autism, also known as Autism Spectrum Disorder (ASD), is a neurological behavioral syndrome that takes hold of children prior to three years of age. Though it strikes boys four times more often than girls, girls tend to be more severely affected. Mental retardation is common with this disorder, up to 75%, according to expert opinion. Personally, I believe this incidence is, in reality, no greater than within the general population. However, due to inherent difficulties associated with testing one afflicted by autism, this number is likely to be grossly exaggerated. Savant (genius) characteristics can also be present.

Statistics vary widely concerning the prevalence of autism. Some studies claim as many as one in 91 children are affected, whereas others suggest more conservative numbers. Thirty years ago the odds were quite different: about one in 10,000. Yet, many experts believe that children were misdiagnosed with schizophrenia at that time. Other studies suggest that there has been a dramatic increase in autism over the last 30 years, but this trend may actually stem from more accurate diagnoses.

Individuals with autism have severely disordered interactions with other people, communication deficits, as well as restricted and stereotyped patterns of interests and behaviors. Autism Spectrum Disorder refers to a wide range of symptoms and characteristics in these areas. Along the continuum, children may exhibit any combination of these behaviors in varying degrees of severity.

Two types of autism have been identified by the psychiatric community. With infantile autism, children fail to reach a multitude of developmental milestones from infancy. Regressive autism, on the other hand, is characterized by a loss of verbal and social skills, usually between 18 months and three years of age.

The American Psychiatric Association diagnostic manual, entitled DSM-IV (Diagnostic and Statistical Manual of Mental Disorders), provides the diagnostic criteria for ASD. A diagnosis of ASD is made based on complete or partial fulfillment of those criteria. According to the DSM-IV, the following are the criteria for Autistic Disorder:

Criterion A: *A total of six (or more) items from sections (1), (2), and (3) with at least two from section (1) and one each from sections (2) and (3):*

(1) Qualitative impairment in social interaction, as manifested by at least two of the following:

Marked impairment in the use of multiple nonverbal behaviors, such as eye-to-eye gazes, facial expressions, body postures, and gestures to regulate social interaction. Our Zack was initially evaluated at two years, eight months of age. He exhibited very poor eye contact and never used gaze shifting (looking back and forth from person to object) for communication. Joint attention (looking at an object when another looks at it) was also absent. Zack did not use any facial expressions or body postures to communicate. Although he had the ability to point, he rarely did so.

Failure to develop peer relationships appropriate to developmental level. Zack had no friends whatsoever, but this was fine with him. While around other children, he would play independently or interact aggressively. He didn't play with them and didn't understand social rules such as sharing and taking turns.

A lack of spontaneous seeking to share enjoyment, interests, or achievements with other people (e.g., by a lack of showing, bringing, or pointing out objects of interest). Zack rarely acknowledged the existence of another person nor shared anything with anyone.

(2) ***Qualitative impairment in communication as manifested by at least one of the following:***

Delay in, or total lack of, development of spoken language (not accompanied by an attempt to compensate through alternative modes of communication, such as gesture or mime). At 32 months of age Zack's receptive language was that of an 11- to 13-month-old and his expressive language was that of a 14- to 16-month-old. With only five to 10 poorly articulated words and phrases at his disposal, Zack would become exceedingly frustrated and unruly when others failed to understand his wants and needs.

In individuals with adequate speech, marked impairment in the ability to initiate or sustain conversation with others. Zack was basically non-verbal at this point. Even if he had been able to speak, it was clear that he had no desire to initiate or sustain a conversation with anyone.

Stereotyped and repetitive use of language or idiosyncratic language, also known as echolalia. This manifestation often includes a sing-song quality, odd jargon, or language used outside of its normal context. This was the only characteristic of autism that Zack did not exhibit to one degree or another. His unrelated speech disorder (apraxia) made it impossible for him to coordinate his tongue movements in the proper sequences. Thus, echolalia was never going to be an issue in our house.

Lack of varied, spontaneous make-believe play or social and imitative play appropriate to developmental level. Young children with ASD often have difficulty imitating motor and verbal activities or play routines. Their play tends to be more mechanical (e.g., building or lining up blocks, pushing cars back and forth) rather than symbolic in nature. Zack had no make-believe play skills;

instead, he loved to open and close doors, tool boxes, latches, and anything else he could open and close. When reading a book, he cared nothing for the story. His only desire was to flip the pages back and forth.

(3) ***Restricted repetitive and stereotyped patterns of behavior, interests, and activities, as manifested by at least one of the following:***

a) Encompassing preoccupation with one or more stereotyped and restricted *patterns of interest that is abnormal either in intensity or focus.* Some children with autism collect common objects such as paper, pens, or garbage with an all-consuming passion. Older children may memorize a multitude of dates and facts about obscure or unusual topics. Zack was obsessive/compulsive about frogs.

b) Apparently inflexible adherence to specific, nonfunctional routines or *rituals.* Zack would only eat white or tan food on a green plate with green utensils and would only drink out of green cups. Huge tantrums and vomiting resulted if I dared to change the color. Only green clothes, shoes, and chairs were acceptable to him.

c) *Stereotyped and repetitive motor mannerisms (e.g., hand or finger flapping, twisting, or complex whole body movements).* Very young children with ASD may not develop repetitive mannerisms or interest in rituals or routines until after the age of three. Therefore, many do not meet this criterion until they are older. More subtle mannerisms such as walking on tiptoes and spinning or loping in circles can be observed earlier. Zack continuously hit things with a stick, wrapped and unwrapped string around his fingers, walked and loped in circles, and flapped his hands.

d) *Persistent preoccupation with parts of objects.* Zack would happily spend hours taking things apart and putting them back together, over and over and over again.

Criterion B: *Delays or abnormal functioning in at least one of the following areas, onset prior to age three: (1) social interaction; (2) language as used in social communication; or (3) symbolic or imaginative play.* As described earlier, Zack had delays and abnormal functioning in all three of these areas.

Criterion C: *The disturbance is not better accounted for by Rett's Disorder or Childhood Disintegrative Disorder. Rett's Disorder presents only in girls and is characterized by very early growth and development that is normal, followed by a deceleration in head growth, development of marked mental retardation, and unusual hand-washing stereotypes and similar features. With childhood disintegrative disorder, there is a prolonged period or normal development. Then irreversible, widespread marked regression develops.* [1]

The other pervasive developmental disorders which fall under the autism umbrella include Asperger's Syndrome and Pervasive Developmental Disorder Not Otherwise Specified (PDD-NOS). With Asperger's, it is not unusual for a diagnosis to surface as late as nine or 10 years of age because early cognitive and language development may appear normal. Social deficits become more prominent as adolescence approaches and the children fail to respond appropriately to peers. As with autism, Asperger's kids generally have unusual interests that are pursued with intensity. (Appendix VII is the Sohn Grayson Rating Scale for Asperger's Syndrome and High-Functioning Pervasive Developmental Disorder, a preliminary tool which may help to identify a child with Asperger's.) With PDD-NOS, also referred to as atypical autism, the child has difficulties in social interaction and other areas consistent with an autism diagnosis but does not

1 Osbourn, Pat, Scott, Fletcher"Guidance on providing supports and services to young children with autism spectrum disorders and their families." *Technical Assistance Manual: Autism Spectrum Disorders.* New Mexico Public Education Department Special Education Bureau TA document – Autism Spectrum Disorders, June 2004.

meet the full criteria in severity or scope.

Young children with ASD are very likely to inconsistently respond to their name. In fact, this trait is often a reliable discriminator between ASD and other developmental disorders. Our Zack definitely did not respond to his name on a regular basis. We often wondered if there was something wrong with his hearing. Yet, at other times we were amazed that he could hear the refrigerator door open from two rooms away. (Selective hearing is common in autistic children, and this is another red flag to look for.)

Many young children with ASD also experience great difficulty transitioning from activity to activity or from place to place. The absence of consistent routines overwhelms their atypical sensory system. Our Zack handled transitions poorly and relied very heavily on structure and routine in order to function.

Some of the most notable early signs of ASD are as follows: no babbling, pointing or gesturing by 12 months; no single words by 16 months; no two-word spontaneous phrases by 24 months; no response to one's own name; and any loss of language or social skills at any age.

Appendices I-IV contain government guidelines for developmental stages for children and youth. There is also a screening instrument known as the (Modified) Checklist for Autism in Toddlers (M-CHAT) that was designed to detect the core features of autism in children as young as 18 months. The list (Appendix V) consists of 23 yes/no questions. Any child who fails three or more items on the entire M-CHAT or two or more of the "critical" items should receive a comprehensive evaluation. The critical items on the M-CHAT include the following: Does your child take an interest in other children? Does your child ever use his/her index finger to point to indicate an interest in something? Does your child ever bring you objects over to you (the parent) to show you something? Does your child imitate you (e.g., if you make a face, will your child imitate?)

Does your child respond to his/her name when you call? If you point at a toy across the room, does your child look at it? Appendix VI is a similar autism screener tool with 40 yes/no red flag questions.

No two children with autism express identical manifestations of the disorder. For this reason, making a formal diagnosis requires a team of professionals, detailed observations, and much input from parents. These unique expressions of autism also make individualized intervention plans necessary. There is no "one-size-fits-all" comprehensive program. General guidelines are available through books and consultation firms, but every strategy must be tweaked to best meet the needs of the particular child.

For instance, our Zack had widespread developmental delays in other areas as well: self-care, fine motor manipulation, oral motor function, cognition, and coping and adapting (sensory regulation and organization). He showed specific sensory preferences in some instances, indicating that he was a sensory seeker, but he also avoided other sensory experiences. His response to pain was inconsistent and abnormal, and he often became hysterical when touched in a loving manner. These specific issues had to be addressed in Zack's intervention program. Appendix IIX, a sensory rating scale questionnaire, will help parents to determine non-typical responses to external stimuli.

Fortunately, not every oddity had to be quashed. Zack did exhibit a few exceptional "splinter skills," sporadic abilities ranging well above typical development. These gifts included most gross motor skills, along with anything relating to problem solving, puzzles, and complex patterns. In fact, his kindergarten teacher told us that in her 20 years of teaching, she had never seen another child who could build intricate designs and patterns like Zack. So far, this is his only savant characteristic. We are waiting to see if any other amazing aptitudes emerge. Perhaps he'll have a future in architecture or organic chemistry.

The superior man...stands erect by bending above the fallen. He rises by lifting others. -- Robert Ingersoll[1]

You hear, O LORD, the desire of the afflicted; you encourage them, and you listen to their cry.
(Psalm 10:17)

1 Copyright 1995 Cook Communications Ministries. God's Little Instruction Book For Dad by Honor Books. Used with permission. All rights reserved.

29

Causes: Theories Abound

No one knows for sure what causes autism. There are a multitude of theories, none of which have been definitively proven. Twenty years ago professionals held the "unloving mother" responsible, as if being the mother of a child with autism isn't difficult enough. Monstrous amounts of guilt were thrust upon those already despairing over a heartbreaking diagnosis. A crueler and more merciless attack I cannot imagine. Thankfully, this antiquated notion has been replaced with more compassionate and more likely possibilities.

One theory suggests that autism occurs as the result of exposure to mercury-containing thimerosal, a preservative once used in MMR (measles/mumps/rubella) vaccinations. Deciding to err on the side of caution, pharmaceutical companies removed thimerosal from shots in the United States and Europe nearly 10 years ago. Yet, the rates of autism continue to skyrocket. Many recent studies have shown no correlation whatsoever between thimerosal and autism; regardless, many still support this theory. The production of thimerosal-MMR vaccinations was discontinued two years before our Zack was born, and I don't believe he was ever exposed to this form of mercury.

I personally never noticed my children reacting adversely to any of their vaccinations. However, I do know how easy it is for parents to want to blame something or someone else for what has happened to their precious child. One family I know was absolutely certain that the vaccinations were responsible for their son's autism. So, when they had another baby, they refused to vaccinate him. Convinced that they had thwarted the risk, they were baffled when their second son was diagnosed on the spectrum as well.

Most experts believe that autism is most likely caused by both a genetic susceptibility and an environmental trigger of some sort—heavy metals or something not yet identified. Although I like fish and surely must have eaten some when I was pregnant, I can't imagine that I would have consumed enough to expose Zack to high levels of heavy metals. Because he didn't eat fish at all during the first two years of his life and we never used lead-based paint for anything, I'm not sure where he could have been exposed to heavy metals. My own mother handled mercury all the time in science class as a young girl before its poisonous nature was well known, but surely that would have affected me—not my child. As a lab technician for NMSU, Los Alamos National Laboratories, and Sandia National Laboratories, I had worked with dangerous chemicals—even radiation. Concerned about such risks, I always used extreme caution and followed OSHA protocol. I have often thought that any dangerous exposure from my working days would be passed along to all three of my kids, but neither of my other children has struggled as Zack has.

Autism tends to run in families, suggesting a genetic link, but neither my husband nor I have any family history of autism. However, now that I'm an expert on this disorder, I often observe spectrum-like quirks in those around me. I have an uncle, for example, who won't look people in the eye while participating in a conversation. Otherwise, he is completely "normal." Also, I have a friend who is obsessive/compulsive about organizing her closet, but this is her only unusual trait. I personally prefer to eat foods individually, rather than filling my mouth with a conglomeration of flavors. My husband is teased by his co-workers when he paces around the same little section of the courtroom during a trial recess. Thus, we all possess minor oddities. For most of us these peculiarities are perceived as silly, even endearing, but they do not prevent us from functioning in society. With autism, these kinds of quirks are all-consuming and rampant to the point of non-functionality. If we could determine their cause, however, perhaps we could find faster, more effective treatments.

Another theory suggests that children with autism have much higher levels of the male hormone testosterone in their system. This overabundance would supposedly diminish impulse control, increase the need for gross motor activity, and increase the analytical functioning of the brain while reducing the desire to communicate verbally. Far-fetched and gender-biased as this hypothesis may be, it might explain why Zack has always been solid muscle. It has been well-established that high testosterone levels support an increase in muscle mass. Although Zack's hormone levels have never been tested, I wouldn't be at all surprised if he had more than his fair share of testosterone.

Rapid growth during the first year of life is another suspected cause of autism. The proponents of this theory believe that the brain grows too fast for the neurological pathways to develop as they should. When our Zack was born, he had gastroesophageal reflux disease (GERD). His pyloric flap located between the esophagus and the stomach wasn't mature; therefore, it didn't work properly. Unable to burp, Zack constantly experienced gas building up in his stomach until the pressure was so great that projectile vomiting was his only release. He couldn't keep any food down until this condition remedied itself at nine months of age. Expelling every meal made him constantly hungry, so I fed him on a nearly continual basis. Because his throat was so raw from throwing up all day, he screamed every night for hours. The screaming was so intense that we didn't feel comfortable leaving him with a babysitter, who might be unable to handle such a trying situation. In fact, things were so stressful around our home that when we told our oldest, Jacob, that he was going to have another baby brother or sister, he protested by pooping in his pants every day for a month. But that is a story for another day.

By the time Zack was nine months old, he was actually able to hold his food down. Absolutely ravenous and making up for lost time, he had a huge growth spurt. In only three months' time he shot up from the 50th percentile to the 95th percentile in height, weight, and head size. When we saw the doctor again a mere three months later, his stats hadn't changed at all. I believe this rapid growth spurt was most likely the cause of Zack's autism, although as a parent I find that I like this very flattering, final supposition the best.

Some experts believe that children with autism are far too smart for their own good. With extraordinary activity taking place within their brains, they fail to integrate external stimuli appropriately and are thus subjected to sensory overloads. I would love to rest in the fact that Zack is highly intelligent. What parent wouldn't? But at what cost? What purpose would this gift serve if he is unable to function in society? Honestly, these amazing brains would still have to make peace with their environment in order to learn, grow, and live up to their greatest potential.

Now that Zack has recovered from autism and I can communicate with and better understand him, I do think his brain seems to work differently. I believe he learns things differently—not poorly, just differently. When we first began therapy, we worked on colors and shapes for a year and a half. I thought he would never get it, so I assumed there must be something very wrong with his brain. What else could be keeping him from learning these concepts after all that time and effort? Now I've come to believe that we just weren't teaching him in a way that he could learn. After all, he seemed to be very bright in other areas. His spatial awareness and problem-solving skills were spectacular, bordering on genius. After a while we realized that we had to tap into his strengths in order to teach him the things kids half his age absorbed naturally and effortlessly. Whether Zack is ultra-smart or not, only time will tell. Regardless, this theory will always be the easiest one for me to embrace.

Findings of the latest autism research studies are easily found on the Internet. My favorite resource is autismspeaks.org. It is easy to sign up for their newsletter, and they have many links to more detailed information. There are many agencies, both private and public, searching with zeal for the cause(s) of autism. One of my greatest hopes is that we are closing in on the answer. Only then can we spare families the pain of having a child with autism.

Every child comes with the message that God is not yet discouraged of man.- Rabindranath Tagore[1]

We have different gifts, according to the grace given us. (Romans 12:6a)

1 Copyright 1995 Cook Communications Ministries. God's Little Instruction Book For Dad by Honor Books. Used with permission. All rights reserved.

30

Initial Evaluation: Two Years, Nine Months

For parents wishing to compare notes and professionals questioning a genuine diagnosis, the final five chapters contain a complete set of our evaluative experiences.

"Kids with autism don't make this kind of progress." I will never forget these words as long as I live. They were spoken by the Early Childhood Evaluative Program (ECEP) experts in Albuquerque. These professionals had diagnosed Zack with Autism Spectrum Disorder/PDDNOS when he was three years old and re-confirmed the diagnosis at four years of age. Zack was now five years and three months old, and they had just shared with me that he no longer met the criteria for autism. Obviously uneasy and dumbfounded, they all but admitted that Zack was misdiagnosed—not once, but twice. If ECEP's conclusions were actually true, my son never actually had autism.

Finding their statement completely preposterous, I asked, "What do you mean, exactly? If he wasn't autistic, why on earth did he exhibit every single characteristic except for the echolalia? One only needs four of the 16 characteristics for an official diagnosis. What have we been enduring for the last three years if it wasn't autism? Can you otherwise explain then why non-stop autism interventions have produced such remarkable results?"

I was absolutely livid that day when they informed me that recovery from autism is an impossibility. These experts were never going to convince me that my child never had autism in the first place. After all, I had immersed myself in autism education since Zack was two years, eight months old. By this point I was an authority in my own right. What we had experienced was undoubtedly autism. I had done more research than I had ever thought possible, performed more therapy than I had ever thought possible, and cried more than I had ever thought possible. My son definitely had autism, and he *did* make this kind of progress!

Before hearing this absurd analysis, I had shared with them about my intentions to apply for a job opening within their organization because the current ECEP autism representative in our hometown was thinking of retiring. Sufficiently knowledgeable and experienced, I desperately wanted to help other families survive this diagnosis. Even the lady leaving the position—who knew me and our family's struggle well— thought I was the perfect candidate. Unfortunately, ECEP's response to me on this subject was just as ridiculous and troubling as their earlier comments. They said that they would never seriously consider my application. Admittedly, my pride took a hit, but I could get over that. What I couldn't get over was their reason: They couldn't risk a family making such assumptions about Zack's recovery from autism; they couldn't risk me offering that kind of hope to anyone. Now it was my turn to be dumbfounded. I thought to myself, "Without hope, all we parents have is complete and utter desperation. How can you live with yourselves, knowing that you are intentionally denying other families hope?"

A year later I learned that these experts may not have believed their own words, but rather may have been bound by the ideological constraints of their profession. (I truly hope that this is indeed the case.) In short, autism is not yet recognized by the American Psychological Association as a reversible condition. By this organization's own definition, autism is a lifelong disorder. Until enough evidence surfaces that recovery is actually possible, this type of reaction from the experts will most likely continue, unfortunately.

I want parents to know that there is hope if you are willing to go through years upon years of excruciating work and heartbreak in order to save your child. I cannot promise you a complete and perfect recovery. Even if your child doesn't fully recover, however, tremendous progress can be made so that your life with your special child can be so much more fulfilling and complete. Striving for the best possible outcome is worth the struggle. I am not going to tell you that it will be easy. I assure you, it won't be. I am not going to tell you that it will be inexpensive. Again, I assure you, it won't be. Will you want to quit? Absolutely, without a doubt. You will probably want to quit every single day. But I beg you, *don't!* Please, whatever you do, don't you dare give up—ever. Your child desperately needs you, so run the good race and persevere. You will be so very glad you did. Consider where Zack started and the progress he has made. Let my words inspire you to fight the good fight.

Zack's first evaluation was performed by our local Birth to Three program. Even though they were not certified to officially diagnose autism, they did provide us with our starting point for Zack. He was 32 months (two years, eight months) old at the time.

The following are the highlights and specifics of their evaluation, paraphrased to facilitate better understanding and reduce redundancy. (My comments are found within the parentheses.)

Many tools were used in their assessment. The Peabody Developmental Motor Scale (PDMS), a motor test for children zero to 83 months of age, is divided into two areas: gross motor (large muscles) and fine motor (small muscles, particularly the hands). Clinical observations include assessment of posture, sensory processing, strength, and quality of movement. The Preschool Language Scale-4 (PLS-4) measures the understanding and use of language through structured tasks. The resulting point score is then compared to that of children in the same age range. The Receptive/Expressive Emergent Language Scale-2 (REEL-2) is another standardized test used to determine understanding and use of language in children zero to 36 months of age. James and I also answered assessment questions in a parent report. (I know we were still influenced a great deal by denial because we had completely convinced ourselves that Zack knew much more than he actually did.) Results of this test are reported in one- to three-month increments.

The cognitive portion of the San Diego HOPE is the developmental scale used to look at the sequence and quality of cognitive development in children zero to 36 months of age. Finally, the Hawaii Early Learning Profile (HELP) is the curriculum-based developmental instrument for children zero to 36 months old. It is useful for obtaining an estimate of developmental levels as well as planning interventions. This is not a standardized test, so the age references in the assessment represented approximations since specific age equivalents could not be given.

Zack's gross motor skills developmental level was 22 months scattered up to 36 months. (Remember that he was 32 months old at the time. This was the only category where he had splinter skills ahead of his chronological age.) He readily threw and caught large balls, rode a tricycle, and walked up and down stairs with alternating feet. His coordinated movements had nice quality; but he refused to imitate all the arm, leg, head, and trunk movements demonstrated for him, including jumping in place and jumping backward.

His fine motor skill level was 22 months. He played with a variety of toys but preferred to do so in his own way. Zack enjoyed stringing beads, stacking blocks, lining up blocks, and completing puzzles. When picking up a marker, he used a fisted grasp pattern and then switched to a fisted grasp with his thumb and forefinger toward the paper. He enjoyed scribbling on the paper, but he did not imitate the evaluator as she drew horizontal or vertical strokes. Yet he did imitate the evaluator dotting the paper. (Being willing to hold a writing utensil without screeching, however, was a skill Zack lost between 32 and 36 months of age.) Zack used both hands equally well during the evaluation, and he held objects in both hands and transferred them from one hand to the other. His favorite activity was pounding objects with a stick.

Zack's receptive language (understanding) tested at 11 to 13 months. He demonstrated an understanding of a specific word or phrase such as "my turn," anticipated what would happen, used more than one object in play, and demonstrated an appropriate use of a ball, a car, and blocks. When presented with bell and/or rattle sounds behind him and to his side, Zack did not respond. It should be noted, however, that he was holding and turning a glitter wand at the time and was not easily distracted from it. He inconsistently responded to his name and often screamed in a very high-pitched voice. His expressive communication skills were judged to be very low for his age; therefore, an audio-logical evaluation was recommended to rule out any hearing difficulties. Zack responded to his parents selectively and could follow simple (one-step) directions at home. When working on a puzzle with the speech pathologist, Zack attended to her use of the sign for "more" and made eye contact during the turn-taking and communication exchange. Very little eye contact was noted otherwise. Zack missed many items on the PLS-4 due to his inattentiveness and failure to answer questions by pointing to specific pictures.

His expressive language (communication) tested at 14 to 16 months. Zack used five to 10 words and a few short phrases to communicate. He also babbled in short syllable strings with inflection. He used pointing with a vocalization or jargon speech to indicate he wanted something. (Pointing was never a particularly consistent skill for Zack, but he was willing to do so during this evaluation.) He was not able to imitate any speech during the evaluation. He was noted to use word approximations for "please" and "thank you." He also used "no," "uh-oh" and "I di it" (I did it). He mostly pointed and became extremely frustrated when he was unable to communicate.

Next, they evaluated his oral motor skills. Zack took the whistles easily and attempted to blow them using voicing. He was very picky about foods, often gagging if the texture was different from the puree consistency. He also ate pretzels, cheese, bread, gummi worms, and fruit roll-ups. Zack stuffed his mouth with Cheetos™ and chewed them with an immature up/down motion. He also enjoyed brushing his teeth. (Many autistic children detest this activity. Here was another little blessing to appreciate.)

The cognition (thinking and learning) portion of the evaluation was next. Zack preferred to play with toys his own way and demonstrated a wide scatter in his cognitive development. He was able to sort small buttons into the corresponding colored cup easily. He needed only verbal assistance to sort circle, square, and triangle shapes. (This skill also disappeared between 32 and 36 months of age. Even after implementing Zack's early intervention program, we still witnessed distinct areas of regression. These areas required painstaking teaching and reviewing to ensure that the skills were mastered sufficiently in order to avoid further regression.) Zack imitated a few actions with toys and body motions at the time. He had a limited amount of vocalizations. He played with objects in an immature way by banging, touching, and waving them, even though he showed a higher cognitive development in his play with some toys. He demonstrated cause-and-effect in his ability to push buttons to produce sounds or an interesting visual effect. Zack looked for objects that he wanted and had understanding of object permanence. He found a small toy hidden beneath one of three cups and was able to find a toy hidden under a cup covered by a cloth. Transitions between objects and toys were difficult, and he became frustrated when the evaluators interrupted his routine. Other than silverware, he did not use objects as tools. Zack understood how familiar objects were used. He enjoyed one and only one book with a very specific associated routine. Other than that, typically he was more interested in turning the pages than the objects and pictures in the book. Zack had an immature play style and preferred to play with toys by shaking and banging them. He had not yet developed any symbolic play that is representative of his real world. He did carry around a small stuffed frog but showed no interest in feeding, hugging, or playing with a stuffed animal in a symbolic pattern.

Zack's social/emotional age equivalent was 18 to 24 months. He played well with his older brother; however, he did not initiate interaction with his eight- month-old sister. While in a group of children, he would play independently or interact aggressively with others. Limited eye contact was observed. He did not attend to what others were doing unless he was highly motivated by specific materials or a familiar routine. Zack paid more attention to his parents and older brother and showed limited attention to other people. He did enjoy roughhousing and touching on his terms. He had limited verbal skills and would often point or throw a tantrum to express his needs. Zack was observed pulling at his father's hand to gain assistance.

Zack's self-help skills age equivalent was 18 to 30 months. He self-fed with utensils with spillage, although he preferred more finger-food and liquid consistencies. He drank from a small cup with spillage and was beginning to help a little with dressing. He was using diapers and occasionally indicated that he was wet or soiled. He required assistance in washing his hands and displayed definite food preferences. He no longer napped, but he had good sleep patterns at night as reported by the parents.

[Next they evaluated his coping and adapting (sensory regulation and organization)]: Zack showed specific sensory preferences, indicating that he was a sensory seeker in some areas and also a sensory avoider in other areas. With touch and movement, he sought out a lot of heavy input. He loved to roughhouse, bang with a stick, play in the sandbox, and engage in gross motor play. Zack did have specific sensory likes and dislikes regarding what he was willing to eat. He had the most difficulty with odd-textured and sticky foods. He was accepting of dry textures such as crackers, bread, and cookies. (Hmm...all of which have gluten.) Zack would swallow and chew hard-textured foods such as hot dogs, gummi bears, apples, and ham, indicating that he liked heavy input in his mouth. He did show immature oral motor awareness, and when placing food in his mouth, he placed his whole hand in his mouth rather than using his tongue and lips to move the food around in his mouth. His response to pain was inconsistent, and he showed atypical awareness of pain. He had banged his head a few times due to frustration, but this has not been a constant behavior.

This is where we began with Zack—with most of his developmental scores that of a child half his age. James and I were absolutely devastated upon receiving this news. Not only were Zack's skills fading right before our very eyes, but our hopes and dreams for our son were fading as well. We wondered, "Would he ever really be able to talk? Would he ever stop screeching and throwing tantrums? Would he ever catch up to his peers? Would he ever be okay?" It was impossible for me to suppress these questions. Every time they surfaced, which was often, I would bawl uncontrollably. I felt as though nothing could curtail my anguish. Our precious son had many more challenges than I had allowed myself to dare to believe. How were we ever going to tackle all of these issues?

Thankfully, the Lord provided our family with Robert as our lead psychologist.. Robert knew what he was doing, and he never steered us wrong. He was our manna from heaven. I know he doesn't see things this way, but we do. As he taught me the therapy methods to carry out with Zack, he encouraged me to execute them continually throughout my son's waking hours. I needed to hear this advice from someone I respected and trusted, and Robert was that someone. There is no doubt in my mind that he was sent by God to work with our family. For this I will be forever grateful.

We should seize every opportunity to give encouragement. Encouragement is oxygen to the soul.
—George M. Adams[1]

He gave you manna to eat in the desert, something your fathers
had never known, to humble and
to test you so that in the end it might go well with you.
(Deuteronomy 8:16)

1 Copyright 1996 Cook Communications Ministries. God's Little Instruction Book For Women by Honor Books. Used with permission. All rights reserved.

31

Evaluation II: Three Years Old

Zack's official autism diagnosis was made by the Department of Pediatrics Center for Development and Disability Early Childhood Evaluative Program (ECEP), affiliated with the University Of New Mexico School Of Medicine located in Albuquerque. He was one day shy of three years old (36 months). The following is an abbreviated description of the tests used and scores revealed as a result of the evaluation. My comments are contained within the parentheses:

Zack's cognitive skills were determined with the Bayley Scales of Infant Development – II, Mental Scale. This test assesses a child's general level of functioning based on typical developmental sequences. A standard score of 85-114 reflects developmental functioning within normal limits when compared to other children of similar ages. Zack received an IQ score of less than 50 with an estimated true score between 50 and 63. (Because it made us feel as though Zack had very little potential to work with, this was by far the most difficult news for us as parents to hear.) These scores placed his performance in the significantly delayed range. In addition, Zack received an average developmental score of 20 months since he performed tasks typical of children between the ages of 15 and 26 months.

His adaptive behavior was evaluated using the Vineland Adaptive Behavior Scales, with his parents as respondents. The Vineland assesses a child's ability to perform day-to-day activities neces-

sary to meet individual needs at home, such as walking, talking, toileting, and getting along with others. Again, a standard score of 85-114 reflects developmental functioning within normal limits when compared to other children of the same age. Zack received the following standard scores and age equivalents: Communication Domain: 62 (1 year, two months); Daily Living Skills Domain: 64 (1 year, six months); Socialization Domain: 72 (1 year, six months); Motor Skills Domain: 72 (1 year, 11 months); and the Adaptive Behavior Composite: 62 (1 year, six months).

Zack's communication skills were assessed using the Rossetti Infant-Toddler Language Scale (RITLS) and the Preschool Language Scale-4 (PLS-4). All tests were administered in a non-standardized format, relying on observations obtained during the evaluation. The RITLS is a criterion-referenced test that measures what a child knows and what he can do in the areas of interaction and attachment, pragmatics, gesture, play, language comprehension, and language expression. The PLS-4 is a communication test that gives standard scores. Again, the standard score of 85-114 is within the normal range. Zack received the following scores: PLS-4 receptive language 51 (1 year, 9 months), and expressive language 61 (1 year, 8 months); RITLS Interaction Attachment was not applicable; Pragmatics (15 months), Gestures (18 months), and Play (21-24 months); Language Comprehension (12-15) months and Language Expression (15 months). His receptive and expressive communication skills were significantly delayed and disordered for his age. In addition to these very poor developmental scores, Zack demonstrated poor quality with social/communicative engagements. Eye contact was fleeting, and interactions were very concrete and self-directed.

To assess Zack's motor skills, the Peabody Developmental Motor Scales, 2nd edition (PDMS-II) was administered. This is a standardized assessment tool that allowed the evaluators to compare Zack's development to that of other children his age. During the testing, he was self-directed. He was reluctant to try items on the assessment and follow directions. Due to his lack of cooperation, Zack's abilities were estimated based on the skills that were observed during the test. On the PDMS-II gross motor scale, he passed items in the 24-36 month age range. In the area of fine motor skills, Zack passed items in the 25-30 month age range. The motor scale of the Bayley Scales of Infant Development, 2nd edition was also administered. This scale combines gross and fine motor skills and assesses somewhat different skills than the PDMS-II. The developmental quotient was 67, equivalent to an age level of 27 months.

Zack had a healthy attachment to his parents. He was affectionate, responded to praise and social smiles, sought his parents' approval, and used some gestures to augment his expressive communication delays. He appeared most happy when others were laughing, playing, and roughhousing with him. He showed objects to his parents and the examiners, but eye contact was frequently absent. Zack made some attempts to request objects, but the attempts were without sustained persistence and were usually observed when a routine was established.

His parents were able to understand his nonverbal communicative intent or requests better than the examiners, but similar to the examiners, they had some difficulties understanding his expressive word approximation because meaningful words and nonsensical jabbering were combined when Zack talked. These vocalizations were directed to others in some but not all settings. He only directed vocalizations toward others on his terms, when he wanted the examiner or his parents to do something for him.

Socially he had difficulty maintaining and utilizing eye contact in order to get his needs met or in conjunction with verbal communication attempts. When his needs and wants were not met, he would protest and attempt to reach for the object himself with few and inconsistent attempts to get help. He was able to get the exam-

iner's attention by using a limited range of gestures and sounds. He did not reliably use joint attention (eye contact focused on desired object) but did use some eye contact to continue an interaction. He was able to give high-fives and play peek-a-boo but with sporadic eye contact. Most good eye contact appeared to be incidental as he attempted to explore his environment.

Zack was willing to point but only when extremely motivated; otherwise, he refused to cooperate. He was very easily distracted; when he was engaged in an activity, he seldom responded to verbal or visual commands. Zack was able to follow familiar one-step direction within a routine, as long as he was attending and processing at the time. Because he is still emerging in his understanding that language is meaningful, he frequently does not appear to pay attention to language. As a result, he doesn't consistently respond to his name or directions given by caregivers. He is currently experiencing clear delays, as well as differences (understanding the purpose of language) in the area of receptive language. Overall, Zack's social development and receptive language deficits are consistent with those characteristics frequently observed in children with pervasive developmental disorders.

Zack's speech is extremely limited. His parents state that he said more words in the past, but he had lost most of them. They are attempting to rebuild his base vocabulary. All pragmatic functions (such as requests, protests, pointing, limited gaze shift, limited facial expression and vocalizations) were demonstrated primarily on his terms and were not related much to others' attempts to engage or direct. He uses non-verbal means to get most of his needs met. Zack's articulation skills were not assessed due to his inability to produce sounds/words with picture stimulus or imitation. He did produce a few words and phrases during the evaluation. Most of these words were approximations, and intelligibility was low to the unfamiliar listener. At this time Zack continues to demon-

> *strate severe expressive language delays and differences. He lacks strategies to express himself and has reduced use of communicative engagements, which is similar to other children with pervasive developmental disorders.*

The experts at ECEP told us that Zack fell on the autism spectrum somewhere between Autism Spectrum Disorder and PDD-NOS (Pervasive Developmental Disorder – Not Otherwise Specified), which is considered to be on the milder end of the spectrum. Most of our team at our local Birth to Three organization considered this diagnosis to be extremely generous. They felt Zack's case was far more severe, deserving of a full-fledged clinical autism diagnosis. Our wonderful lead psychologist Robert was our one holdout. He was very encouraged by Zack's obvious bonding with me, Dad, and his older brother. Because of his attachment to us, it was Robert's opinion that Zack was too social to be diagnosed as clinically autistic. Zack may not have appeared to have much academic potential at the time, but he had enormous potential to further develop his heart. This was a strength we could encourage and build upon. Regardless of semantics, Zack was definitely somewhere on the autism spectrum. The road ahead was undoubtedly going to be long and arduous, but we loved him dearly. Our precious Zack was worth every struggle, every heartbreak, and every teardrop we encountered along the way.

When God measures a man, He puts the tape around the heart instead of the head.—Unknown [1]

The LORD is close to the brokenhearted and saves those who are crushed in spirit.
(Psalm 34:18)

---

1 Copyright 1995 Cook Communications Ministries. God's Little Instruction Book For Dad by Honor Books. Used with permission. All rights reserved.

32

Evaluation III: Four Years Old

Shortly after Zack turned four (48 months) he was re-evaluated by the Department of Pediatrics Center for Development and Disability Early Childhood Evaluative Program (ECEP). These were their findings. My comments are provided within the parentheses:

Zack's cognitive skills were assessed with the Mullen Scales of Early Learning. This test evaluates a child's general level of functioning based on typical developmental sequences. As was the case a year previously, a standard score of 85-114 reflects developmental functioning within normal limits when compared to other children of a similar age. Zack received a standard score of 77 with an estimated true score between 70 and 84. (When Zack was three, his score was less than 50 with an estimation between 50 and 63.) *This number placed his performance in the descriptive category of "below average."* Even still, we were somewhat encouraged by the progress made. *He performed tasks typically performed by children between the ages of 34 and 52 months.*

His adaptive behavior was evaluated using the Vineland Adaptive Behavior Scales with his mother as respondent. This test assesses a child's ability to participate in day-to-day activities to meet individual needs at home, such as walking, talking, toileting, and getting along with others. Again, a standard score of 85-114 reflects developmental functioning within normal limits. Zack received the following standard scores and age equivalents on the Vineland: Communication Domain: 77 (2 years, eight months); Daily Living Skills Domain: 86 (3 years, three months); Socialization Domain: 82 (2 years, 10 months); and the Adaptive Behavior Composite: 76 (2 years, 11 months). Based on these scores, Zack's adaptive behavior skills were moderately low.

Zack's communication skills were assessed using the Preschool Language Scale-4 (PLS-4), a communication test with standard scores (85-114 indicates skills within normal limits). It evaluates how much language a child understands and how well a child communicates with others. These tests assess the communication skills Zack exhibited during the evaluation and those his family reported having seen at home. He received the following scores: Receptive Language: 76 (3 years, four months); Expressive Language: 69 (2 years, nine months); and Total Language: 70 (2 years, 11 months). Zack's receptive communication skills were moderately delayed for his age. His expressive communication skills were significantly delayed for his age. His articulation skills were disordered, characterized by inconsistent consonant errors and decreased intelligibility with increased utterance length (increased number of words strung together). Oral motor skills were disordered, characterized by poor jaw-tongue dissociation and an immature chewing pattern.

His motor skills were assessed with the Peabody Developmental Motor Scales, 2nd edition (PDMS-2) and the Infant/Toddler Sensory Profile. The PDMS-2 is a standardized test that allowed the evaluators to compare Zack's motor skills to other children his age. On the Gross Motor Subtests, his skills were scattered, with some skills close to what is typical for his age. However, his age equivalent was 21-36 months, which was in the 4th percentile for his age category. On the Fine Motor Subtests, his fine motor age equivalent was 20-34 months, which places him in the 1st percentile. Zack's total motor skills were classified as very poor for his age on the standardized test, less than two (2) deviations below the mean of the test. The Infant/Toddler Sensory Profile is a caregiver questionnaire identifying sensory processing differences. Zack did demonstrate differences in his oral-sensory processing, as well as subtle differences in other areas.

Zack presented today as a friendly and playful little boy. His parents are very observant and responsive. Throughout the session Zack checked in visually and physically with both parents. He used movement and roughhousing with Dad to take breaks from testing. Although Zack demonstrated a willingness to participate in the testing activities (a huge change for the better compared to the previous year), the evaluators needed to make some accommodations in order to assist Zack in completing them. He was able to focus when presented with novel activities and was not frustrated when he was not able to perform a task. He was playful and engaging and even enlisted the help of one evaluator to play a trick on his dad, locking the door when Dad left the room. Through actions, gestures, and words Zack communicates his wants, needs, and intentions. He asks for help and can direct adults in a game he invents. Once, he decided it was time for him to "test" the evaluator. Zack is using multiple-word sentences, but his articulation errors affect his overall intelligibility.

He currently attends a specialized preschool and a Head Start program within his community. Mom reports that he is working on his social skills at school, including communicating with peers. By report he follows the school routines well and shows a preference for some friends over others. Mom reports that Zack thrives in novel environments so much that his teachers find providing him with a continuous supply of innovative activities quite challenging.

Zack enjoys gross motor movement and roughhouse type of play. Taking these types of breaks help him focus and organize. He enjoys engaging others in play and inventing new games. In fact, he provided an example of constructive play, having an end goal in mind that required the transformation of objects into a new configuration. He demonstrated simple dramatic/representational play. The schemes comprised of uncomplicated routines of one or two steps. In the playroom Zack focused mostly on manipulative- and mechanical-type toys. He did not spontaneously talk into the phone when modeled for him; instead, he left to find another mechanical toy. While at the child-friendly kitchen center, he repeatedly opened and closed the doors to the oven and microwave without exploring the inside. He imitated sedentary play with a doll briefly and then put the doll in the cart to push it around, thereby turning the activity into one with movement. Gross motor activities appear to be the focus of Zack's play: his need to move "big" interferes with his ability to expand on object use and play schemes.

He is still a picky eater but uses both a fork and spoon with ease. He often asks, "Down, please," during a meal and needs encouragement to sit and finish. Zack does not have difficulty falling asleep, and he sleeps 10 to 10.5 hours per night. He takes care of his own toilet needs (Praise the Lord, Hallelujah!). Zack bathes with minimal assistance and brushes his own teeth. He had been to the dentist twice and has done very well. He dresses and undresses himself (another big milestone accomplished).

Zack was observed imitating words, gestures, and actions. When Mom asked him to repeat single words in order to enhance articulation, he stopped, looked at Mom, and repeated the word with better accuracy. He imitated crayon strokes and copied a four-block train design. (These two skills were part of our intervention program for nearly a year and a half, during which time I seriously wondered if we would ever be successful.)

On the Visual (nonverbal problem-solving) Reception Scale of the Mullen Scales of Early Learning, Zack placed at the 52-month level (four months ahead of his chronological age). He demonstrated continued development in visual memory and spatial orientation and was able to discriminate and memorize details of drawings and printed letters and words. On the Receptive Language and Expressive Language Scales, Zack is functioning at the 34- and 36-month-old level, respectively. He comprehends simple questions and can follow related commands. He has more difficulty following through with unrelated or multiple-step commands. Zack has understanding of size concepts but not length and height concepts. Today he counted to five and identified most of the primary colors. (We had been working on colors since the first week of the intervention program. Yet, it still wasn't solid.) Zack uses multiple-word sentences to question, comment, and respond but intelligibility is decreased in longer utterances. He asks "where," "when," and "who" questions.

Since Zack's last ECEP evaluation, his parents have engaged him in an intensive program of therapies and social interactions that have resulted in notable increases in his social communication abilities. During today's evaluation, Zack spontaneously used gestures, eye contact, facial expressions, body movements, and short phrases to interact with his parents and evaluators. He appropriately solicited and directed the adults' attention, chose activities and playmates, responded to questions, and took turns during interactions with the evaluators. Using eye contact, shifting his gaze to reference people and objects during interactions, and coordinating gestures, speech, and eye contact continues to be somewhat challenging for Zack. However, his social communication skills now appear mildly delayed rather than disordered.

Zack understands descriptive concepts involving objects in relation to one another, such as *under* and *behind*, the comparative *most* and shapes (another maddening skill that took nearly a year and a half to master). He understood expanded sentences with embedded clauses such as "Show me the white kitten that is sleeping." He can group objects into categories, understand analogies, and make inferences from simple stories. Zack understands "more" as a way to ask for something, but not as a comparative term (i.e., Who has more candy?).

He usually communicated using words and phrases. As the language demands increased during the expressive language-testing tasks, Zack began to resort more to pantomime and gestures, as if it was easier for him to demonstrate concepts than to use words. He usually talked in two to four word phrases and often coordinated some gestures with his speech. Zack spontaneously used quantity concepts, plurals, a verb + ing ending, and possessive pronouns "mine" and "your" but not the possessive with an ('s). He demonstrated how common objects were typically used and performed the appropriate actions when asked "What would you do?" questions.

Zack's articulation skills were screened from his spontaneous speech and using the Preschool Language Scale - 4 Articulation Screener. Multiple Consonant errors were noted. (Children have rules for pronouncing words.) These rules were tested using a phonological process analysis. Results showed that Zack used the following phonological processes inconsistently: final consonant omission, prevocalic voicing, fronting velars, backing, stopping, and consonant cluster reduction. He also inconsistently used and assimilated consonants across words. When examined from a motor planning aspect, Zack demonstrated the following characteristics of a speech motor planning and programming disorder (such as apraxia of speech): 1) Receptive language skills, while delayed, were better than expressive language skills by almost one full standard deviation on the PLS-4. 2) Consonant errors were inconsistent across and within words. 3) No significant difference in articulation accuracy was noted between spontaneous and imitated single syllable words. 4) Zack's articulation accuracy decreased as the number of syllables in an utterance increased. Most utterances over four to five words/syllables in length were difficult or impossible to understand. 5) Vowel distortions were noted occasionally but were not considered significant. 6) Difficulty with certain food textures (scratchy, slimy, pulpy), immature chewing pattern, and tongue posturing.

When snacking, Zack chewed with an open mouth, using an immature up-and- down munching pattern. He seemed unaware of crumbs on the outside of his mouth and did not use his tongue to remove the crumbs. As he drank from his sippy cup, Zack consistently demonstrated a protruding tongue despite frequent reminders from Mom to keep his tongue in his mouth. Occasionally Zack demonstrated a moderate tongue-thrust when he swallowed. He demonstrated delayed and disordered oral motor skills that impact his eating, drinking, and articulation skills.

Next, Zack's sensory integration responses were tested. He used his hands well during the various activities of the session. However, his atypical grasping pattern with markers reflects some sensory feedback issues. In the touch and movement area, his family is aware of Zack's need for breaks involving deep pressure. Proprioceptive input and movement both help him organize his system, thereby helping him attend better during tabletop activities. This is an excellent strategy for Zack that can be useful in the classroom and modified appropriately as he matures. Over the past year his mom has channeled his sensory-seeking behavior to more socially appropriate activities. It is encouraging to see that he has responded so well to redirecting his behaviors while simultaneously meeting his needs for deep pressure and movement. He continues to squint as a result of sensory overload; an ophthalmologist has ruled out all problematic eye conditions.

Zack is a delightful little boy who has made good gains in his overall development in the past year with the support of his family and specialized programs through the public schools. His parents have worked very hard to provide consistent therapy to Zack and are proud of the progress he has made. In addition to developmental gains, his parents report that daily home life has become less stressful. He now interacts and communicates more effectively and has learned appropriate means for getting his sensory needs met. Zack has benefited from a consistent program of techniques used to support children with autism. However, he continues to demonstrate weaknesses in social interaction and functional communication. The diagnosis of autism spectrum disorder or pervasive developmental disorder – not otherwise specified (PDD-NOS) continues to be a diagnosis that fits Zack's profile.

He also demonstrates a pattern of disordered articulation and oral motor differences showing some degree of speech motor planning and programming disorder in addition to a diagnosis of autism spectrum disorder/PDD-NOS. It has been our pleasure to work with Zack and his family. His successes are a tribute to their consistency, hard work, and positive attitude.

Don't be discouraged; everyone who got where he is, started where he was.— Richard L. Evans [1]

As he went along, he saw a man blind from birth. His disciples asked him, "Rabbi, who sinned, this man or his parents, that he was born blind?" "Neither this man nor his parents sinned," said Jesus, "but this happened so that the work of God might be displayed in his life. As long as it is day, we must do the work of him who sent me."

(John 9:1 – 4a)

---

1 Copyright 1996 Cook Communications Ministries. God's Little Instruction Book For Men by Honor Books. Used with permission. All rights reserved.

33

Evaluation IV: Five Years, Three Months Old

The Department of Pediatrics Center for Development and Disability Early Childhood Evaluative Program only assesses children under the age of five. Because Zack was five years, three months old at the time of his last evaluation, he was referred to the Southwest Autism Network (SWAN), the agency that provides testing for older children. Since both agencies are affiliated with UNM, and both occupy the same business location, crossover of employees is common. Therefore, Zack's team consisted of the same group of professionals who had diagnosed him at three and four years of age.

In my opinion, the lead paragraph describing their behavioral observations is a bit guarded. Remember, these experts told me, "Children with autism don't make this kind of progress" after having diagnosed Zack with ASD/PDD-NOS twice before. I believe they felt the need to do some back-pedaling with their disclaimer. Here are their findings. My comments are found within the parentheses:

> *Behavioral Observations: When evaluating children with possible autism spectrum disorder, it is often difficult to get responses to formal test items. In addition, there is no test that will show whether or not a child has autism spectrum disorder. The criti-*

cal areas in evaluating the presence or absence of this disorder include a child's communication strategies, social interactions, and types of behaviors. As a result, the content of this evaluation is primarily based upon informal interactions with the clinicians in these areas.

After Zack accompanied a clinician to the evaluation room, he scanned the room, picked out a dinosaur book and spontaneously offered, "I like dinosaurs" to the clinician. When curious about what a particular object was, Zack stated, "What is this?" The clinician replied that the item was a whirlybird. When the clinician showed him how to operate the toy, Zack spontaneously stated, "It flew" and, "It went over your head." He then pointed to a specific part and continued with, "You see that part? It does this." The whirlybird landed on the clinician and Zack said, "I got you." He smiled appropriately and definitely understood that he was sharing this experience with the clinician.

Zack continued with, "I'm better at this than you are," when this clinician failed to make the whirlybird fly very well. And, when this clinician intentionally withheld a verbal response, Zack would turn and look at the clinician, persistently repeating the question until the clinician gave a response.

Later on in the evaluation process, Zack physically initiated play with the examiner by starting with, "I'm coming to fire you," and then play-acted shooting this clinician with a play gun. When the clinician reciprocated with play-acting, Zack continued the pretend-play scenario, stating, "I'm coming to caught (get?) you. I got your shoulder." Then he physically interacted in a playful manner with the clinician. This theme continued with much reciprocation until a theme was established; the clinician was playing the "bad guy," Zack the "good guy". (I suspect Zack had come to see all clinicians as "bad guys" after all those years of difficult, demanding therapy. . .just kidding.)

Testing results: Zack's developmental abilities were evaluated by the Mullen Scales of early learning (AGS Edition). The Mullen's scores are reported in T-scores, which have a mean of 50 and a standard deviation of 10. Given the fact that Zack had a cold and was heavily medicated on the day of testing, we believe these scores are valid but a low estimate of his abilities. Zack received the following T-scores and age equivalents on the Mullen: (He was almost 63 months old at the time of testing.) Visual Reception (29): 46 months, which falls in the "below average" category. (At four, Zack tested advanced for his chronological age in this area; therefore, I consider this particular test result suspect). Fine Motor (46): 59 months, "average" category. Receptive Language (43): 57 months, "average" category. Expressive Language (40): 51 months, "average" category.

Zack's Early Learning Composite was 80, which places him in the "below average" category. During the testing Zack made multiple reversal errors on visual tasks and letter identification tasks. These reversals significantly affected his Visual Receptive score. This needs to be interpreted very cautiously, given these reversal errors. (None of Zack's therapists had ever encountered significant reversal errors; we were very surprised by SWAN's findings in this area.)

Adaptive behavior was evaluated using the Vineland Adaptive Behavior Scales with his mother as a respondent. The Vineland assesses a child's ability and skills to do day-to-day activities and get along with others. A standard score of 85-114 reflects developmental functioning within normal limits when compared to other children of the same age. Zack received the following standard scores and age equivalents on the Vineland: Communication Domain (104), "adequate" adaptive level; Daily Living Skills Domain (95), "adequate" adaptive level; Socialization Domain (101), "adequate" adaptive level; Motor Skills Domain

(100), "adequate" adaptive level; Adaptive Behavior Composite (100), "adequate" adaptive level.

Impression Statement: Based on our evaluation, Zack does not meet the diagnostic criteria for Autistic Disorder, Pervasive Developmental Disorder-Not Otherwise Specified (PDD-NOS) or Asperger's Syndrome. It is important to note that Zack continues to display disordered language that is affecting others' ability to understand him and subtle social-emotional delays that can impact his ability to effectively negotiate complex social interactions with same-age peers. Zack is demonstrating a speech/language disorder characterized by difficulties in oral-motor production of sounds in sequence as well as syntactic language errors. Although Zack is showing social immaturity, his social skills are not disordered and do not appear to present as a core disability.

Recommendations: If Zack shows signs of learning challenges as he gets older, his parents might seek a comprehensive psycho-educational evaluation to determine if he has a specific learning disability.

When these professionals shared their opinions about the potential of children with autism, they also informed me that my Zack would always have "issues" of one sort or another, despite his astonishing evaluation. Our Zack may indeed have some lingering issues at this time, but I refuse to accept that he will always have limitations. These experts have been mistaken in the past. Who knows what the future holds?

We will just keep working hard until there are no more "issues." After all, Zack will always be my precious, little miracle boy. I can't and won't let him down if he is still depending on me. And I know my Lord will be right beside me, helping and carrying me through every conceivable storm. He has proved this to me over and over. He will never leave me nor forsake me. So great is the love of God!

Measure wealth not by the things you have, but by the things you have for which you would not take money. —Unknown[1]

For I am convinced that neither death nor life, neither angels nor demons, neither the present or the future, nor any powers, neither height nor depth, nor anything else in all creation, will be able to separate us from the love of God that is in Christ Jesus our Lord. (Romans 8:38)

34

Final Evaluation: Five Years, Seven Months Old

From the first day of Zack's intervention plan, our highest priority and long-term goal was to enroll him in a standard kindergarten class. Three years of grueling therapy later, it was time for his final evaluation. Now five years, seven months old, the public school system needed to determine his eligibility for all-inclusion into a typical kindergarten class. Because of Zack's struggles with apraxia, his eligibility for speech therapy was also assessed. Desiring the least-restrictive learning environment possible for our son, speech therapy was the only special education service we had requested. These are the results of Zack's multidisciplinary educational assessment report. (My comments are found within the parentheses.):

Referral: Zack was referred for evaluation by his IEP (Individual Education Plan) committee to address present levels of performance before promotion to kindergarten. Zack's current IEP lists his primary special education exceptionality as Autism, secondary special education exceptionality as Speech-Language Impaired.

Universal Nonverbal Intelligence Test (UNIT): The UNIT is an individually administered test of general intelligence and cognitive abilities of children and adolescents ages five through 17 who may be disadvantaged by traditional verbal and language-loaded measures. The UNIT yields standard scores that have a mean of 100 and a standard deviation of 15, producing an average range of scores from 85-115. Subtest scores are reported with a mean of 10 and a standard deviation of 3, which yields average scores in the range of seven to 13. Zack received the following scores:

Scaled Scores were as follows: Symbolic Memory (12), Cube Design (11), Spatial Memory (10), and Ana-logic Reasoning (13). Standard Scores, Percentiles, and Descriptors were as follows: Memory Quotient (106), 66th percentile, "Average"; Reasoning Quotient (112), 79th percentile, "High Average"; Symbolic Quotient (115), 84th percentile, "High Average"; Non-symbolic Quotient (103), 58th percentile, "Average"; and Full Scale (110), 75th percentile, "High Average."

The Full Scale Intelligence Quotient (FSIQ) is an index of overall cognitive and intellectual functioning (traditional IQ score) that can predict an individual's ability to learn and think about both familiar and new information. Zack's score of 110 is in the "High Average" range. (They sprung this IQ score on us right in the middle of our IEP meeting. If you recall, Zack's first formal evaluation determined his IQ to be 50. Over the next two years, his evaluations never suggested anything close to an average IQ score. Here we were, sitting in the middle of our meeting, being told that our son's IQ was slightly above average. I couldn't believe it at first. I was in a state of complete shock. For three years I had hoped and prayed for Zack to be average with every fiber of my being, knowing full well that the odds were not in his favor. What kind of a parent desperately hopes and prays for average for their child? A parent of a child with autism, that's who. All of those prayers had been answered with an added measure of grace. Irrepressible sobs of happiness burst forth. So long had I cried out of sadness and desperation. What *a foreign experience this was for me, and what a welcome one at that. Overwhelmed with abundant joy, I felt that this miraculous occurrence was surpassed only by my own salvation experience.)*

The Memory Quotient is a measure of memory for content (what is seen), location (where it was seen), and sequence (the order in which it was seen). It measures short-term recollection and recognition of both meaningful and abstract material. Memory includes attending, organizing, encoding, storing, and recalling information and experiences. The Memory Quotient is comprised of Symbolic Memory and Spatial Memory. Zack's score of 106 is within the "Average" range.

The Reasoning Quotient is a measure of pattern processing, understanding of relationships, and planning abilities. It is an index of thinking and problem-solving abilities, for both familiar and unfamiliar situations. The Reasoning Quotient is comprised of Cube Design and Ana-logic Reasoning. Zack scored in the "High Average" range with a standard score of 112.

The Symbolic Quotient is an index of an individual's ability to solve problems that involve meaningful material and whose solutions lend themselves to internal verbal mediation, including labeling, organizing, and categorizing. The Symbolic Quotient is comprised of Symbolic Memory and Ana-logic Reasoning. Zack's score of 115 is within the "High Average" range of ability.

The Non-symbolic Quotient measures an individual's ability to solve problems involving abstract material or material that is not very meaningful and whose solutions are not conducive to verbal mediation. Non-symbolic mediation includes perception, recognition, sequencing, organization, and integration and encompasses aspects of cognition including reasoning and memory. This quotient is comprised of Cube Design and Spatial Memory. Zack's standard score of 103 falls within the "Average" range.

Analysis of the subtest scores reveals no significant strengths and/or weaknesses relative to Zack's own individual mean on the UNIT subtest. There were also no significant inter-scale cognitive differences between Zack's assessed memory, reasoning, symbolic and non-symbolic abilities; these abilities are similarly developed.

Bracken Basic Concept Scale-Revised (BBCS-R): The Bracken Basic Concept Scale-Revised is used to assess the basic concept development of children two years, six months through 7 years, 11 months. The BBCS-R is used to measure comprehension of 308 foundational and functionally relevant educational concepts in 11 subtests or concept categories: Colors, Letters, Numbers/Counting, Sizes, Comparisons, Shapes, Direction/Position, Self/Social Awareness, Texture/Material, Quantity, and Time/Sequence. This test is individually administered, and the concepts are presented orally within the context of completed sentences and visually in a multiple-choice format. Of the 11 subtests on the BBSC-R the first six compose the School Readiness Composite (SRC). Here are Zack's subtest scores and classifications: SRC (11), "Average"; Direction/Position (10), "Average"; Self-Social Awareness (10), "Average"; Texture/Material (10), "Average"; Quantity (10), "Average"; and Time/Sequence (8), "Average." Here are Zack's Composites, Standard Scores, Percentiles, and Classifications: Total Test (101), 50th percentile, "Average"; SRC (106), 63rd percentile, "Average."

Zack's performance in the area of school-readiness skills was within the "Average" range. His total test score of 106 is considered in the "Average" range. He was able to identify and label 11 colors and all upper and lower-case letters. He was able to count and identify "how many" questions with the aid of pictures. He was able to demonstrate the concepts of addition and subtraction with the use of visual aids. He was able to identify single-digit numbers, and double-digit numbers. He demonstrated knowledge of concepts such as big, little, small, tall, short, large, wide, and shallow. He demonstrated knowledge of comparison concepts and identified 10 shapes. He was able to indicate which child was crying, laughing, and sick in the area of self/social awareness. (All of these concepts were drilled for months, if not years.) After a verbal command he was able to identify which picture showed specifics such as "part" of an orange, "both" dogs, and "which" person is alone. In the area of time/sequence he was able to put a series of pictures in order. (This was yet another skill requiring a great deal of drilling to master.)

Developmental Tests of Visual-Motor Skills: This test is used to help identify significant difficulties that some children have in integration or coordinating their visual perceptual and motor (finger and hand movement) abilities. Visual perception is the child's interpretation of visual stimuli, not visual acuity. The Visual Motor Integration subtest is a developmental sequence of geometric forms to be copied with paper and pencil. It requires integration among sensory inputs and motor output. Zack had an overall standard score of 102, placing him at the 50th percentile or in the "Average" range.

A speech language evaluation indicated that Zack continues to meet criteria for Speech-Language Impaired, Articulation and Oral Language Impaired. Due to Zack's speech-language impairment, it appears he might benefit educationally with special education support in the academic areas impacted by language as well as speech-language services. Eligibility: Based upon evaluation procedures completed, as defined by the New Mexico PED Technical Evaluation Assistance Manual (TEAM), it appears that Zack continues to meet the criteria for Speech-Language Impaired, defined as a communication disorder such as stuttering, impaired articulation, language impairment, or voice impairment which adversely affects a child's educational performance.

This last bit of news may have been frightening for a parent of an otherwise typically developing child, but for us it was.not. Zack had come so far, and we had all survived his autism. Also, his speech deficits were still obvious to everyone; they were impossible to ignore or deny. We knew that we still had a lot of work to do. Even without this evaluation we knew this to be true. Dealing with Zack's apraxia and the possibility of related learning disabilities was still far less daunting compared to the struggles of his autism. Our family had already endured the worst trial imaginable. It seems reasonable to assume that what lies ahead is bound to be more manageable. Of course, as we have learned all too well, God has His own plans. If our future holds more misery, we can be certain that our struggles will glorify Him and His purpose.

God has a history of using the insignificant to accomplish the impossible. —Richard Exley[1]

"For my thoughts are not your thoughts, neither are your ways my ways," declares the LORD. "As the heavens are higher than the earth, so are my ways higher than your ways and my thoughts than your thoughts."
(Isaiah 55:8, 9)

1 Copyright 1996 Cook Communications Ministries. God's Little Instruction Book For Men by Honor Books. Used with permission. All rights reserved.

Resources

We wanted to keep the suggested resources as current as possible, so for this publication we've opted to provide current web addresses rather than the charts themselves.

Appendix I,II,III, IV: Developmental Stages for Children/ Youth 0 – 6years
(http://www.edu-cyberpg.com/teachers/time.html)

Appendix V: (Modified) M-CHAT Autism Questionnaire
(http://www.firstsigns.org/screening/tools/rec.htm#dev_screens)

Appendix VI: Autism Screener Questionnaire on Behavior and Social Communication
(http://www.firstsigns.org/screening/tools/rec.htm#dev_screens)

Appendix VII: Sohn Grayson Rating Scale for Asperger's Syndrome and High- Functioning Pervasive Developmental Disorder
(http://vrosario.bol.ucla.edu/forms/Sohn_Grayson.pdf)

Appendix VIII: Sensory Rating Scale
(http://www.tsbvi.edu/Outreach/seehear/fall97/sensory.htm)

Appendix IX: Tips for Easing Transitions
(http://www.typeamom.net/seven-ways-to-ease-transitions-for-children-with-autism.html)

Tatianna Dickens

Tatianna Dickens

Tatianna Dickens

LaVergne, TN USA
07 March 2010

175109LV00003B/1/P

9 780978 679644